Thomas Gabel

**Learning in Cooperative Multi-Agent Systems**

Thomas Gabel

# Learning in Cooperative Multi-Agent Systems

## Distributed Reinforcement Learning Algorithms and their Application to Scheduling Problems

**Südwestdeutscher Verlag für Hochschulschriften**

**Impressum / Imprint**
Bibliografische Information der Deutschen Nationalbibliothek: Die Deutsche Nationalbibliothek verzeichnet diese Publikation in der Deutschen Nationalbibliografie; detaillierte bibliografische Daten sind im Internet über http://dnb.d-nb.de abrufbar.
Alle in diesem Buch genannten Marken und Produktnamen unterliegen warenzeichen-, marken- oder patentrechtlichem Schutz bzw. sind Warenzeichen oder eingetragene Warenzeichen der jeweiligen Inhaber. Die Wiedergabe von Marken, Produktnamen, Gebrauchsnamen, Handelsnamen, Warenbezeichnungen u.s.w. in diesem Werk berechtigt auch ohne besondere Kennzeichnung nicht zu der Annahme, dass solche Namen im Sinne der Warenzeichen- und Markenschutzgesetzgebung als frei zu betrachten wären und daher von jedermann benutzt werden dürften.

Bibliographic information published by the Deutsche Nationalbibliothek: The Deutsche Nationalbibliothek lists this publication in the Deutsche Nationalbibliografie; detailed bibliographic data are available in the Internet at http://dnb.d-nb.de.
Any brand names and product names mentioned in this book are subject to trademark, brand or patent protection and are trademarks or registered trademarks of their respective holders. The use of brand names, product names, common names, trade names, product descriptions etc. even without a particular marking in this work is in no way to be construed to mean that such names may be regarded as unrestricted in respect of trademark and brand protection legislation and could thus be used by anyone.

Verlag / Publisher:
Südwestdeutscher Verlag für Hochschulschriften
ist ein Imprint der / is a trademark of
ICS Morebooks! Marketing SRL
4, Industriala street, 3100 Balti, Republic of Moldova
Email: info@omniscriptum.com

Herstellung: siehe letzte Seite /
Printed at: see last page
**ISBN: 978-3-8381-1036-3**

Zugl. / Approved by: Osnabrück, Universität, Diss., 2009

Copyright © Thomas Gabel
Copyright © 2009 ICS Morebooks! Marketing SRL
Alle Rechte vorbehalten. / All rights reserved. Balti2009

# Preface

Decentralized decision-making has become an active research topic in artificial intelligence. In a distributed system, a number of individually acting agents coexist. If they strive to accomplish a common goal, i.e. if the multi-agent system is a cooperative one, then the establishment of coordinated cooperation between the agents is of utmost importance. With this in mind, our focus is on multi-agent reinforcement learning methods which allow for automatically acquiring cooperative policies based solely on a specification of the desired joint behavior of the whole system.

Research in distributed systems has pointed out that the decentralization of the control of the system and of the observation of the system among independent agents has a significant impact on the complexity of solving a given problem. Therefore, we address the intricacy of learning and acting in multi-agent systems by the following complementary approaches.

Many practical problems exhibit some structure whose exploitation may ease the task of finding solutions. For this reason, we are going to identify a subclass of general decentralized decision-making problems that features regularities in the way the agents interact with one another. We will show that the complexity of optimally solving a problem instance from this class is provably lower than solving a general one.

Even though a lower complexity class may be entered by sticking to certain subclasses of a general multi-agent problem, the computational complexity may be still so high that optimally solving it is infeasible. This holds, in particular, when intending to tackle problems of larger size that are of relevance for practical problems. Given these facts, our goal will be not to develop optimal solution algorithms that are applicable to small problems only, but to look for techniques capable of quickly obtaining approximate solutions in the vicinity of the optimum. To this end, we will develop and utilize various model-free reinforcement learning approaches. In contrast to offline planning algorithms which aim at finding optimal solutions in a model-based manner, reinforcement learning allows for employing independently learning agents and, hence, for a full decentralization of the problem.

As a matter of fact, many large-scale applications are well-suited to be formulated in terms of spatially or functionally distributed entities. Thus, multi-agent approaches are of high relevance to various real-world problems. Job-shop scheduling is one such application stemming from the field of factory optimization and manufacturing control. It is our particular goal to interpret job-shop scheduling problems as distributed sequential decision-making problems, to employ the multi-agent reinforcement learning algorithms we will propose for solving such problems, and, moreover, to evaluate the performance of our learning approaches in the scope of various established scheduling benchmark problems.

# Contents

**1 Introduction**     **1**
    1.1 Motivation . . . . . . . . . . . . . . . . . . . . . . . . . . . . . . . 1
    1.2 Objectives . . . . . . . . . . . . . . . . . . . . . . . . . . . . . . . . 4
    1.3 Outline . . . . . . . . . . . . . . . . . . . . . . . . . . . . . . . . . 5

**2 Single- and Multi-Agent Reinforcement Learning**     **7**
    2.1 The Reinforcement Learning Framework . . . . . . . . . . . . . . . 7
        2.1.1 Markov Decision Processes . . . . . . . . . . . . . . . . . . 8
        2.1.2 Learning Optimal Behavior . . . . . . . . . . . . . . . . . . 9
        2.1.3 On Actors and Critics . . . . . . . . . . . . . . . . . . . . . 10
        2.1.4 Policy Search-Based Reinforcement Learning . . . . . . . . . . . . 11
        2.1.5 Value Function-Based Reinforcement Learning . . . . . . . . . . . 12
    2.2 From One to Many Agents . . . . . . . . . . . . . . . . . . . . . . . 14
        2.2.1 Cooperative and Non-Cooperative Multi-Agent Systems . . . . . . 14
        2.2.2 Application Fields of Learning Multi-Agent Systems . . . . . . . . 15
    2.3 Cooperative Multi-Agent Systems with Partial Observability . . . . . . . . 16
        2.3.1 The Multi-Agent Markov Decision Process Model . . . . . . . . . 17
        2.3.2 Partially Observable Markov Decision Processes . . . . . . . . . . 18
        2.3.3 The Framework of Decentralized Markov Decision Processes . . . . 18
        2.3.4 The Price of Decentralization . . . . . . . . . . . . . . . . . 21
    2.4 Decentralized Markov Decision Processes with Changing Action Sets . . . 22
        2.4.1 On Transition Dependencies . . . . . . . . . . . . . . . . . . 22
        2.4.2 Variable Action Sets and Partially Ordered Transition Dependencies 23
        2.4.3 Implications on Complexity . . . . . . . . . . . . . . . . . . 26
        2.4.4 Example Applications . . . . . . . . . . . . . . . . . . . . . 28
    2.5 Related Work on Learning in Cooperative Multi-Agent Systems . . . . . . 29
        2.5.1 Alternative Frameworks for Distributed Control . . . . . . . . . . 29
        2.5.2 Optimal Solution Algorithms . . . . . . . . . . . . . . . . . . 29
        2.5.3 Subclasses with Reduced Problem Complexity . . . . . . . . . . . 30
        2.5.4 Search for Approximate Solutions . . . . . . . . . . . . . . . 31

# Contents

**3 Distributed Scheduling Problems**     **35**
- 3.1 Foundations . . . . . . . . . . . . . . . . . . . . . . . . . . . . . . . . 36
  - 3.1.1 The Classical Job-Shop Scheduling Problem . . . . . . . . . . . 36
  - 3.1.2 The Disjunctive Graph Model . . . . . . . . . . . . . . . . . . 39
  - 3.1.3 Classical Benchmark Problems . . . . . . . . . . . . . . . . . . 40
- 3.2 Multi-Agent Job-Shop Scheduling . . . . . . . . . . . . . . . . . . . . . 40
  - 3.2.1 Discussion of Distributed Scheduling . . . . . . . . . . . . . . 41
  - 3.2.2 Job-Shop Scheduling as Decentralized Markov Decision Process . . 42
- 3.3 Related Work on Solving Job-Shop Scheduling Problems . . . . . . . . . . 45
  - 3.3.1 Optimal and Near-Optimal Solution Algorithms . . . . . . . . . . 45
  - 3.3.2 Dispatching Priority Rules . . . . . . . . . . . . . . . . . . . 46
  - 3.3.3 Artificial Intelligence-Based Approaches . . . . . . . . . . . . 48

**4 Policy Search-Based Solution Approaches**     **51**
- 4.1 Foundations . . . . . . . . . . . . . . . . . . . . . . . . . . . . . . . . 51
  - 4.1.1 Policy Performance . . . . . . . . . . . . . . . . . . . . . . . 52
  - 4.1.2 Multi-Agent Policy Search Reinforcement Learning . . . . . . . . 53
- 4.2 Joint Equilibrium Policy Search . . . . . . . . . . . . . . . . . . . . . . 55
  - 4.2.1 Learning Joint Policies . . . . . . . . . . . . . . . . . . . . . 55
  - 4.2.2 Global Action Parameterization . . . . . . . . . . . . . . . . . 58
  - 4.2.3 Theoretical Properties . . . . . . . . . . . . . . . . . . . . . 60
  - 4.2.4 Discussion . . . . . . . . . . . . . . . . . . . . . . . . . . . 62
  - 4.2.5 Empirical Evaluation . . . . . . . . . . . . . . . . . . . . . . 63
- 4.3 Gradient-Descent Policy Search . . . . . . . . . . . . . . . . . . . . . . 68
  - 4.3.1 Gradient-Descent Policy Learning . . . . . . . . . . . . . . . . 69
  - 4.3.2 Independent Agents and Decentralized Policy Gradient . . . . . . 72
  - 4.3.3 Policy Gradient under Changing Action Sets . . . . . . . . . . . 75
  - 4.3.4 Discussion . . . . . . . . . . . . . . . . . . . . . . . . . . . 78
  - 4.3.5 Empirical Evaluation . . . . . . . . . . . . . . . . . . . . . . 80
- 4.4 Discussion . . . . . . . . . . . . . . . . . . . . . . . . . . . . . . . . . 89
  - 4.4.1 Related Work . . . . . . . . . . . . . . . . . . . . . . . . . . 89
  - 4.4.2 Advantages and Limitations of JEPS and GDPS . . . . . . . . . . 90

**5 Value Function-Based Solution Approaches**     **93**
- 5.1 Foundations . . . . . . . . . . . . . . . . . . . . . . . . . . . . . . . . 93
  - 5.1.1 The Issue of Generalization . . . . . . . . . . . . . . . . . . . 94
  - 5.1.2 Batch-Mode Reinforcement Learning . . . . . . . . . . . . . . . 95
- 5.2 Distributed and Approximated Value Functions . . . . . . . . . . . . . . . 98

|       | 5.2.1 | Independent Value Function Learners . . . . . . . . . . . . . . . . . | 98  |
|-------|-------|------------------------------------------------------------------------|-----|
|       | 5.2.2 | Neural Fitted Q Iteration . . . . . . . . . . . . . . . . . . . . . . . | 100 |
|       | 5.2.3 | Heuristic NFQ Enhancements . . . . . . . . . . . . . . . . . . . . . | 102 |
| 5.3   | Fitted Q Iteration with Neural Networks and Optimistic Assumption . . . | 105 |
|       | 5.3.1 | Optimistic Q Learning . . . . . . . . . . . . . . . . . . . . . . . . . | 105 |
|       | 5.3.2 | Optimism Under Partial State Observability . . . . . . . . . . . . | 108 |
|       | 5.3.3 | Batch-Mode Learning of Distributed Q Values . . . . . . . . . . . | 110 |
| 5.4   | Empirical Evaluation . . . . . . . . . . . . . . . . . . . . . . . . . . . . | 112 |
|       | 5.4.1 | Experimental Set-Up . . . . . . . . . . . . . . . . . . . . . . . . . . | 113 |
|       | 5.4.2 | Example Benchmarks . . . . . . . . . . . . . . . . . . . . . . . . . . | 117 |
|       | 5.4.3 | Benchmark Suites . . . . . . . . . . . . . . . . . . . . . . . . . . . . | 122 |
|       | 5.4.4 | Generalization Capabilities . . . . . . . . . . . . . . . . . . . . . . | 125 |
| 5.5   | Discussion . . . . . . . . . . . . . . . . . . . . . . . . . . . . . . . . . . | 128 |
|       | 5.5.1 | Related Work . . . . . . . . . . . . . . . . . . . . . . . . . . . . . . | 128 |
|       | 5.5.2 | Advantages and Limitations of OA-NFQ . . . . . . . . . . . . . . | 131 |

# 6 Communicating Agents and Optimal Schedules     133
  6.1  Foundations . . . . . . . . . . . . . . . . . . . . . . . . . . . . . . . . . . . 133
      6.1.1  Reactive Policies and Their Limitations . . . . . . . . . . . . . . . 134
      6.1.2  Interaction Histories . . . . . . . . . . . . . . . . . . . . . . . . . . 134
  6.2  Resolving Transition Dependencies . . . . . . . . . . . . . . . . . . . . . 135
      6.2.1  Interaction History Encodings . . . . . . . . . . . . . . . . . . . . 135
      6.2.2  Communication-Based Awareness of Inter-Agent Dependencies . . . 138
  6.3  Empirical Evaluation . . . . . . . . . . . . . . . . . . . . . . . . . . . . . 142
      6.3.1  Example Benchmark . . . . . . . . . . . . . . . . . . . . . . . . . 142
      6.3.2  Benchmark Suites . . . . . . . . . . . . . . . . . . . . . . . . . . . 144
  6.4  Discussion . . . . . . . . . . . . . . . . . . . . . . . . . . . . . . . . . . . 149

# 7 Conclusion     151
  7.1  Summary . . . . . . . . . . . . . . . . . . . . . . . . . . . . . . . . . . . . 151
  7.2  Outlook . . . . . . . . . . . . . . . . . . . . . . . . . . . . . . . . . . . . 154

# Glossary     157

# Bibliography     159

# List of Figures     175

# Contents

# 1 Introduction

The last century has witnessed an enormous technological progress that today allows for solving computational problems that were far out of reach a few decades ago. In spite of this advancement, there are various significant hurdles that render the search for optimal solutions of many practical problems impossible. A major difficulty is represented by the fact that in practice complete and certain information about the system, its environment, and all interfering influences cannot be expected to be known. Instead, decisions very often have to be taken under partial knowledge of the situation. Another complicating factor is that in "real-world" problems the environment may be changing dynamically, mainly due to the influence of other parties. Finally, the issue of problem complexity must also be acknowledged. Even if it can be proved that a certain problem can be solved within a finite amount of computational steps, this number may be astronomically high and, thus, finding an optimal solution practically intractable.

The application of ideas and methods from the research fields of artificial intelligence (AI) and machine learning represents one option to tackle the above-mentioned challenges. The basic idea is to develop systems that are capable of adapting their behavior with respect to the situation they find themselves in, and that allow for utilizing learned capabilities under altered conditions as well. The learning algorithms behind these ideas typically interpret the given task as an optimization problem and improve the learner's behavior successively, yielding near-optimal, approximate solutions within reasonable time at the cost of abandoning the goal of finding the respective problem's best solution possible.

In the book at hand, we consider learning systems that are composed of multiple, independently acting and learning entities – frequently called agents – that aim collectively at solving a given task. They do so by steadily adapting and improving their behaviors using different variants of machine learning algorithms we are going to develop. Why this problem setting is an interesting one, what are the special problems and challenges arising, and why this is of relevance to practical problems, shall be discussed in the next section. Thereafter, we provide an overview of the objectives and contents of this book.

## 1.1 Motivation

It has been a long-standing goal of research in artificial intelligence to create intelligent decision-making agents. In this context, decision-making typically refers to the process of selecting an action out of a set of alternatives, whereas the decision maker denotes the agent around which the decision-making process is centered. Although in the literature there is no distinct definition of the agent concept, it is generally accepted that an agent can perceive observations of its environment, act upon that environment by executing actions, and, ultimately does so in order to accomplish a certain goal. However, for many practical

# 1 Introduction

problems it is unrealistic to expect that some goal can be accomplished by executing a single action. Instead, in most cases a specific sequence of actions may be required, thus rendering the problem for the agent as a sequential decision-making one.

Systems inhabited with just one single agent are a case apart. In the more general, and for many practical applications very relevant case, multiple agents coexist and interact with one another. This is also the scenario we are focusing on in this work. We consider multi-agent systems where the independent decision makers must work together, i.e. sequentially make the right decisions in order to achieve a common goal. More importantly, we define the agents to be autonomous and capable of learning. By autonomy, we mean that the agents do not rely on a substantial amount of prior knowledge provided by the designer of the system. By learning, we indicate that the agents are adaptive and compensate their lack of knowledge by learning through trial and error, i.e. through repeated interaction with their environment. To accomplish the latter, we will employ the machine learning framework of reinforcement learning, more specifically, of multi-agent reinforcement learning.

Decentralized decision-making is required in many real-life applications. Examples include distributed sensor networks or teams of autonomous robots for monitoring and/or exploring a certain environment, rescue operations where units must decide independently which sites to search and secure, or production planning and factory optimization where machines may act independently with the goal of achieving optimal joint productivity. Notably, the latter shall shift into the center of our interest shortly. After all, the growing interest in analyzing and solving decentralized learning problems is to a large degree evoked by their high relevance for practical problems.

However, the step from one to many agents raises a number of interesting challenges. On the one hand, the total number of joint action combinations grows exponentially with the number of agents involved. On the other hand, the agents may have different perceptions of the world and, furthermore, their action choices may influence one another. Viewed in this light, the main motivation for this book is to develop distributed learning algorithms that reliably work under these conditions. Moreover, we are interested in the practical utility of the approaches we are going to present. As indicated above, many practical problems (e.g. NP-hard and more complex ones) are too complex to be tractably solvable. This means, from a certain problem size on, either the number of calculations necessary for finding the optimal solution or the corresponding memory requirements for storing it are too extensive, which renders optimally solving such problems infeasible. Following a divide and conquer approach, there are in fact various practical problems that may benefit from a distributed solution approach using a system of autonomously learning agents.

## Scope

Let us illustrate the scope of this book with the help of a simple, yet instructive example. The production of many complex goods involves a large number of processing steps and may require inputs from different sources. Coordinated cooperation between a company's subunits, as well as with affiliated companies, is essential for optimizing the overall efficiency of production. Assume that in a shop floor of a company's subunit, there are a number of orders waiting to be processed. The decision as to which order to dispatch first

## 1.1 Motivation

may be not an easy one: So, it may be known that the affiliated company belonging to order A needs the finished product urgently in order to continue manufacturing. But, the same may hold true for order B, with the difference that the corresponding processing step necessary is much more time-consuming and expensive. Furthermore, it is expected that another subunit is soon going to supply intermediate products to which an important processing step must be applied (order C). Apparently, there are a number of dependencies between the units that are difficult to take into consideration if there is no omniscient observer of the entire plant.

This is an example of a distributed production planning problem, though admittedly a restricted one. However, it serves us for two purposes. First, it suggests a number of research challenges that arise when dealing with learning in multi-agent systems and, thus, points to some of the problem characteristics and conditions that shall be of relevance throughout this book, such as:

- First of all, the considered subunit is a member of a corporation. It, as well as other subunits, aim collectively at several collaborate goals. For example, if a final product is manufactured in time, this is a win for the company as a whole. If we endow each subunit with some autonomy, then – in the notion of distributed artificial intelligence – each subunit represents an agent in a cooperative multi-agent system.

- There is a (varying) set of tasks that must be accomplished by each unit. The decision as to which out of the set of orders to serve next must be taken by the subunit (or some intelligent entity residing in it) where, obviously, the fulfillment of some orders may be more rewarding than others.

- Several issues do complicate the decision to pick one of the waiting tasks. First, the subunit is basically well-informed only about its own current situation (its work load, priorities, state of processing tools etc.), not about that of other units or affiliated companies. Second, there are many dependencies between the subunits. e.g. products may have to traverse different units in a certain order, where at each spot a specific processing step must be applied. Consequently, new tasks may arrive at all times. Third, each subunit acts in principle independently (i.e. chooses its next task to be executed on its own), which is why it is not guaranteed that the collective of subunits as a whole acts in a coordinated manner.

  Obviously, concerning some of these issues, communication between different subunits and affiliated companies may be very beneficial, but instant information flow cannot be generally assumed.

- The ultimate goal in this scenario would be to have an adaptive (dispatch) decision-making agent at each subunit that improves its capabilities through learning, i.e. by taking into consideration previous experiences made (earlier decisions, their outcomes, and costs incurred). If a human is to be included in the decision-making process, then the learning agent may be realized as a decision support system that provides advice to the human. However, an entirely independent decision-making agent can also be envisioned.

# 1 Introduction

The second purpose of the introductory example is that it hints at a concrete application of multi-agent systems. Production planning and scheduling problems arise frequently in practice and have long been in the focus of Operations Research. Besides their practical relevance, they are known for their intricacy, which makes them appealing as a research test bed. In particular, we are going to focus on a specific class of scheduling problems, viz on job-shop scheduling problems, which can be easily posed as multi-agent problems and to which the foregoing manufacturing example belongs. Although the modelling and learning approaches we are going to propose in the context of this book are of a general nature and can be deployed for different applications, distributed job-shop scheduling problems depict the target application domain in the context of which we will test, analyze, and validate all approaches.

## 1.2 Objectives

The utilization of multi-agent systems provides a number of advantages compared to centralized solution approaches. Among those is the ability to distribute the required computations over a number of entities, an increased amount of robustness, flexibility, and scalability due to the possibility of exchanging individual agents, or the benefit of allowing for spatial distribution of the work.

As argued above, however, various problems and challenges arise if it is desired that the agents involved make optimal and coordinated decisions despite their independence of one another and despite their lack of omniscience. In fact, it has been shown that endowing agents in such a decentralized system with optimal behaviors, resulting in optimal solutions for the respective task, is computationally intractable except for the smallest problem sizes.

Taking this into consideration, it is a first goal of this work to identify a subclass of general distributed sequential decision-making problems, that features certain regularities in the way the agents interact with one another, as well as to exploit those regularities such that the problem complexity can be decreased significantly.

Second, it is our overall goal to tackle decentralized problems of moderate and larger size that are of practical interest. This involves settings with ten and more agents, which is why optimal solution methods can hardly be applied. Therefore, we aim at employing multi-agent reinforcement learning approaches, where the agents are independent learners and do their learning online in interaction with their environment. The disadvantage of choosing this learning approach is that agents may take potentially rather bad decisions until they learn better ones and that, hence, only an approximate joint policy may be obtained. The advantage is, however, that the entire learning process is done in a completely distributed manner, with each agent deciding on its own local action based on its partial view of the world state and on any other information it eventually gets from its teammates. So, to this end, the objective is to enable the agents to obtain high quality solutions in the vicinity of the optimal one as quickly and efficiently as possible.

A complementing goal is depicted by studying the impact achieved when revealing to the agents some information regarding their teammates and their interdependencies, as opposed to the learning situation where each agent considers only its own local state, ignoring the desires or needs of others.

A final objective spanning the entire book is to put an emphasis on application scenarios from manufacturing, production control, or assembly line optimization where, as indicated above, the production of a good typically involves a number of processing steps that must be performed in a specific order. In terms of this application area, we are assuming that the decision to further process semi-finished products can only be taken if all preceding processing steps are finished and that a company usually manufactures a variety of products concurrently, which is why an appropriate sequencing and scheduling of individual operations is of crucial importance. To this end, it is our goal to model problem instances from the class of job-shop scheduling problems as sequential decision-making problems that are targeted in a distributed fashion using a multi-agent approach and that correspond to the above-mentioned subclass of general distributed decision problems. Thus, we aim at factorizing job-shop scheduling problems by attaching independent and learning agents to each of the processing units. In applying the above-mentioned learning approaches to various scheduling benchmark problems, our objective is to evaluate the performance of multi-agent learning algorithms and to emphasize their usefulness for problems of high practical relevance.

## 1.3 Outline

This book is divided into seven chapters. In addition to the introduction and conclusion, there are two chapters (Chapters 2 and 3) that mainly focus on foundational issues, problem modelling, and related work, as well as three chapters (Chapters 4-6) where we develop various distributed learning algorithms, analyze their properties, and evaluate their performance with empirical experiments in the domain of job-shop scheduling. Figure 1.1 depicts an attempt to provide a graphical overview of this work.

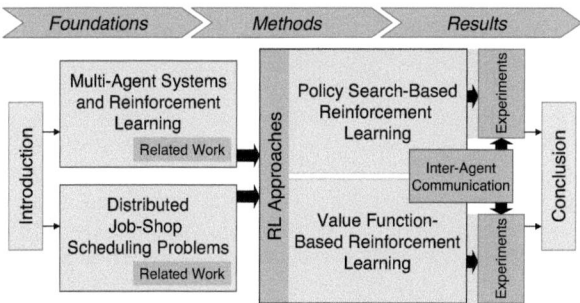

Figure 1.1: The Big Picture: Overview of this Book

In Chapter 2 we, generally speaking, focus on multi-agent systems and on reinforcement learning. We start with a summary of the core concepts of single-agent reinforcement learning and discuss a generally accepted distinction of reinforcement learning approaches that can be found in the literature. We then make the transition from single-agent to multi-agent problems and emphasize why this transition yields a significant increase in

# 1 Introduction

problem complexity. Next, we argue that, in particular in practice, it is unrealistic to assume that each agent in a multi-agent system has a full overview of its environment and of the state of the other agents. Hence, cooperative multi-agent systems with partial state observability shift into our interest, concerning which it is well-known that they are appealing from a practical point of view, but that solving them is computationally intractable. The latter issue provides the motivation for us to identify a specific subclass of distributed decision problems that is provably less complex than general ones. In so doing, in Section 2.4 we define the class of decentralized Markov decision processes with changing action sets and partially ordered transition dependencies which will play a central role within all following chapters of this book.

Complementing Chapter 2, Chapter 3 introduces our intended application domain of job-shop scheduling problems. We discuss their problem complexity, existing benchmark problems and established solution approaches. Moreover, we argue why we aim at solving scheduling problems in a distributed fashion using a multi-agent approach and we show how we can fruitfully utilize the problem class identified in the previous chapter for this purpose.

We are going to stress that – despite the reduction of problem complexity brought about by the problem class specification mentioned – the types of problems we are addressing are far beyond trivial and, particularly when it comes to solving larger-sized problem instances, finding optimal solutions is infeasible in most cases. Therefore, in Chapters 4 and 5, we will develop approximate solution approaches based on model-free reinforcement learning techniques by means of which we target at finding near-optimal solutions within reasonable time. In Chapter 4, we develop two distributed learning algorithms that are tailored for solving approximately single instances of decentralized decision processes and that exploit the characteristics of the problem class with changing action sets we identified before. These algorithms perform a directed search in the space of policies the agents can represent and comply with certain convergence properties. By contrast, in Chapter 5, we develop decentralized learning algorithms that enable each agent to aim at determining a so-called value function for the problem at hand from which a corresponding behavior can easily be derived. Moreover, our goal here is also on the issue of generalization which means that the agents learn behavior policies that capture general problem-solving knowledge and, hence, can be successfully applied for altered or entirely different problem settings as well.

What is common to the investigations we make in both chapters mentioned previously is that all approaches suggested rely on learning agent behaviors that can be described as purely reactive, that is that the agents do not explicitly take into account their histories and do not specifically address certain inter-agent dependencies. With the aim of enhancing the capabilities of purely reactively acting and learning agents, in Chapter 6, we study two approaches that enable the agents to make more deliberate decisions. In particular, we are going to utilize communication between agents as a tool to resolve certain dependencies between agents. In this chapter as well as in the two preceding chapters, we empirically evaluate all the approaches proposed in the context of our targeted application domain: We model intricate job-shop scheduling problems as multi-agent problems, make the agents learn good scheduling policies, and evaluate their performance using various established job-shop scheduling benchmark problems.

# 2 Single- and Multi-Agent Reinforcement Learning

One of the general aims of machine learning is to produce intelligent software systems, sometimes called *agents*, by a process of learning and evolving. For the notion of an agent, however, there exists no generally accepted formal definition. According to Russell and Norvig (2003), "An agent is anything that can be viewed as perceiving its environment through sensors and acting upon that environment through actuators." Agents are typically presumed to inhabit some environment within which they have to strive for fulfilling some specific task. To do so, they must sequentially take decisions which actions to execute next, they ought to try to adapt their policies of actions such that to behave optimally, and they may be required to reason about the existence of other agents with which to cooperate or compete.

In this chapter, we will start off (Section 2.1) by presenting the idea of reinforcement learning which represents one of the most popular frameworks for modelling intelligent agents and for making them learn to solve a given task by repeatedly sensing and acting within their environment. Subsequently, in Section 2.2 we will draw a bow from systems with single agents to those with multiple agents that collectively, yet independently must learn to achieve a common goal. Since, typically, in a multi-agent system not every agent gets hold of a global view over the entire environment including other agents, we specifically have to address the issue of partial observability: To this end, we summarize the framework of decentralized partially observable Markov decision processes (DEC-POMDPs, Bernstein et al., 2002), which is frequently used for modelling multi-agent problems (Section 2.3). Since general DEC-POMDPs are known to be intractable except for the smallest problem sizes, in Section 2.4 we propose a sub-class of such problems that builds the foundation for most of the ideas and methods to be presented in the remainder of this book. Specifically, this sub-class is well suited to model a wide range of practical multi-agent problems, including the scheduling tasks that are in the particular center of our interest, and solving problem instances of this class is provably less complex than solving general DEC-POMDPs. We end this chapter by a review of related work in Section 2.5.

## 2.1 The Reinforcement Learning Framework

Reinforcement learning (RL, Sutton and Barto, 1998) follows the idea that an autonomously acting agent obtains its behavior policy through repeated interaction with its environment on a trial-and-error basis.

In each time step an RL agent observes the environmental state and makes a decision for

# 2 Single- and Multi-Agent Reinforcement Learning

a specific action, which, on the one hand, may incur some immediate reward (also called reinforcement) generated by the agent's environment and, on the other hand, transfers the agent into some successor state. The agent's goal is not to maximize the immediate reward, but its long-term, expected reward. To do so, it must learn a decision policy that is used to determine the best action for a given state. Such a policy is a function that maps the current state the agent finds itself in to an action from a set of viable actions.

This idea of learning through interaction with the environment can be rendered by the following steps that must be performed by an RL agent (illustrated and refined in Figure 2.1):

1. The agent perceives an input state.

2. The agent determines an action using a decision-making function (policy).

3. The chosen action is performed.

4. The agent obtains a scalar reward from its environment (reinforcement).

5. Information about the reward that has been received for having taken the recent action in the current state is processed.

The basic reinforcement learning paradigm is to learn the mapping from states to actions only on the basis of the rewards the agent gets from its environment. By repeatedly performing actions and observing resulting rewards, the agent tries to improve and fine-tune its policy. The respective reinforcement learning method (step 5) specifies how experience from past interaction is used to adapt the policy. Assuming that a sufficient amount of states has been observed and rewards have been received, the optimal decision policy will have been found and the agent following that policy will behave perfectly in the particular environment. After this intuitive introduction, in the remainder of this section we will more formally introduce some central concepts of reinforcement learning.

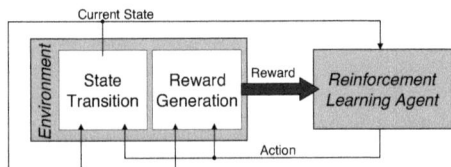

Figure 2.1: Schematic View on Reinforcement Learning: An Agent Interacts with its Environment

## 2.1.1 Markov Decision Processes

Basic reinforcement learning problems are usually formalized as Markov Decision Processes (Puterman, 2005).

## 2.1 The Reinforcement Learning Framework

**Definition 2.1** (Markov Decision Process, MDP)**.**
*A Markov decision process (MDP) is a 4-tuple $M = [S, A, p, r]$ where $S$ denotes the set of environmental states and $A$ the set of actions the agent can perform. Function $r : S \times A \times S \to \mathbb{R}$ denotes immediate rewards $\mathcal{R}_{ss'}^a = r(s, a, s')$ that arise when taking action $a \in A$ in state $s \in S$ and transitioning to $s' \in S$. The probability $\mathcal{P}_{ss'}^a = p(s, a, s')$ of ending up in state $s'$ when performing action $a$ in state $s$ is specified by the probability distribution $p : S \times A \times S \to [0, 1]$.*

For MDPs, the Markov property assures that the transition from $s$ to $s'$ and the corresponding payout of reward $\mathcal{R}_{ss'}^a$ depends only on the starting state $s$ and the action $a$ taken, not on the history of previous states and actions.

The behavior of the agent that interacts with its environment modelled as an MDP is specified in terms of a policy function that is defined as follows.

**Definition 2.2** (Policy (MDP case))**.**
*Given an MDP according to Definition 2.1, an agent's policy $\pi : S \times A \to [0, 1]$ specifies a probability distribution over actions, where $\pi(s, a)$ tells the probability of executing action $a$ in state $s$. In this general case, this mapping from state-action pairs to probabilities is called a* stochastic *policy.*

A special case of a general, stochastic policy is a *deterministic* one which, for a given state $s$, always picks the same action $a$ and, hence, is written as $\pi : S \to A$.

### 2.1.2 Learning Optimal Behavior

When interacting with the MDP, an RL agent passes through a sequence of states $s(t)$, that are coupled to one another by the transition probabilities $\mathcal{P}_{s(t),s(t+1)}^{a(t)}$, and receives a sequence of immediate rewards $r(t) = \mathcal{R}_{s(t),s(t+1)}^{a(t)}$. The goal of reinforcement learning is to maximize the expected value $\mathbb{E}[R_t|s_0, \pi]$ of the discounted sum

$$R_t = \sum_{k=0}^{\infty} \gamma^t r(t+k) \tag{2.1}$$

of rewards the agent obtains over time, where $\gamma \in [0, 1)$ is a factor that determines to which amount future rewards are discounted compared to immediate ones.

When conditioned on some specific state $s \in S$, the expected value mentioned is called the value $V^\pi$ of state $s$ under policy $\pi$ and is recursively defined as

$$\begin{aligned} V^\pi(s) &= \mathbb{E}[R_t|s_t = s, \pi] \\ &= \sum_{a \in A} \pi(s, a) \sum_{s' \in S} \mathcal{P}_{ss'}^a (\mathcal{R}_{ss'}^a + \gamma V^\pi(s')). \end{aligned} \tag{2.2}$$

Accordingly, function $V^\pi$ is called the *value function* for policy $\pi$.

In a similar manner, the value $Q^\pi(s, a)$ of a state-action pair is defined, which is meant to express the expected return after taking action $a$ in state $s$ and following policy $\pi$

subsequently:

$$Q^\pi(s,a) = \mathbb{E}[R_t|s_t = s, a_t = a, \pi]$$
$$= \sum_{s' \in S} \mathcal{P}^a_{ss'}(\mathcal{R}^a_{ss'} + \gamma V^\pi(s')) \quad (2.3)$$

In stochastic shortest path problems, the discount factor $\gamma$ can be safely set to 1 because the existence of a termination state $s^f$ is assumed. Once the agent reaches that state it remains there and receives no further rewards. Problems of that type are structured such that reaching $s^f$ is inevitable. Consequently, the goal is to reach the final state with maximal expected reward[1].

During learning the agent is in search of an optimal policy $\pi^\star$ that outperforms all other policies $\pi$ in being capable of accumulating as much reward as possible. It has been shown (Bertsekas and Tsitsiklis, 1996) that for each MDP there exists an optimal policy $\pi^\star$ such that for any policy $\pi$ it holds $V^{\pi^\star}(s) \geq V^\pi(s)$ for all states $s \in S$. If we assume to be in possession of an "optimal" value function $V^\star$, it is easy to infer the corresponding optimal (deterministic) policy by exploiting the value function greedily according to

$$\pi^\star(s) = \arg\max_{a \in A} \{ \sum_{s' \in S} \mathcal{P}^a_{ss'}(\mathcal{R}^a_{ss'} + \gamma V^\star(s')) \}.$$

### 2.1.3 On Actors and Critics

Considering the basic enumeration of steps a reinforcement learning agent performs (cf. the beginning of Section 2.1), the most interesting part lies probably in step 5. Here, the agent is faced with the task of processing recent experience to obtain an improved version of its behavior policy. In order to coarsely distinguish different approaches for achieving that, the *actor-critic architecture* can be employed (Witten and Corbin, 1973; Barto et al., 1983).

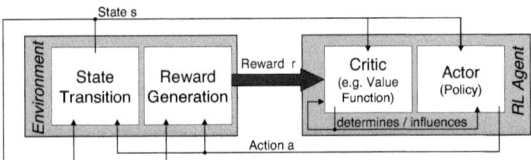

Figure 2.2: The Actor-Critic Architecture

In actor-critic methods it is assumed that there are separate memory structures for the action-taking part of the agent, i.e. the policy (actor), and a component, the critic, that monitors the performance of the actor and determines when and how the policy ought to be changed. The critic very often takes the form of a value function.

---

[1]Reinforcement learning literature uses the terms rewards and costs interchangeably where costs, intuitively, correspond to negative rewards. Hence, if the goal is to get to a terminal state under maximal reward, this could be formulated also as getting there under minimal costs.

Building upon the presence or absence of these two components, Heidrich-Meisner et al. (2007) distinguish between actor-only, actor-critic, and critic-only methods. Because the distinction between the former two is rather subtle, in this book, we adopt a slightly different view and differentiate between the following:

**Policy Search-Based Methods** comprise actor-only and actor-critic variants and are characterized by the fact that an explicit representation of an agent's policy is present.

**Value Function-Based Methods** correspond to critic-only methods in that they basically rely on learning a value function and on (implicitly) inducing a policy from this function.

As the work at hand deals with both types of learning systems, we provide some corresponding foundations in the next two subsections.

### 2.1.4 Policy Search-Based Reinforcement Learning

A policy search-based reinforcement learning agent employs an explicit representation of its behavior policy and aims at improving it by searching the space $\mathbb{P}$ of possible policies. This is feasible only, if it restricts its search space to a reasonable subset of $\mathbb{P}$. Typically, this is done by representing the agent's policy with a set of real-valued parameters $\theta$ such that the search is to be performed in the set of representable policies $\mathbb{P}_\theta \subset \mathbb{P}$ only. In so doing, a large portion of prior knowledge can be integrated into the learning task and, hence, the search complexity be heavily reduced.

Although this option seems appealing at first glance, it must be noted that incorporating large amounts of background knowledge is hard to accomplish, if, for example, the task at hand is not well enough understood for specifying an appropriate subclass of policies.

A prominent class of direct policy search methods (actor-only) are evolutionary reinforcement learning algorithms. Evolutionary algorithms are search algorithms based on the mechanics of natural selection, natural genetics, and the principle of the survival of the fittest (Holland, 1975). When combined with reinforcement learning, EA methods are primarily employed for searching in the space of policies (Moriarty et al., 1999), but may also be used as an enhancement, for example for evolving neural networks as actors (Chellapilla and Fogel, 1999; Metzen et al., 2008) or for improving the structure of the function approximation mechanism used (Stanley and Miikkulainen, 2002; Whiteson and Stone, 2006).

Policy gradient reinforcement learning methods (Williams, 1992; Baxter and Bartlett, 1999), that can be cast both as actor-only as well as actor-critic methods, rely on stochastic policies that are assumed to be differentiable with respect to their parameters $\theta$. They focus on the performance of the current policy

$$\begin{aligned} J(\pi_\theta) &= \mathbb{E}_\theta[\sum_t \gamma^t r(t)] \\ &= \sum_{s,s' \in S, a \in A} d^{\pi_\theta}(s) \pi(s,a) \mathcal{P}_{ss'}^a \mathcal{R}_{ss'}^a \end{aligned}$$

where $d^{\pi_\theta}(s) = \lim_{t \to \infty} Pr(s = s_t|s_0, \pi_\theta)$ is the starting state distribution of the process, and aim at improving the policy by following the ascent of this performance measure.

To do so, the performance gradient $\nabla_\theta J(\pi_\theta)$ with respect to the policy parameterization $\theta$ is estimated from interaction with the environment and the parameter vector $\theta$ is adjusted accordingly. Policy gradient methods explicitly allow the consideration of an approximate value function, i.e. a critic component, which basically supports a faster and more accurate determination of the gradient and, in so doing, improves learning performance. Besides a direct policy search approach, policy gradient-based reinforcement learning methods will be in the center of our interest in Chapter 4 where we develop and analyze multi-agent policy gradient algorithms for distributed scheduling problems.

### 2.1.5 Value Function-Based Reinforcement Learning

In contrast to policy search-based learning algorithms, the majority of research in the field of reinforcement learning has focused on value function-based methods, following the idea of first learning the optimal value function (cf. Section 2.1.2) for the task at hand and then derive the agent's policy from this value function.

So, the crucial question is, how to obtain the optimal state value function. To perform that task, dynamic programming methods, e.g. *value iteration* (Bellman, 1957), may be employed which converges under certain assumptions to the optimal value function $V^\star$ of expected rewards. Value iteration is based on successive updates of the value function for all states $s \in S$ according to

$$V_{k+1}(s) = max_{a \in A}\{\sum_{s' \in S} \mathcal{P}^a_{ss'}(\mathcal{R}^a_{ss'} + \gamma V_k(s'))\}, \tag{2.4}$$

where index $k$ denotes the sequence of approximated versions of $V$, until convergence to $V^\star$ is reached.

As a convenient shorthand notation, the operator $T$ is used to denote a mapping between cost-to-go functions according to Equation 2.4, i.e. $(TV_k)(s) = V_{k+1}(s)$ for all $s \in S$.

Speaking in terms of state-action values, i.e. Q values, using relation 2.3 and knowing that Bellman's equation can be interpreted as $V^\star(s) = \max_{a \in A(s)} Q^\star(s, a)$, the value iteration algorithm from above can be written as

$$Q_{k+1}(s,a) = \sum_{s' \in S} \mathcal{P}^a_{ss'}(\mathcal{R}^a_{ss'} + \gamma \max_{b \in A(s')} Q_k(s', b))$$

and, again, in operator notation this update scheme is abbreviated as $(HQ_k)(s,a) = Q_{k+1}(s,a)$ for all states and actions.

If there are no explicit transition model $p$ of the environment and of the reward structure $r$ available, *Q learning* is one of the reinforcement learning methods of choice to learn a state-action value function for the problem at hand (Watkins and Dayan, 1992). It updates directly the estimates for the values of state-action pairs according to

$$Q(s,a) = (1-\alpha)Q(s,a) + \alpha(\mathcal{R}^a_{ss'} + \gamma max_{b \in A(s')}Q(s',b)) \tag{2.5}$$

where $\alpha$ denotes the learning rate and where the successor state $s'$ and the immediate reward $\mathcal{R}^a_{ss'}$ are generated by simulation or by interaction with a real process. For the

## 2.1 The Reinforcement Learning Framework

case of finite state and action spaces where the Q function can be represented using a look-up table, there are convergence guarantees that say that Q learning converges to the optimal value function $Q^\star$, assumed that all state-action pairs are visited infinitely often and that $\alpha$ diminishes appropriately. Given convergence to $Q^\star$, the optimal policy $\pi^\star$ can be induced by greedy exploitation of $Q$ according to

$$\pi^\star(s) = \arg\max_{a \in A(s)} Q^\star(s, a).$$

As outlined, the determination of an optimal state value function is crucial to most reinforcement learning methods. Intending to show the functioning of some new RL technique in principle, one usually chooses typical benchmark problems (grid worlds) that are very limited in terms of state and action space size. In those cases, having to deal with only a finite number of states, it is feasible to store $V(s)$ for each single state $s \in S$ explicitly using a tabular function representation with $|S|$ table entries. However, interesting reinforcement learning problems have typically large, high-dimensional or even continuous state spaces, such that computational and/or memory limitations inhibit the use of a tabular function representation. Instead, the employment of a function approximator becomes inevitable. Thus, we have to turn to "suboptimal" methods that target the evaluation and approximation of the optimal value function $V^\star(s)$ or $Q^\star(s,a)$: We replace the optimal value function by an appropriate approximation $\tilde{V}(s,w)$, where $w$ determines the set of the approximator's parameters. In particular, our focus will be on the use of neuro-dynamic approaches, where multilayer perceptron (MLP) neural networks are used as approximation architecture (Bertsekas and Tsitsiklis, 1996) which have shown to be a as a suitable and robust technique to approximate $V^\star$.

Networks of this type are known to be capable of representing any function that is continuous and closed on a bounded set arbitrarily close (Hornick et al., 1989), and they feature good generalization capabilities. Although most theoretical results regarding the convergence behavior of RL algorithms do not generally hold in the presence of value function approximation, impressive results could be obtained in the past, for example Tesauro's milestone TD-Gammon (Tesauro, 1995).

Value iteration and Q learning, as outlined in this section, are just two prominent examples for a model-based and model-free reinforcement learning method, respectively. Research in RL, however, has generated a variety of methods that extend those well-known optimization techniques, aiming at applicability also in situations where large state spaces must be handled or where the absence of a transition model $p$ and reward model $r$ prevent the usage of simple value iteration. It is beyond the scope of this book to provide a comprehensive review on progress and state of the art in RL. Instead, in later chapters, we will selectively relate our work to other well-known reinforcement learning algorithms and, if needed, briefly describe them.

Value function-based reinforcement learning methods will be in the center of our interest in Chapter 5 where we develop and deploy multi-agent reinforcement learning algorithms for distributed scheduling problems.

## 2.2 From One to Many Agents

As pointed out by Littman (1994), no agent lives in a vacuum, but typically must interact with other agents to achieve its goals. Distributed artificial intelligence (Weiss, 1999) is the subfield of artificial intelligence that focuses on complex systems that are inhabited by multiple agents. The main goal of research in this area is to provide principles for the construction and application of multi-agent systems as well as means for coordinating the behavior of multiple independent agents (Stone and Veloso, 2000).

Taking the step from a single-agent to a multi-agent system brings about significant changes in several aspects:

- From an individual agent's point of view, the environment's dynamics can no longer be influenced by itself only, but also by other agents taking their actions. This superimposes with the uncertainty of the environment.

- The presence of other agents may require an agent to explicitly reason about their goals, actions, and to, eventually, coordinate appropriately.

- In addition to the single-agent temporal credit assignment problem, the multi-agent credit assignment problem arises, which corresponds to answering the question of whose agent's local action contributed how much to a (corporate) success.

- When multiple agents learn and, hence, adapt their behavior in parallel, each individual agent faces the difficulty of learning in a non-stationary environment. Consequently, convergence guarantees, such as the convergence of the Q learning mentioned in Section 2.1.5, may no longer hold.

In the following, we will approach these challenges from different sides. We start off by providing a coarse classification of multi-agent systems and also discuss their relevance for practical applications.

### 2.2.1 Cooperative and Non-Cooperative Multi-Agent Systems

The literature on multi-agent systems makes a distinction regarding the level of cooperativeness of the agents inhabiting the same environment (Tan, 1993). Much work has been devoted on systems with agents with competing or opposing goals, meaning that the reward functions of the agents are coupled in a complementary way: If one agent succeeds (e.g. gets a large reward), then the other one fails (e.g. gets a large negative reward). Such multi-agent systems have frequently been modelled as Markov Games (Filar and Vrieze, 1996), in particular as zero-sum games, and a number of corresponding multi-agent reinforcement learning algorithms have been suggested (Littman, 1994; Tesauro, 2003). Assuming full knowledge of the actions taken by the opponent agent, those algorithms are typically guaranteed to converge to optimal solutions. Moreover, extensions to those algorithms yielding faster learning progress were suggested while still featuring guaranteed (Bikramjit et al., 2001) or approximate convergence (Brafman and Tennenholtz, 2001).

By contrast, in the universal case of general multi-agent systems each agent possesses its own, arbitrary reward function which may be entirely unrelated to the rewards other agents receive. Fundamental work for this realm of problems, sometimes referred to as general-sum games, was done by Hu and Wellman (1998, 2003) who developed the Nash-Q learning algorithm with certain appealing theoretical properties (Bowling, 2000), but assumed an environment where each agent has full knowledge over the actions taken by other agents. Aiming at the reduction of necessary preconditions to be met for this algorithm to be applicable, Littman (2001) proposed the Friend-or-Foe Q learning algorithm, which, however, requires every other agent to be classified as cooperative or competitive a priori, and Greenwald and Hall (2003) developed correlated Q learning which generalizes Nash-Q and FoF-Q.

Completing the distinction started at the beginning of this section, we emphasize that the case of multi-agent systems with cooperative agents which collectively aim at achieving a common goal (so far, we briefly reviewed algorithms for competing agents only) is to be found very frequently in practical applications and, thus, of special importance. The book at hand targets cooperative multi-agent systems exclusively which is why in Section 2.3 we are going to focus in detail on such problems. Prior to this, we shortly highlight the relevance of multi-agent systems research for practice by paying tribute to a number of successful applications and relevant industrial problems.

### 2.2.2 Application Fields of Learning Multi-Agent Systems

There is a variety of application fields for multi-agent systems and, what is of special interest to us, multi-agent reinforcement learning systems. We here provide only a brief and, for sure, incomplete overview of practical applications for learning approaches used in the scope of cooperative multi-agent systems. Reinforcement learning and related approaches have been applied to optimize agent behavior in the scope of

- mobile telephony (e.g. for channel allocation (Singh and Bertsekas, 1997) or ad-hoc networks (Chang et al., 2004)),

- network technology (e.g. for data packet routing (Boyan and Littman, 1994; Ferra et al., 2003)),

- elevator control (e.g. for adaptive elevator dispatching (Barto and Crites, 1996)),

- energy and oil distribution (e.g. for electric power generation networks (Schneider et al., 1999) or for optimizing pipeline operations (Mora et al., 2008)),

- computing power management (e.g. for load balancing across servers (Tumer and Lawson, 2003), for distributed computing (Tesauro et al., 2005), or for constrained job dispatching in mainframe systems (Vengerov and Iakovlev, 2005)),

- autonomous robots (e.g. for robotic soccer (Riedmiller and Merke, 2003; Gabel et al., 2006; Riedmiller and Gabel, 2007) or for exploration of unknown territory (Low et al., 2008)) and computer games (e.g. for first-person shooter games (Smith et al., 2007)),

- rescue operations (e.g. for enabling units to decide independently which sites to search and secure (Settembre et al., 2008)),
- or surveillance and security tasks (e.g. for distributed sensor networks (Marecki et al., 2008) or for patrolling tasks (Santana et al., 2004) or for military applications (Pita et al., 2008)).

This numeration of mostly real-life applications misses another important area – the field of production planning and factory optimization, where machines may act independently with the goal of achieving maximal joint productivity – which shall move into the center of our interest in the successive chapters. Before we explore this application and related work in more detail (Chapter 3), we devote the following sections to providing a more fine-grained categorization of cooperative multi-agent systems as well as to the identification of an appealing model for learning in multi-agent systems.

## 2.3 Cooperative Multi-Agent Systems with Partial Observability

Speaking about different kinds of multi-agent systems, up to this point we assumed that each agent possesses full knowledge over the global system state, i.e. it is aware not just of its own *local* state, but also of the local states of all other agents as well. Moreover, decision-making for an agent is simplified, if it has full or at least partial information about the actions its teammates are taking. Especially in the light of practical applications, these assumptions appear rather unrealistic, which is why a more fine-grained classification of multi-agent systems with respect to the observation capabilities of the agents is required. In the following, we are going to focus on fully cooperative multi-agent systems and explore three specific dimensions along which the observability of the environment and of the other agents can be restricted. This discussion is accompanied by Figure 2.3 which gives a comprehensive overview of the corresponding frameworks and formal models.

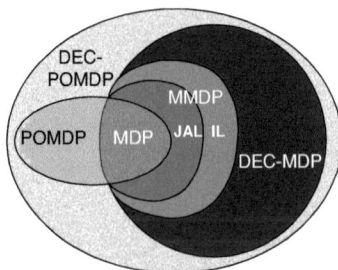

Figure 2.3: Overview of Modelling Frameworks for Handling Learning in Single- and Multi-Agents Systems

## 2.3 Cooperative Multi-Agent Systems with Partial Observability

### 2.3.1 The Multi-Agent Markov Decision Process Model

Boutilier (1999) introduced a straightforward extension of standard Markov decision processes to the multi-agent case. He assumes that a collection of agents controls the system by their individual actions: The effects of one agent's actions blend with those taken by others, while all agents share the same reward function.

**Definition 2.3** (Multi-Agent Markov Decision Process, MMDP).
*A multi-agent Markov decision process (MMDP) is a 5-tuple $M = [Ag, S, A, p, r]$ where $Ag = \{1, \ldots, m\}$ is a set of $m$ agents and $A = A_1 \times \cdots \times A_m$ is the set of joint actions to be executed by the agents. Each agent $i \in Ag$ has at its disposal its own set $A_i$ of individual, or local actions. The components $S$, $p$, and $r$ are as in Definition 2.1 except that functions $p$ and $r$ are now defined over joint actions $(a_1, \ldots, a_m) \in A$.*

An MMDP cannot be interpreted as a single-agent MDP by equating the entire team with a single agent, because in an MMDP the behavior of the system is influenced by simultaneously and independently acting agents – distributed decision-making and distributed learning take place. Consequently, because the agents are not inherently forced to harmonize their behaviors, it is the task of the designer of the learning algorithm to ensure that cooperative behavior arises.

In addition to the problem of coordinating with one another, also the question arises to which extent each agent is informed about the local actions taken by other agents. Boutilier (1999) distinguishes between two types of learners:

**Joint Action Learners (JAL)** aim at learning the value of their own actions in conjunction with their teammates' actions. To do so, they must know at each instant of time which action other agents have taken, which renders this approach even closer to the standard MDP case, although the challenge of inter-agent coordination persists.

A joint action learner processes experience tuples of the kind $\langle s, a, r, s' \rangle$ where $a$ corresponds to a joint action. Hence, when learning a Q function for example, values for the space of states and joint actions would have to be stored, which becomes quickly intractable with increasing numbers of agents, as the amount of joint actions grows exponentially with $|Ag|$.

**Independent Learners** may be aware of the existence of other agents in the environment, but get no hold of information regarding their actions. Insofar this case bears some resemblance for practical problems (Claus and Boutilier, 1998; Hu and Wellman, 1998; Riedmiller and Merke, 2003; Gabel and Riedmiller, 2006a). Experience tuples $\langle s, a_i, r, s' \rangle$ they process contain the local actions of agent $i$ only.

Finally, a key characteristic of the MMDP framework is that all agents, by definition, receive the same reward (which enforces cooperation), and that all agents are capable of fully observing the global system state. In particular, the latter strongly restricts the applicability of the multi-agent Markov decision process model since this assumption rarely holds in practice. Insofar, the MMDP model has paved the way towards defining more powerful modelling mechanisms that also cover partial state observability to which we

## 2 Single- and Multi-Agent Reinforcement Learning

will turn soon (Section 2.3.3). Summing up, the type of agents we will deal with in the remainder of this work can be characterized as independent learners that are obstructed by several further constraining restrictions.

### 2.3.2 Partially Observable Markov Decision Processes

In the real world, an agent may not be able to accurately observe the current state of its environment. This may be caused, for instance, by faulty or noisy sensors that disturb the true observation according to some probability distribution. Another reason may be that the agent's observation capabilities are restricted to certain features of the world state only, which results in that the agent perceives certain different states as identical. In order to handle problems such as uncertain observations or perceptual aliasing, the model of partially observable Markov decision processes (POMDPs, cf. Figure 2.3) has been introduced which extends the MDP model by considering observations and their probabilities of occurrence depending on the current state.

**Definition 2.4** (Partially Observable Markov Decision Processes, POMDP).
*A partially observable Markov decision process (POMDP) is a 6-tuple $M = [S, A, p, r, \Omega, O]$ where $S$, $A$, $p$, $r$ are defined as for an MDP (Definition 2.1). The set of possible observations the agent can make is denoted by $\Omega$, and $O : S \times A \times S \times \Omega \to [0, 1]$ is a probability distribution over observations where $O(s, a, s', o)$ denotes the probability that the agent observes $o \in \Omega$ upon executing action $a \in A$ in state $s \in S$ and transitioning to $s' \in S$.*

In the work at hand, (single-agent) POMDPs are no further investigated since our main interest is on multi-agent systems. We briefly refer to relevant and surveying literature (e.g. by Lovejoy (1991), Kaelbling et al. (1998), or Timmer (2008)).

### 2.3.3 The Framework of Decentralized Markov Decision Processes

We are interested in systems with full decentralization: The system is cooperatively controlled by a group of independent decision makers which do not have a global view of the system state and where none of the agents can influence the whole system state by its actions. Nevertheless, those agents share the same objectives and aim at maximizing the utility of the team as a whole. In order to study decentralized decision-making under the conditions mentioned, Bernstein et al. (2002) proposed the framework of decentralized partially observable Markov decision processes.

**Definition 2.5** (Decentralized Partially Observable Markov Decision Process). *A decentralized partially observable Markov decision process (DEC-POMDP) is defined as a 7-tuple $M = [Ag, S, A, p, r, \Omega, O]$ with*

- *$Ag = \{1, \ldots, m\}$ as the set of agents,*
- *$S$ as the set of world states*

## 2.3 Cooperative Multi-Agent Systems with Partial Observability

- $A = A_1 \times \ldots \times A_m$ as the set of joint actions to be performed by the agents ($a = (a_1, \ldots, a_m) \in A$ denotes a joint action that is made up of elementary actions $a_i$ taken by agent $i$),

- $p$ as the transition function with $p(s, a, s')$ denoting the probability that the system arrives at state $s'$ upon executing joint action $a$ in $s$,

- $r$ as the reward function with $r(s, a, s')$ denoting the reward for executing $a$ in $s$ and transitioning to $s'$,

- $\Omega = \Omega_1 \times \cdots \times \Omega_m$ as the set of all observations of all agents ($o = (o_1, \ldots, o_m) \in \Omega$ denotes a joint observation with $o_i$ as the observation for agent $i$),

- $O$ as the observation function that determines the probability $O(o_1, \ldots, o_m | s, a, s')$ that agent 1 through $m$ perceive observations $o_1$ through $o_m$ upon the execution of $a$ in $s$ and entering $s'$.

For DEC-POMDPs it is assumed that the states possess the Markov property. This means that the next global state $s'$ depends only on the current state $s$ and on the joint action $a$ executed, but not on the history of states and actions:

$$Pr(s_{t+1} | a_t, s_t, a_{t-1}, s_{t-1}, \ldots, a_0, s_0) = Pr(s_{t+1} | a_t, s_t).$$

The literature on DEC-POMDPs typically assumes that the world state can be factored into components relating to individual agents. In so doing, it is possible to separate features of the world state belonging to one agent from those that belong to others. Such a factorization is strict in the sense that a single feature of the global state can correspond to one agent only.

**Definition 2.6** (Factored DEC-POMDP).
*A factored, m-agent DEC-POMDP is defined such that the set $S$ of states can be factored into $m$ agent-specific components: $S = S_1 \times \cdots \times S_m$.*

We refer to the agent-specific components $s_i \in S_i$, $a_i \in A_i$, and $o_i \in \Omega_i$ as the local state (also denoted as the partial view), local action and local observation of agent $i$, respectively.

Concerning the degree of observability, a number of cases must be distinguished. If the observation function is defined in such a manner that each agent's local observation always truly identifies the global state, then the problem is said to be *fully observable*. In this case, which we will not consider any further, a DEC-POMDP effectively reduces to an MMDP (cf. Definition 2.3). The opposite extreme is when the agents do not obtain any information at all related to the current state. Non-observing agents may be modelled by letting $\Omega_i = \emptyset$ for all $i$. Between these two extreme cases, there are many nuances concerning the degree of partial state observability. A prominent special case – moving into our focus from now on – is when the joint observation of all agents collectively identifies the world state, which gives rise to the definition of DEC-MDPs:

## 2 Single- and Multi-Agent Reinforcement Learning

**Definition 2.7** (Decentralized Markov Decision Processes, DEC-MDP).
*A DEC-POMDP is said to be* jointly observable, *if the current state s is entirely determined by the amalgamation of all agents' observations: if $O(o|s, a, s') > 0$, then $Pr(s'|o) = 1$. A DEC-POMDP that is jointly observable is called a* decentralized Markov decision process *(DEC-MDP)*.

Apparently, a DEC-POMDP generalizes a POMDP by allowing for controlling the system state in a decentralized manner using a set $Ag$ of agents that each have a local view, and hence partial observability, on the system state only. In a similar manner, a DEC-MDP generalizes standard Markov decision processes.

Notice, however, although the combination of the agents' local observations tells the global system state, each agent individually may still be uncertain regarding its own local state $s_i$.

**Definition 2.8** (Locally Fully Observable DEC-MDP).
*A factored m-agent DEC-MDP has* local full observability, *if for all agents i and for all local observations $o_i$ there is a local state $s_i$ such that $Pr(s_i|o_i) = 1$.*

It is important to note that joint observability of a DEC-POMDP $M$ (i.e. it is a DEC-MDP) in combination with local full observability (i.e. fully known local states) do *not* imply that $M$ is fully observable (i.e. that it was an MMDP). As a matter of fact, in many practical multi-agent systems it holds that the observations of all agents, when combined, reveal with certainty the global state, and each such observation determines with certainty the partial view of an agent, but, none of the agents knows the complete state of the system – typically vast parts of the global state are hidden from each of the agents.

Figure 2.3 visualizes the relationships between the models defined so far and highlights how the decentralized frameworks generalize and subsume the single-agent ones. In accordance to the step towards decentralization taken, we may also define local and joint policies for decentralized Markov decision processes:

**Definition 2.9** (Local and Joint Policies, Deterministic and Reactive Local Policies).
*Given a decentralized (partially observable) Markov decision process according to Definitions 2.6/2.7, a* local policy $\pi_i$ *of agent i is defined as a mapping from local sequences of observations $\bar{o}_i = o_{i,1}, \ldots, o_{i,t}$ over $\Omega_i$ to a probability distribution over actions from $A_i$, i.e. $\pi_i : \overline{\Omega}_i \times A_i \to [0, 1]$.*

*A* joint policy $\pi$ *is defined as the tuple of m local policies, i.e. $\pi = \langle \pi_1, \ldots, \pi_m \rangle$. Additionally, we define two special cases of general, stochastic local policies:*

1. *A* deterministic *local policy, for a given observation sequence $\bar{o}_i$, always picks the same action $a \in A_i$ and, hence, is written as $\pi_i : \overline{\Omega}_i \to A_i$.*

2. *A* reactive *local policy $\pi_i$ ignores the observation sequence $\bar{o}_i$ and picks its action based solely on its most recent observation $o_i$. Hence, it is written as $\pi_i : \Omega_i \times A_i \to [0, 1]$.*

We note that a local policy for agent $i$ acting in a locally fully observable DEC-POMDP (Definition 2.8) is a mapping from sequences $\bar{s}_i \in \overline{S}_i$ of local states in agent $i$'s partial view to local actions, i.e. $\pi_i : \overline{S}_i \times A_i \to [0,1]$. This differs from locally non-fully observable DEC-POMDPs where local policies are defined on top of sequences of local observations.

In the remainder of this book, we primarily consider multi-agent systems with joint full observability (DEC-MDPs), since a factorization of the world state is natural in many practical and real-world problems. Right away, however, this ostensible simplification does not bring about a reduction of the complexity of the problems considered, as we will see in the next section.

### 2.3.4 The Price of Decentralization

Research on distributed systems has pointed out that decentralizing control and observability among agents has a significant impact on the complexity of solving a given problem. In particular, it is well-known that solving optimally a DEC-POMDP (and, equally, a DEC-MDP) is NEXP-complete[2], even in the benign case of two agents: A non-deterministic Turing machine requires $O(2^{p(n)})$ time, with $p(n)$ as an arbitrary polynomial and problem size $n$, and unlimited space for deciding such a problem (Bernstein et al., 2000).

On the one hand, this stands in clear contrast to the bounds for MDPs (P-completeness, i.e. decidable by a deterministic Turing machine within $O(p(n))$ time, (Papadimitriou and Tsitsiklis, 1987)) and for POMDPs (PSPACE-completeness, i.e. decidable by a deterministic Turing machine using $O(p(n))$ space, (Mundhenk et al., 2000)). On the other hand, this increase in complexity can be elucidated when considering that the size of an agent's local policy grows exponentially with the number of observations it can make, because a local policy is a mapping from local observation histories to actions. Therefore, there are $|A_i|^{|\Omega_i|^T}$ possible policies, if we denote by $T$ the time horizon considered. In order to solve the DEC-MDP at hand optimally, each agent $j$ would be required to build a belief-state MDP for each one of agent $i$'s local policies. The number of states in any of these belief-state MDPs would be exponential in the number $|\Omega_j|$ of observations agent $j$ can make, as it must consider its observation histories. Although this argument is informal (for a formal reduction proof see Bernstein et al. (2000)), it hints to the doubly exponential complexity of this class of problems.

In this book, we address the intricacy of learning and acting in general decentralized Markov decision processes by the following two orthogonal approaches.

**Exploitation of Problem Structure** Many practical problems exhibit some structure whose exploitation may ease the task of finding solutions. In the subsequent section (Section 2.4), we are going to identify a subclass of general DEC-MDPs that features regularities in the way the agents interact with one another. For this class, we can show that the complexity of optimally solving an instance of such a DEC-MDP is provably lower than the general problem. Moreover, this class is of high relevance for many real-world applications. Correspondingly, in Chapter 3 we show how it can be employed for problems from the application field of production planning.

---
[2] Also referred to as NEXPTIME-complete or NPEXP-complete, see Bovet and Crescenzi (1994) for details on complexity classes.

**Approximate Solutions** Even though a lower complexity class may be entered by sticking to certain subclasses of the general problem, the computational complexity of a problem instance of such a DEC-(PO)MDP may be still so high that optimally solving it is infeasible. This holds, in particular, when intending to tackle problems of larger size that are of relevance for practical problems. Given these facts, our goal will be not to develop optimal solution algorithms that are applicable to small problems only, but to look for techniques capable of quickly obtaining approximate solutions in the vicinity of the optimum.

For this task, we will develop and utilize various model-free reinforcement learning approaches in subsequent chapters. In contrast to offline planning algorithms which aim at finding optimal solutions in a model-based manner, reinforcement learning allows for employing independently learning agents and, hence, for a full decentralization of the problem.

## 2.4 Decentralized Markov Decision Processes with Changing Action Sets

The enormous computational complexity of solving decentralized cooperative Markov decision processes conflicts with the fact that real-world tasks do typically have a considerable problem size. In this section, we identify a new subclass of general DEC-MDPs whose complexity is provably lower (NP-hard) and discuss its characteristics (Gabel and Riedmiller, 2008a).

### 2.4.1 On Transition Dependencies

Speaking about interactions between agents, one must distinguish between independent local actions (also called non-interacting) and dependent local actions (also called interacting ones). Independent actions influence the local state and observation of the agent only which is executing those actions, whereas the local observations and state transitions of its teammates remain unaffected. By contrast, dependent local actions interfere with other agents and have an influence on their local observations and transitions. We formalize this concept by defining transition and observation independence.

**Definition 2.10** (Transition and Observation Independence).
*A factored m-agent DEC-MDP is called (a)* transition-independent *and (b)* observation-independent, *if there exist functions (a) $p_1, \ldots, p_m$ and (b) $O_1, \ldots, O_m$ such that*

(a) $p(s'_i|(s_1, \ldots, s_m), (a_1, \ldots, a_m), (s'_1, \ldots, s'_{i-1}, s'_{i+1}, \ldots, s'_m)) = p_i(s'_i|s_i, a_i)$

(b) $O(o_i|(s_1, \ldots, s_m), (a_1, \ldots, a_m), (s'_1, \ldots, s'_m), (o_1, \ldots, o_{i-1}, o_{i+1}, \ldots, o_m))$
$= O_i(o_i|s_i, a_i, s'_i)$

*for all agents $i = 1, \ldots, m$.*

## 2.4 Decentralized Markov Decision Processes with Changing Action Sets

Thus, transition independence implies that the new local state of agent $i$ depends only on its previous local state and its recent local action. Consequently, the transition function $p$ of the multi-agent system's underlying MDP can be factored such that

$$p(s'_1,\ldots,s'_m|(s_1,\ldots,s_m),(a_1,\ldots,a_m)) = \Pi_{i=1}^m p_i(s'_i|s_i,a_i).$$

Similarly, observation independence means that the observation an agent $i$ sees depends exclusively on $i$'s recent and new local state as well as on its action taken.

Clearly, transition and observation independence represent rather strong assumptions on a multi-agent system, implying that the agents act very much decoupled from one another and never interfere.

**Definition 2.11** (Reward Independence).
*A factored $m$-agent DEC-MDP is called* reward-independent, *if there is a local reward function $r_i : S_i \times A_i \times S_i \to \mathbb{R}$ for all $i \in Ag$ as well as a function $R : \mathbb{R}^m \to \mathbb{R}$ that amalgamates the global reward value from the local ones, such that maximizing each $r_i$ individually also yields a maximization of $R$. Thus,*

$$r((s_1,\ldots,s_m),(a_1,\ldots,a_m),(s'_1,\ldots,s'_m)) = R(r_1(s_1,a_1,s'_1),\ldots,r_m(s_m,a_m,s'_m)))$$

*and for all $i \in Ag$*

$$r_i(s_i,a_i,s'_i) \leq r_i(s_i,a'_i,s''_i)$$
$$\Leftrightarrow R(r_1,\ldots,r_i(s_i,a_i,s'_i),\ldots,r_m) \leq R(r_1,\ldots r_i(s_i,a'_i,s''_i)\ldots,r_m).$$

If, in addition to transition and observation independence, a locally-fully observable DEC-MDP is also reward-independent, then it actually decomposes into $m$ separate local MDPs with independent learners and, hence, corresponds to an MMDP (cf. Equation 2.3, P-complete). Subsequently, we will drop the assumptions of transition, observation, and reward independence, presume some characteristics of the agents' local action sets, and, in so doing, define a class of DEC-MDPs that is considerably more general than MMDPs, but does not feature the NEXP-hard complexity of general DEC-MDPs.

### 2.4.2 Variable Action Sets and Partially Ordered Transition Dependencies

The set of actions available to an agent may very well be non-stationary. For example, if an agent has to accomplish some task that can be decomposed into several subtasks, then, when thinking of a subtask as an action, there is no more cause to perform some subtask again, if it has already been done. More specifically, in the application domain of job-shop scheduling that we will target throughout this book (starting in Chapter 3), jobs are composed of a number of operations that have to be processed in a specific order on different machines. Here, it is natural to think of these operations as the actions and, logically, their availability depends on whether all predecessor operations have already been processed or not.

Generalizing this idea, we define what it means for an agent to dispose of changing action sets.

## 2 Single- and Multi-Agent Reinforcement Learning

**Definition 2.12** (DEC-MDP with Changing Action Sets).
*An m-agent DEC-MDP with factored state space $S = S_1 \times \cdots \times S_m$ is said to feature changing action sets, if the local state of agent i is fully described by the set of actions currently selectable by that agent: $s_i = A_i \setminus \{\alpha_0\}$.*

*The set of all potentially executable actions of agent i is denoted by $\mathcal{A}_i = \{\alpha_0, \alpha_{i1} \ldots \alpha_{ik}\}$ such that it holds $A_i \subset \mathcal{A}_i$ and[3] $S_i = \mathcal{P}(\mathcal{A}_i \setminus \{\alpha_0\})$.*

*Here, $\alpha_0$ represents a null action that does not change the state and is always in $A_i$. Subsequently, we abbreviate $\mathcal{A}_i^r = \mathcal{A}_i \setminus \{\alpha_0\}$ and let $\mathcal{A}^r = \cup_{i=1}^m \mathcal{A}_i^r$.*

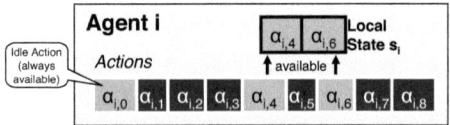

Figure 2.4: DEC-MDPs with Changing Action Sets: Local State of Agent $i$

Figure 2.4 shows an agent whose set of all available actions contains eight elements, $\alpha_{i,1}$ through $\alpha_{i,8}$, plus the null action $\alpha_0$. However, only two actions, $\alpha_{i,4}$ and $\alpha_{i,6}$, are currently at disposal by agent $i$. Correspondingly, the local state of this agent is $s_i = A_i(s_i) = \{\alpha_{i,4}, \alpha_{i,6}\}$

Concerning state transition dependencies, one can distinguish between dependent and independent local actions. While the former influence an agent's local state only, the latter may additionally influence the state transitions of other agents. As pointed out, our interest is in non-transition independent scenarios. In particular, we assume that an agent's local state can be affected by an arbitrary number of other agents, but that an agent's local action affects, besides its own local state, the local state of maximally one other agent.

**Definition 2.13** (DEC-MDP with Partially Ordered Transition Dependencies).
*A factored m-agent DEC-MDP with changing action sets is said to have partially ordered transition dependencies, if there exist functions $\sigma_i$ for each agent i with*

1. $\sigma_i : \mathcal{A}_i^r \to Ag \cup \{\emptyset\}$ *and*

2. $\forall \alpha \in \mathcal{A}^r$ *the directed graph $G_\alpha = (Ag \cup \{\emptyset\}, E)$ with $E = \{(j, \sigma_j(\alpha)) | j \in Ag, \sigma_i(\alpha) \neq \emptyset\}$ is acyclic and contains only one directed path*

*and it holds*

$$Pr(s'_i|s, (a_1 \ldots a_m), (s'_1 \ldots s'_{i-1}, s'_{i+1} \ldots s'_m))$$
$$= Pr(s'_i|s_i, a_i, \{a_j \in \mathcal{A}_j | i = \sigma_j(a_j), j \neq i\})$$

*The influence exerted on another agent always yields an extension of that agent's action set: If $\sigma_i(\alpha) = j$, i takes local action $\alpha$, and the execution of $\alpha$ has been finished, then $\alpha$ is added to $A_j(s_j)$, while it is removed from $A_i(s_i)$.*

---
[3]By $\mathcal{P}(X)$, we denote the power set of set $X$.

## 2.4 Decentralized Markov Decision Processes with Changing Action Sets

That is, the dependency functions $\sigma_i$ indicate whose other agents' states are affected when agent $i$ takes a local action. Figure 2.5 exemplarily shows the dependency functions $\sigma_2$ for agent 2 and $\sigma_3$ for agent 3 (in part). For the ease of illustration and notation, this example assumes that $\mathcal{A}_i = \{\alpha_0, \ldots, \alpha_8\}$ for all $i \neq j$ (so we can drop index $i$, when referring to local actions $\alpha_{i,k}$). By definition, the idle action $\alpha_0$ does not affect any other agent, $\sigma_2(\alpha_0) = \emptyset$. Equally, do action $\alpha_3$, $\alpha_5$, and $\alpha_8$, when executed by agent 2. While these three actions influence the local state of agent 2 solely, the remaining actions of agent 2's action set $\mathcal{A}_2$ do have an impact on other agents' state transitions. For example, action $\alpha_2$ influences – when executed by agent 2 – besides its own local state also the local state of agent 4, i.e. $\sigma_2(\alpha_2) = 4$.

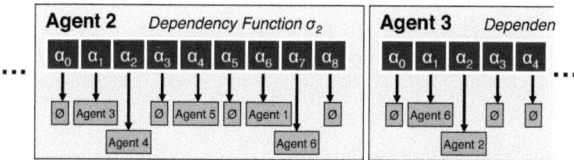

Figure 2.5: Exemplary Dependency Functions

Furthermore, condition 2 in Definition 2.13 implies that for each local action $\alpha$ there is a total ordering of its execution by the agents. While these orders are total, the global order in which actions are executed is only partially defined by that definition and subject to the agents' policies.

Figure 2.6 tries to illustrate this fact by further developing the running example from the preceding figures. For three elementary actions from $\mathcal{A}^r$, it shows the corresponding dependency graphs. Apart from recognizing that all graphs $G_\alpha$ shown are acyclic with one directed path, one may also read the values of the dependency functions from this illustration: For example, the fact that the execution of action $\alpha_4$ by agent 2 influences the local state of agent 5 (i.e. $\sigma_2(\alpha_4) = 5$) corresponds to having an arc between agent 2 and agent 5 in the dependency graph $G_{\alpha_4}$.

The following lemma states that for the problems considered any local action may appear only once in an agent's action set and, thus, may be executed only once.

**Lemma 1.** *In a factored m-agent DEC-MDP with changing action sets and partially ordered transition dependencies it holds: $\forall i \in Ag, \forall \alpha \in \mathcal{A}_i^r, \forall t \in \{1 \ldots T\}$ and $\forall \bar{s}_i = (s_i^1 \ldots s_i^t)$: If there is a $t_a$ $(1 \leq t_a < T)$ with $\alpha \in s_i^{t_a}$ and a $t_b$ $(t_a < t_b \leq T)$ with $\alpha \notin s_i^{t_b}$, then $\forall \tau \in \{t_b \ldots T\} : \alpha \notin s_i^\tau$.*

*Proof.* By contradiction. Let $t_a$, $t_b$ and $\alpha \in \mathcal{A}_i^r$ with $\alpha \in s_i^{t_a}$, $\alpha \notin s_i^{t_b}$ as required by the lemma. Then, there is an $f \in Ag \cup \{\emptyset\}$ such that $\sigma_i(\alpha) = f$, and hence edge $(i, f) \in E$. Assume there is a $t_c > t_b$ with $\alpha \in s_i^{t_c}$. Then, there is an agent $j \in Ag$ such that $\sigma_j(\alpha) = i$, and hence edge $(j, i) \in E$. Since graph $G_\alpha$ is acyclic, it follows that the time when $\alpha$ joins $s_f$ is after the time that $\alpha$ leaves $s_j$, i.e. $t_a > t_c$. Contradiction. □

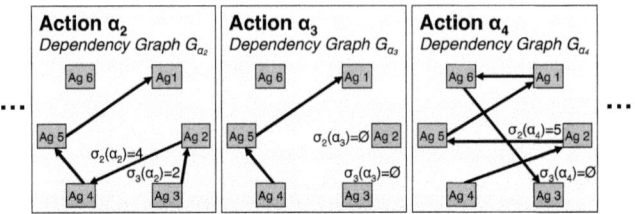

Figure 2.6: Exemplary Dependency Graphs

### 2.4.3 Implications on Complexity

While it has been proven that the complexity of solving general DEC-MDPs is NEXP-complete (Bernstein et al., 2000; Goldman and Zilberstein, 2004), a number of authors has tried to identify subclasses of the general problem that yield lower (e.g. NP-complete) complexity (for example, Becker et al. (2004b) or Goldman and Zilberstein (2003)). As shown by Shen et al. (2006), a key factor that determines whether the problem complexity is reduced to NP-completeness is whether the agents' histories can be compactly represented. In particular, there must exist an encoding function $Enc_i : \overline{\Omega}_i \to E_i$ such that

1. a joint policy[4] $\pi = \langle \pi_1 \ldots \pi_m \rangle$ with $\pi_i : E_i \to \mathcal{A}_i$ is capable of maximizing the global value and

2. the encoding is polynomial, meaning that $|E_i| = O(|S|^{c_i})$.

For our class of factored $m$-agent DEC-MDPs with changing action sets and partially ordered transition dependencies we can define an encoding that adheres to both of these conditions, thus showing that those problems are NP-complete.

The interaction history of a DEC-MDP is the sequence of local observations $\overline{o}_i \in \overline{\Omega}_i$ which in our case correspond to the history of local states $\overline{s}_i \in \overline{S}_i = \times_{t=1}^{T} S_i$, since we assume local full observability (where $T$ refers to the finite problem horizon and $S_i = \mathcal{P}(\mathcal{A}_i^r)$ as before).

**Definition 2.14** (Interaction History Encoding).
*Given a local action set $\mathcal{A}_i = \{\alpha_0 \ldots \alpha_k\}$ and a history $\overline{s}_i = (s_i^1, \ldots, s_i^t) \in \overline{S}_i$ of local states of agent $i$, the encoding function is defined as $Enc_i : \overline{S}_i \to E_i$ with $E_i = C_{\alpha_1} \times \cdots \times C_{\alpha_k}$ and $C_{\alpha_j} = \{0, 1, 2\}$. And it holds $Enc_i(\overline{s}_i) = (c_{i,\alpha_1} \ldots c_{i,\alpha_k}) \in E_i$ with*

$$c_{i,\alpha_j} = \begin{cases} 0 & \text{if } \nexists \tau \text{ with } \alpha_j \in s_i^\tau \\ 1 & \text{if } \alpha_j \in s_i^t \\ 2 & \text{else} \end{cases}$$

---

[4] We focus on deterministic policies here, though the argument could be easily extended to stochastic policies $\pi_i : E_i \times \mathcal{A}_i \to [0, 1]$.

## 2.4 Decentralized Markov Decision Processes with Changing Action Sets

Basically, the encoding guarantees that each agent knows whether some local action has not yet been in its action set, is currently in its action set, or had been in its action set. The encoding idea is visualized in Figure 2.7: Here, agent $i$ has currently two actions at its disposal (part a). Part b shows the preceding interaction history (sequence of recent local states) storing which is exponential in the state space size and doubly exponential in $k = |\mathcal{A}_i|$. As can be seen, actions $\alpha_7$ as well as $\alpha_2$ were previously executed while $i$'s local state has also been influenced by other agents such that other actions, $\alpha_4$ and $\alpha_6$, became available. The encoding (part c) provides a way of representing agent $i$'s history in a compact manner. Proving that this encoding is capable of representing the optimal policy and showing that it is a polynomial encoding, we can conclude that the subclass of DEC-MDPs we identified is NP-complete.

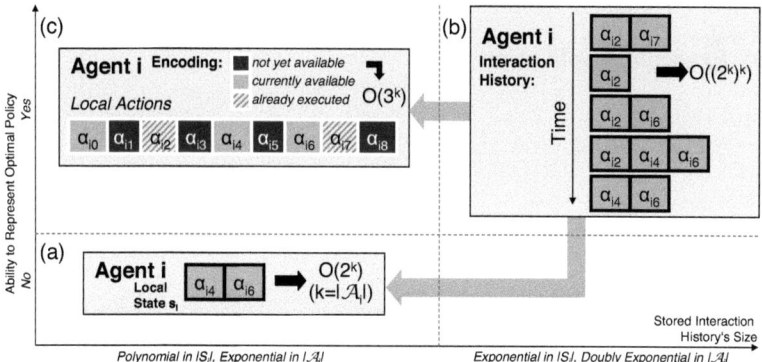

Figure 2.7: Interaction History and Encoding Function

**Lemma 2.** $Enc_i$ *provides a polynomial encoding of agent $i$'s observation history.*

*Proof.* Because of $S_i = \mathcal{P}(\mathcal{A}_i^r)$, it holds $|S_i| \in O(2^k)$, if $|\mathcal{A}_i| = k$. The encoding $E_i$ provided by $Enc_i$ is of size $|E_i| \in O(3^k)$. Since $O(3^k) = O((2^n)^{log_2 3})$, this encoding is polynomial in the size of $S_i$, i.e. $|E_i| \in O(|S_i|^{c_i})$ with constant $c_i = log_2 3$. □

**Lemma 3.** $Enc_i$ *provides an encoding of agent $i$'s observation history such that a joint policy $\pi = \langle \pi_1 \ldots \pi_m \rangle$ with $\pi_i : E_i \rightarrow \mathcal{A}_i$ is sufficient to maximize the global value.*

*Proof.* Let $\pi = \langle \pi_1 \ldots \pi_m \rangle$ be a set of local policies for a factored $m$-agent DEC-MDP with changing action sets and partially ordered transition dependencies. Because each local action can be performed only once by each agent (Lemma 1), $\pi$ defines a total execution order over the elements of $\mathcal{A}_i^r$ for all agents $i$. Thus, each local policy must allow for realizing any possible such order. Since $E_i$ contains the historical information which actions $\alpha \in \mathcal{A}_i^r$ have already been executed, each $\pi_i$ can select the next $\alpha_x \in \mathcal{A}_i$ to be executed depending on $e_i$: If $\alpha_x \in s_i$ ($s_i$ as current action set), i.e. $e_{i,x} = 1$, then that action is taken, otherwise ($\alpha_x$ is not yet in the action set, $c_{i,x} = 0$) the null action $\alpha_0$ is selected. □

## 2 Single- and Multi-Agent Reinforcement Learning

Because deciding a polynomially encodable DEC-MDP is NP-complete (Shen et al., 2006), solving a factored $m$-agent DEC-MDP with changing action sets and partially ordered transition dependencies is so, also.

**Theorem 1.** *Solving a factored $m$-agent DEC-MDP with changing action sets and partially ordered transition dependencies is NP-complete.*

*Proof.* This follows directly from the fact that deciding a polynomially encodable DEC-MDP is NP-complete (Shen et al., 2006) and from Lemma 2 and 3. □

### 2.4.4 Example Applications

Factored DEC-MDPs with changing action sets and partially ordered transition dependencies may seem to represent a small set of domains, but it turns out that the class of problems we address is quite general. This class of problems involves cooperative agents, each having its local view and its local set of tasks to perform, with specific structured interactions and dependencies between them. Those dependencies can model the locking of a shared resource as well as temporal enabling constraints, both of which arise frequently in practical applications.

It should be noted that distributed problem solving in practice is often characterized by a factored system state description where the agents base their decisions on local observations. Also, our assumptions that local actions may influence the state transitions of maximally one other agent and that any action has to be performed only once are frequently fulfilled. Sample real-world applications include scenarios from manufacturing, production planning, or assembly line optimization, where typically the production of a good involves a number of processing steps that have to be performed in a specific order. In a factory, however, usually a variety of products is assembled concurrently, which is why an appropriate sequencing of single operations is of crucial importance for overall performance. Thus, the class of factored $m$-agent DEC-MDPs with changing action sets and partially ordered transition dependencies covers a variety of such scheduling problems, for example flow-shop and job-shop scheduling scenarios (Pinedo, 2002). We will focus in very detail on these types of problems in the next chapter.

Our framework also allows for modelling problems where actions are to be executed multiple times (yet, a finite number of times), if we add a virtual action for each required execution of the considered action. Therefore, practical problems with recirculating tasks can also be modelled. Beyond that, a big portion of supply chain problems where complex items are assembled through a series of steps are covered.

Other practical application domains to which our model is of relevance include network routing (e.g. sub-task of determining the order of forwarding packets), railway traffic control (e.g. task of allowing trains to pull into the station via agent-based track switches), or workflow management.

## 2.5 Related Work on Learning in Cooperative Multi-Agent Systems

Research on reinforcement learning in cooperative multi-agent systems distinguishes, similarly as in the single-agent case (cf. Section 2.1.2), between model-based and model-free approaches. If the agents are aware of the probabilities of state transitions and observations, they can contemplate about expected transitions and rewards and aim at finding an optimal policy. In the literature, this way of solving decentralized Markov decision processes in a model-based manner is sometimes called offline planning and somehow contrasted with (model-free) reinforcement learning.

### 2.5.1 Alternative Frameworks for Distributed Control

Besides decentralized partially observable Markov decision processes (DEC-POMDPs, Definition 2.5), also a number of alternative modelling frameworks have been introduced recently which all aim at formalizing the problem of decentralized control of multiple agents. Nearly contemporaneously to Bernstein et al.'s (2000) DEC-POMDPs, Pynadath and Tambe (2002a) suggested the multi-agent team decision problem (MTDP) which contains the assumption of perfect recall, i.e. assumes that any agent has full access to all the information it received (observation and reward histories as well as received communicative messages). As shown by Seuken and Zilberstein (2008), both, the DEC-POMDP and MTDP model, are equivalent in terms of expressiveness as well as in terms of complexity. Additionally, frameworks have been proposed that do explicitly model inter-agent communication, e.g. the DEC-POMDP-COM model (Goldman and Zilberstein, 2003) or the COM-MTDP model (Pynadath and Tambe, 2002b). However, Goldman and Zilberstein (2004) has shown that the explicit consideration of communicative actions does not change the respective model's expressiveness.

Other frameworks that have been developed or utilized for handling distributed control problems include interactive partially observable Markov decision processes (I-POMDPs, Gmytrasiewicz and Doshi, 2005) and partially observable identical payoff stochastic games (POIPSGs, Peshkin et al., 2000), as well as partially observable stochastic games (POSGs, Fudenberg and Tirole, 1991) which allow for private reward function and, hence, non-cooperative behavior. A thorough discussion of these models, which both explicitly build upon and extend the POMDP model, is beyond the scope of this work.

### 2.5.2 Optimal Solution Algorithms

Model-based algorithms that aim at finding the optimal solution of a general decentralized Markov decision process are limited by the extreme (NEXP-complete) intricacy of these problems, and can be applied only for very small problem sizes (typically no more than two agents involved). Furthermore, they must assume that the problems under consideration are characterized by a finite problem horizon (by contrast, infinite horizon problems are undecidable as shown by Madani et al., 2003).

The most straightforward approach is to enumerate all possible joint policies, evaluate them using the model of the system, and choose the best one. Although this idea is sound, since there exists an optimal deterministic joint policy for any general DEC-POMDP for problems with a finite horizon (Oliehoek et al., 2008a), it becomes quickly intractable as the number of possible joint policies grows doubly exponentially with the horizon of the problem.

Therefore, most of the algorithms suggested so far rely on some kind of policy search technique. Multi-agent A* (Szer et al., 2005) is a heuristically guided policy search method that performs an A*-like search through the space of partially defined policies. It prunes away parts of the policy search space that are for sure worse than the best performing policy found till then, utilizing an admissible heuristic function. The first optimal solution method for general DEC-POMDPs was suggested by Hansen et al. (2004), employing dynamic programming techniques to incrementally build up optimal joint policies (starting from the last decision stage of the problem). In order to counteract the doubly exponential growth of the set of $k$-step-to-go policy trees for each agent, the authors suggest to eliminate sub-trees of policies using a test based on linear programming. Subsequently, several extensions to this dynamic programming approach for DEC-POMDPs have been proposed, among those optimal algorithms (e.g. point-based dynamic programming, Szer and Charpillet, 2006) as well as approximate ones.

### 2.5.3 Subclasses with Reduced Problem Complexity

While the approaches mentioned before address the general problem, another body of related work aims at exploiting particular structural or independence properties of the problems under consideration. In so doing, a number of specific subclasses with lower complexity than NEXP-completeness could be identified. For example, Becker et al. (2004b) introduce the class of transition independent DEC-(PO)MDPs, in which no agent affects state transitions of other agents and where the agents are tied together by a so-called joint reward structure. The authors show that solving transition independent DEC-MDPs is NP-complete and Wu and Durfee (2006) suggest a solution method based on mixed integer linear programming. Networked distributed POMDPs (Nair et al., 2005) drop the assumption of joint observability (Definition 2.1), but still rely on full transition independence and additionally assume a spatial neighborhood relation between agents. A different approach is taken by Goldman and Zilberstein (2003) who allow the agents to exchange their full local states with all other agents from time to time. The resultant class of DEC-MDPs with this kind of synchronizing communication protocol could also been shown to be in NP.

While these subclasses are quite distinct, our identified class of factored $m$-agent DEC-MDPs with changing action sets and partially ordered transition dependencies features some commonalities with event-driven DEC-MDPs (Becker et al., 2004a), where the latter, however, focus on systems with two agents and assume less regularities in the inter-agent dependencies. Also related to our approach is the work by Oliehoek et al. (2008b), who try to exploit localities of interaction by formalizing the propagation of inter-agent dependencies through time and, in so doing, building up interaction graphs for each state.

Other special cases that have been discussed in the literature, but bear less relevance to our work include goal-oriented DEC-MDPs (Goldman and Zilberstein, 2004), DEC-

MDPs with time and resource constraints (Beynier and Mouaddib, 2005, 2006; Marecki and Tambe, 2007), or DEC-MDPs with either non-interacting or interdependent, but fully communicated states (Spaan and Melo, 2008).

### 2.5.4 Search for Approximate Solutions

Even though a lower complexity class may be entered by sticking to certain subclasses of the general problem, the computational complexity of a problem instance of such a DEC-(PO)MDP may be still so high that optimally solving it is infeasible. Therefore, finding approximate solutions seems to be a more viable option. However, as shown by Rabinovich et al. (2003), finding $\varepsilon$-optimal history-dependent joint policies for both DEC-POMDPs and DEC-MDPs is still NEXP-complete. Consequently, when speaking about approximate solutions, it typically holds:

- Calculating the approximate solution must be tractable, i.e. should be accomplished in polynomial time.

- Finding the global optimum is sacrificed in order to lower complexity and to be able to handle larger-scale problems.

- While $\varepsilon$-optimal solutions provide a guarantee for finding a joint policy that is within an $\varepsilon$ of the optimal one, in the AI community it is generally accepted that approximate algorithms provide no performance guarantees at all (e.g. no bound on the quality of the solution with respect to the optimum).

**Model-Based Approximative Solution Approaches**

Substantially relying on the knowledge of the full model, joint equilibrium-based search for policies (Nair et al., 2005) guarantees to find at least a locally optimal joint policy: Here, each agent's local policy is a best response to the policies employed by the remaining agents (Nash equilibrium). This method relies on alternating maximization, a technique where a single agent's policy is improved while all other local policies are fixed and, after some time, another agent is chosen to optimize its policy in the same manner. This process is repeated until convergence to a local optimum is reached.

Seuken and Zilberstein (2007b,a) introduced memory-based dynamic programming, a technique that employs heuristics to detect those parts of the space of possible beliefs regarding the global state, that seem relevant to be further investigated. For this bounded set of interesting belief states established dynamic programming techniques are employed for searching through the space of potential joint policies, evaluating them, and selecting the best one.

Oliehoek et al. (2008a) infer approximate Q value functions for DEC-POMDPs, use them as admissible heuristics in the context of multi-agent A* search as well as payoff functions for a series of Bayesian games as which they model the decentralized decision-making problem.

Other model-based approaches make use of finite-state controllers (FSCs) for the purpose of representing policies, a technique that is also well applicable to infinite-horizon

DEC-POMDPs. For instance, Bernstein et al. (2005) assume and optimize controllers of fixed size, i.e. with a fixed number of internal states, which results in the controllers finding themselves in the same internal state for different observation sequences and, hence, suboptimal action choices. Amato et al. (2007) also utilize finite state controllers of fixed size, but employ the model for defining a quadratically constrained linear program whose solution yields an optimal fixed-size controller. While FSCs are stochastic in general, Szer and Charpillet (2005) suggest an optimal best-first search algorithm for approximately solving infinite-horizon DEC-POMDPs, searching in the space of deterministic controllers of fixed size.

**Model-Free Approximative Solution Approaches**

A further body of related work aims at learning approximate solutions for decentralized multi-agent systems without the support of a model. These model-free methods are of higher relevance to us, since in the following chapters we also do not assume knowledge of the model for the problems considered.

Because, as argued, even for small size problems, model-based algorithms can fail to compute optimal policies or near-optimal approximations thereof due to, for example, lack of memory space, model-free multi-agent reinforcement learning approaches have established as a promising alternative. Despite the fact that the nice convergence properties of several (single-agent) reinforcement learning algorithms are traded off against tractability, various impressive approaches and applications have been presented in the literature.

Addressing the inherent challenges an independently learning agent faces (such as the multi-agent credit assignment problem, the task of inter-agent coordination, and the problem of partial state observability, cf. Section 2.2), a number of approaches assume and exploit independencies between subsets of the agents and, in so doing, tackle certain subclasses of general DEC-POMDPs (similarly, but less formally as in Section 2.5.3). For example, agents may be arranged in a structure of local neighborhoods where they can exchange freely value function estimates (Schneider et al., 1999; Chades and Bouteiller, 2005) or local policies (Yagan and Tham, 2007) with one another or where they are granted full access to the local observations and actions of all other neighbors (Laumonier and Chaib-draa, 2007).

This kind of information sharing might be made explicit, but may also be modelled by the use of communication. The latter approach is pursued, for instance, by Aras et al. (2004) where agents repeatedly exchange different types of messages to reveal certain local information to their teammates. The use of communication is also necessary, if the interaction between the agents is modelled with the help of coordination graphs (Kok and Vlassis, 2004). In order for coordinated behavior to be established several sweeps over the graph structure are required which corresponds to passing multiple messages between agents (Guestrin et al., 2002).

In order to address the challenge of local and, hence, partial observability several authors rely on policy gradient approaches, which have turned out to provide robust results in model-free POMDP settings. For example, multi-agent network routing problems are tackled using distributed policy gradient algorithms where the task is modelled as an episodic (Peshkin and Savova, 2002) or non-episodic (Tao et al., 2001) problem. Yagan and Tham (2007) enhance this approach by additionally applying finite state controllers for coping with potentially large observation-action history sequences.

Finally, a number of authors try to combat the multi-agent credit assignment problem by investigating and crafting different variants of agent-specific reward (or utility) functions, an approach that sometimes is referred to as reward shaping. For example, the Collective Intelligence framework (Wolpert and Tumer, 2002; Tumer et al., 2002; Agogino and Tumer, 2005) aims at adapting reward functions and forming clusters of agents to build multi-agent systems in which global welfare is maximized. Bagnell and Ng (2005) point out that learning based solely on global rewards is generally compromised insofar as more interaction with the environment is required when compared to local rewards, although defining the latter requires significantly more prior knowledge on the problem. Alternatively, Chang et al. (2003) propose a filtering method that is geared to extract an approximation of a local reward signal from the global one for a model-free learning scenario.

As already indicated, model-free solution approaches to decentralized Markov decision processes are also in the center of our interest. In this spirit, in the next chapter we will present an application domain from the realm of production planning for which we will argue that finding solutions using model-free multi-agent reinforcement learning approaches is an appropriate and promising idea.

# 3 Distributed Scheduling Problems

Scheduling and sequencing have emerged as crucial decision-making tasks to support and enhance the productiveness of manufacturing enterprises as well as logistics and service providers. The general goal of scheduling is to allocate a limited number of resources to outstanding tasks over time such that one or several objectives are optimized. Here, resources and tasks, respectively, depict abstractions of real-world entities that may take very different forms depending on the application scenario considered. For example, in warehousing they may correspond to storages and stored goods, in personell management to employees and working shifts, in computer program scheduling to CPU cores and processes, and, most prominently, in manufacturing production control to machines on a working floor and operation steps of a production process.

Choosing scheduling problems as the application domain to be targeted in the scope of this work was motivated by various reasons.

- Scheduling is a decision-making process that is of high importance to various real-world problems. It plays a crucial role in many production and manufacturing systems as well as in the context of supply chain management, logistics, or information processing.

- As we will show, many scheduling problems suggest a natural formulation as distributed decision-making tasks. Hence, the employment of learning multi-agent systems represents an evident approach. Furthermore, given the well-known inherent intricacy of solving scheduling problems, decentralized approaches for solving them may yield a promising option.

- Scheduling is a highly active research field. Therefore, over the years numerous benchmark problems of varying sizes have been proposed and have been frequently used to compare different solution approaches. To this end, we can benefit from employing standardized benchmarks for the purpose of experimental evaluation and, hence, avoid the need of designing artificial, hand-crafted test problems.

The dissertation at hand focuses in depth on one particular type of scheduling problems, for which the argument made above holds in every respect, namely *job-shop scheduling*. We emphasize, however, that although the remainder of this work particularly targets job-shop scheduling problems (JSSPs), the methods and algorithms we develop may be employed for different multi-agent problems and, thus, for different kinds of scheduling problems as well. Among those are, for example, single-machine models, flow-shop problems, and even flexible shop problems (Pinedo, 2002).

We start this chapter by providing the necessary foundations and notation used for job-shop scheduling problems (Section 3.1). In Section 3.2, we focus on how to cast JSSPs

# 3 Distributed Scheduling Problems

as multi-agent learning problems and, in so doing, create the link between the concepts concerning decentralized decision-making introduced in Chapter 2 and our scheduling application domain. We finish this chapter (Section 3.3) with related work on solving JSSPs and, thus, bridge to the learning methods for cooperative multi-agent systems that we will present in Chapters 4 and 5.

## 3.1 Foundations

Job-shop scheduling problems are among the most studied scheduling problems. A great deal of research has been invested into the development of JSSP solution methods both in the Operations Research and artificial intelligence communities. Subsequently, we outline the main characteristics of this class of scheduling problems.

### 3.1.1 The Classical Job-Shop Scheduling Problem

In many application scenarios from manufacturing, production planning, or assembly line optimization, the production of a good involves a number of processing steps that have to be performed in a specific order. Obviously, the decision to further process some good can only be taken, if all preceding steps are finished. In a factory, however, it is usually the case that not just a single, but a variety of products is assembled concurrently. Therefore, an appropriate sequencing and scheduling of individual processing operations is crucial, if maximal joint productivity is desired.

Problems of that type are formalized as *classical* job-shop scheduling problems. Intuitively, in job-shop scheduling $n$ jobs (sometimes called tasks) must be processed on $m$ resources (sometimes called machines) in a pre-determined order. Each job $j$ consists of $\nu_j$ operations that are denoted as $o_{j,1} \ldots o_{j,\nu_j}$ and that have to be handled on a certain resource $\varrho(o_{j,k})$ for a specific duration $\delta(o_{j,k})$. A job is finished after completion of its last operation (completion time $c_j$).

**Definition 3.1** (Job-Shop Scheduling Problem).
*A job-shop scheduling problem is defined by a 6-tuple $\mathbb{J} = [\mathcal{J}, \mathcal{R}, \mathcal{O}, \iota, \varrho, \delta, \mathcal{T}]$ where $\mathcal{J} = \{1, \ldots, n\}$ is the set of jobs, $\mathcal{R} = \{r_1, \ldots, r_m\}$ is the set of resources, and $\mathcal{O}$ is the set of operations that the jobs consist of. Function $\iota : \mathcal{O} \to \mathcal{J}$, $\varrho : \mathcal{O} \to \mathcal{R}$, and $\delta : \mathcal{O} \to \mathbb{N}^+$ tell for each operation to which job it belongs, on which resource it must be processed, and how many time steps its processing takes, respectively.*

*Furthermore, $\mathcal{T} = \{\mathcal{T}_1, \ldots, \mathcal{T}_n\}$ denotes a set of strict total orders where $\mathcal{T}_j$ is defined over the set $\mathcal{O}_j = \{o \in \mathcal{O} | \iota(o) = j\}$ of operations in job $j$. The number of operations of job $j$ is denoted as $\nu_j = |\mathcal{O}_j|$, and the total order $T_j$ ensures that for each $o \in \mathcal{O}_j$ there is a $k \in \{1, \ldots, \nu_j\}$ such that $o$ can be bijectively referenced by $o_{j,k}$ with $(o_{j,k}, o_{j,l}) \in \mathcal{T}_j$ for all $k < l$.*

Each resource may process one job at a time, and all required processing times are assumed to be integer. Moreover, it may be assumed $\varrho(o_{j,k}) \neq \varrho(o_{j,l})$ for all $j \in \{1, \ldots, n\}$ and for all $k \neq l$. This characteristic of JSSPs says that recirculation is not allowed, i.e. that each job has to be processed maximally once on each resource. Often, it is also assumed that each job has to be processed exactly once on each resource, which implies that $\nu_j = m$.

Figure 3.1 shows a $6 \times 6$ (6 resources and 6 jobs, $m = n = 6$) problem instance from Muth and Thompson (1963). In this example, job 2 must first be processed on resource 2 for 8 time units, then go to resource 3 for 5 time steps, and so on. Resource 3 may start processing with job 1, 3, or 5.

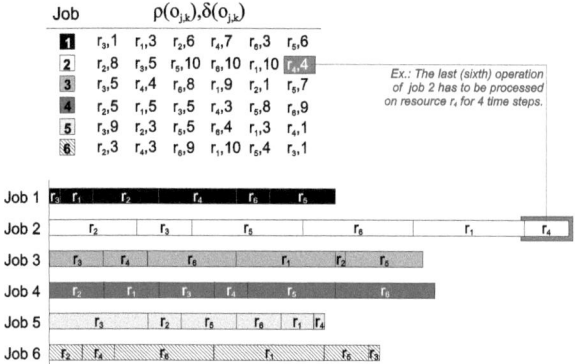

Figure 3.1: Example of a Classical Job-Shop Scheduling Problem (problem instance FT6)

A schedule for a given problem is denoted by the set of starting times of all operations and it is called *feasible*, if it fulfills all constraints regarding the resources (no more than one job can be executed at a time) and regarding the precedences of the jobs' operations (operation orders must be adhered to). In the scope of this book, a number of classes of schedules are of interest which are based on assumptions that are made with respect to what the scheduler is or is not allowed to do during generating a schedule:

**Semi-Active Schedules:** A feasible schedule is called semi-active, if an earlier completion of any operation could be achieved only by changing the processing order on at least one resource.

**Active Schedules:** A feasible schedule is called active, if a change to the processing orders on the resources does not result in finishing at least one operation earlier and no operation later.

**Non-Delay Schedules:** A feasible schedule is called non-delay, if no resource is kept idle, while there is at least one operation waiting for further processing on that resource.

The relation between these classes is visualized in Figure 3.2. It is well known, that the optimal schedule for a given job-shop scheduling problem is to be found in the set of active schedule, but not necessarily in the class of non-delay schedules.

Speaking about optimality, scheduling objectives to be optimized all relate to the completion times of the jobs. An objective function is considered to be a regular performance

3 Distributed Scheduling Problems

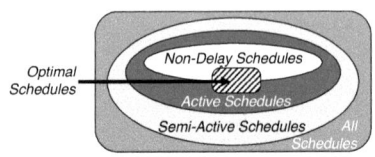

Figure 3.2: Classes of Schedules: A job-shop scheduling problem's optimal solution is to be found within the class of active schedules, but not necessarily among the non-delay schedules.

measure, if it is non-decreasing in $c_j$. In practice, for example, it may be desired to minimize the jobs' due date violations or the number of jobs that are late. For job-shop scheduling problems, however, the objective function most frequently used aims at minimizing maximum makespan $C_{max}$, which corresponds to the length of the resulting schedule:

$$C_{max} = \max_{j=1,\ldots,n} \{c_j\}.$$

Finding the optimal schedule for a classical job-shop scheduling problem is known to be NP-hard (Pinedo, 2002; Brucker and Knust, 2005). It means that, unless P=NP, there exists no polynomial time algorithm that finds the optimal solution of a given JSSP instance. Emphasizing the intricacy of job-shop scheduling, Lawler et al. (1993) proved that there is even no good polynomial time approximation of an optimal scheduling algorithm, if $C_{max}$ is the optimization criterion.

The Gantt chart in Figure 3.3 shows an optimal solution for the 6×6 benchmark FT6 depicted in Figure 3.1. Here, the schedule's makespan is 55, i.e. $C_{max} = 55$. In fact, the optimal solution sketched is a delay schedule: After 6 processing steps resource $r_3$ remains idle and waits until (at $t = 8$) it can process the second operation of job 2 ($o_{2,2}$), although it immediately could have continued to process job 5 which had been waiting at resource $r_3$ from the beginning on.

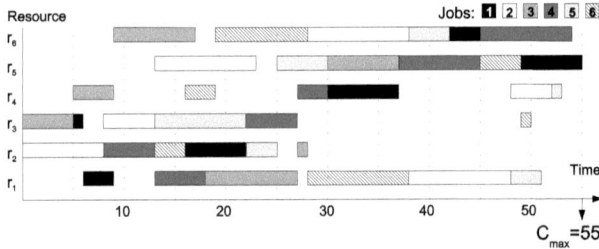

Figure 3.3: Visualization of an Optimal Schedule for the Scheduling Problem FT6 (cf. Figure 3.1) Using a Gantt Chart

## 3.1.2 The Disjunctive Graph Model

The disjunctive graph model, that was developed by Roy and Sussmann (1964), can be used to formulate job-shop scheduling problems and to represent schedules. A disjunctive graph $G = (V, C, D)$ is a mixed graph consisting of a set $V$ of nodes, a set $C$ of directed edges (conjunctions), and a set $D$ of undirected edges (disjunctions). With regard to a given job-shop scheduling problem $\mathbb{J}$, a disjunctive graph is defined as follows:

- The set $V$ of nodes represents the set $\mathcal{O}$ of all operations of $\mathbb{J}$. Moreover, $V$ contains two additional nodes corresponding to two virtual operations $o_s$ and $o_e$: The source node $o_s$ represents the start of the schedule and the sink node $o_e$ its end. Thus, $V = \mathcal{O} \cup \{o_s, o_e\} = \{o_s, o_{1,1}, \ldots, o_{1,\nu_1}, \ldots, o_{n,1}, \ldots, o_{n,\nu_n}, o_e\}$.

- The set $C$ of conjunctions represents the precedence constraints of the operations within the same job, i.e. it reflects the strict total orders $\mathcal{T}_j$ for each $j$. $C$ contains a directed edge $o_{j,k} \rightarrow o_{j,k+1}$ for each $j \in \mathcal{J}$ and $k \in \{1, \ldots, \nu_j - 1\}$. Additionally, there are arcs $o_s \rightarrow o_{j,1}$ and $o_{j,\nu_j} \rightarrow o_e$ for all $j$.

- Each directed edge $o \rightarrow o'$ is weighted with the processing time of its starting node's operation, i.e. with $\delta(o)$, where $\delta(o_s) = 0$ is assumed.

- The set $D$ of disjunctions reflects the different orders according to which jobs may be executed on the different resources. It comprises undirected edges $o - o'$ between all pairs of operations that must be processed on the same machine, i.e. $D = \{o - o' | \varrho(o) = \varrho(o'), o \neq o', \iota(o) \neq \iota(o')\}$.

- Each undirected edge $o - o'$ is associated with a pair of processing times $(\varrho(o), \varrho(o'))$.

Intuitively, conjunctive edges can be seen as a mean to enforce that in a feasible schedule any operation cannot be started before its predecessor operation has not been finished. Similarly, the disjunctions reflect the constraint that in a feasible schedule on any resource a new operation cannot be started before the resource has finished processing another operation, i.e. each resource can process only one job at a time.

If we fix a direction for the disjunctive edges from $D$, then the resulting graph corresponds to a schedule for the given problem. While a set $\mathcal{S}$ of fixed directions is called a selection, a selection is denoted as complete, if for each edge from $D$ a direction has been settled. Moreover, a selection is called consistent, if and only if the resulting graph $G(\mathcal{S}) = (V, C \cup \mathcal{S})$ corresponding to selection $\mathcal{S}$ is acyclic.

On the one hand, given a consistent and complete selection $\mathcal{S}$ of disjunctive edges with fixed directions, it is straightforward to construct the corresponding feasible schedule with earliest starting times for all operations (earliest start schedule, ESS). When fixing the direction of an edge $o - o'$ to $o \rightarrow o'$ or $o' \rightarrow o$, respectively, then the respective edge weight $\varrho(o)$ or $\varrho(o')$ becomes relevant. The makespan of the schedule corresponding to $G(\mathcal{S})$ is equal to the length of a longest path from $o_s$ to $o_e$ (also called critical path).

On the other hand, any feasible schedule specifies an order according to which all operations $o$ with $\varrho(o) = r_i$ are processed on resource $r_i$ ($i = 1, \ldots, m$), which in turn induces a complete and consistent selection. Using a regular objective function (like $C_{max}$, as

## 3 Distributed Scheduling Problems

we do), a complete and consistent selection always exists that corresponds to an optimal schedule, which is why it suffices to focus on schedules only that are defined by complete consistent selections in disjunctive graphs (Brucker and Knust, 2005).

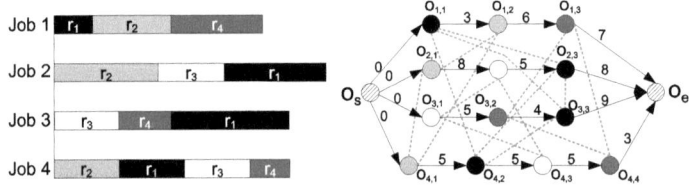

Figure 3.4: A Small JSSP and its Corresponding Disjunctive Graph Model: Operations and nodes are colored according to the resources on which they must be processed. Conjunctions are shown in black color, disjunctions in dashed gray. No selection is made, i.e. all disjunctive edges have no fixed direction. For readability, disjunctive edge weights are omitted.

### 3.1.3 Classical Benchmark Problems

Over the years, numerous benchmark instances of job-shop scheduling problems have been proposed and have been frequently used to compare different solution approaches. They were provided by different authors and strongly vary in their problem sizes. A compilation of important benchmarks is provided by the Operations Research Library (Beasley, 2005).

An example for such a benchmark problem is the FT6 instance mentioned in Section 3.1.1. Most of them are, of course, much more complex and certain examples remained unsolved for decades. For other, larger-scale instances there is still no optimal solution known. We will make extensive use of those scheduling benchmark problems, when evaluating the algorithms we are going to propose in the next chapters.

## 3.2 Multi-Agent Job-Shop Scheduling

In scheduling theory, a distinction between *predictive* production scheduling (also called analytical scheduling or offline-planning) and *reactive* scheduling (or online control) is made (Blazewicz et al., 1993). A predictive scheduler assumes complete knowledge over all tasks to be accomplished, e.g. over entire production floors, tries to take all constraints into account and aims at finding a globally coherent solution that maximizes an objective function. By contrast, reactive scheduling can be regarded as an approach to making local scheduling and dispatching decisions based on a shorter planning horizon and on less problem knowledge, and as an approach where decisions are taken during execution (which is why it is sometimes referred to as online production control). In particular, it allows for a larger degree of independence between the entities involved in the decision process.

In this section, we argue that reactive scheduling allows for adopting a multi-agent perspective on scheduling problems. We discuss advantages and drawbacks of this approach and show that job-shop scheduling problems are well suited to be modelled using the framework of decentralized Markov decision processes with changing action sets and partially ordered transition dependencies that we proposed in Section 2.4. In so doing, we provide a sound foundation for employing multi-agent reinforcement learning techniques for production management and, particularly, scheduling problems.

### 3.2.1 Discussion of Distributed Scheduling

Manufacturing environments have for a long time been known to require distributed solution approaches for finding high-quality solutions, because of their intrinsic complexity and, possibly, due to an inherent distribution of the tasks involved (Wu et al., 2005). Accordingly, the natural distributed character of multi-agent systems may be exploited in a purposive manner when addressing scheduling problems. This has led to the application of a number of agent-based approaches to resource allocation and scheduling problems, including market- and auction-based systems, hybrid systems extending standard scheduling methods by agent techniques, as well as reinforcement learning techniques.

Using a multi-agent system for a scheduling task corresponds to performing reactive scheduling as both inherently support decentralized decision-making. On the one hand, this may be considered detrimental since a globally optimal solution cannot be yielded by doing reactive scheduling. By contrast, predictive schedulers – benefiting from full knowledge of the entire scheduling problem to be solved – typically attain the optimum. On the other hand, however, the list of potential merits of performing reactive scheduling using a multi-agent approach is not to be underestimated:

- Reactive scheduling features the advantage of being able to react to unforeseen events (like a machine breakdown) appropriately without the need to do complete re-planning.

- Operations Research has to the bigger part focused on predictive scheduling and yielded numerous excellent centralized algorithms capable of finding an optimal schedule in reasonable time. This works well for small and medium-sized JSSPs; for larger problem dimensions, however, computational complexity makes the application of centralized algorithms infeasible.

- The application of a centralized predictive scheduling algorithm in practice may require enormous communication between the entities involved in the problem. Hence, limited bandwidth or communication delays may render the use of a centralized approach impossible.

- Many resource allocation or scheduling problems are intrinsically distributed in nature, meaning that there exists no central authority with all the necessary information to formulate and solve a centralized optimization problem. Stated from a practical point of view, a centralized control cannot always be instantiated, which is

3 Distributed Scheduling Problems

why a decentralized problem interpretation using a multi-agent system may at times be of higher impact to real-world applications.

- By combining partial solutions as provided by the agents involved for local problems they are facing, it may be feasible to find a more efficient solution for the global problem. Although in this way generally only near-optimal results will be obtained – as job-shop scheduling problems are known to be tightly interacting and non-decomposable (Liu and Sycara, 1997) – that kind of divide and conquer strategy may be of high efficiency.

- Further advantages that can be claimed for taking a multi-agent approach to (practical) manufacturing and scheduling problems include increased flexibility, reduced costs, fault tolerance, and the fact that multi-agent systems may facilitate humans and agent-based machinery to work together as colleagues.

Baker (1998) survey in detail the utility of multi-agent systems for factory control, resource allocation, and scheduling problems. While they name various different ways for utilizing agents for distributed production control (e.g. for deciding what and how much to produce, or when to release jobs into a factory), we subsequently focus on their use for deciding upon job routing and operation sequencing. In so doing, we associate to each of the $m$ resources an agent $i$ that locally decides which operation to process next. How this idea relates to DEC-MDP with changing action sets is the subject of the next section.

### 3.2.2 Job-Shop Scheduling as Decentralized Markov Decision Process

Job-shop scheduling problems are well suited to be modelled using factored $m$-agent DEC-MDPs with changing action sets and partially ordered transition dependencies (see Definitions 2.12 and 2.13). We reinforce this claim by showing how the components of a JSSP can be employed to construct a corresponding DEC-MDP.

**Factored World State** The world state of a job-shop scheduling problem $\mathbb{J}$ (cf. Definition 3.1) can be factored: We assume that to each of the resources one agent $i$ is associated that observes the local state at its resource and controls its behavior. Consequently, we have as many agents as resources in the JSSP ($|Ag| = |\mathcal{R}| = m$).

**Local Full Observability** The local state $s_i$ of agent $i$, hence the situation of resource $r_i$, is fully observable (thus, local observations and local states are identical). Additionally, the composition at all resources fully determines the global state of the scheduling problem. Therefore, the system is jointly observable, i.e. it is a DEC-MDP (cf. Definition 2.7).

**Factored Actions** Actions correspond to the starting of jobs' operations (job dispatching). So, a local action of agent $i$ reflects the decision to further process one particular job (more precisely, the next operation of that job) out of the set $A_i \subseteq \mathcal{J}$ of jobs currently waiting at $r_i$.

## 3.2 Multi-Agent Job-Shop Scheduling

**Changing Action Sets** If actions denote the dispatching of waiting jobs for further processing, then, apparently, the set of actions available to an agent varies over time, since the set of jobs waiting at a resource changes. While $A_i \subseteq \mathcal{A}_i^r$ denotes[1] the currently available actions for agent $i$, $\mathcal{A}_i^r$ is the set of all potentially executable actions for this agent.

Hence, $\mathcal{A}_i^r$ corresponds to the set of jobs $j$ that contain an operation $o_{j,k}$ which must be processed on resource $r_i$, i.e. $\varrho(o_{j,k}) = i$. Accordingly, it holds

$$\mathcal{A}^r = \cup_{i=1}^m \mathcal{A}_i^r = \mathcal{J}. \tag{3.1}$$

Furthermore, the local state $s_i$ of agent $i$ is fully described by the changing set of jobs currently waiting at resource $r_i$ for further processing. Thus, $s_i = A_i$ and $S_i = \mathcal{P}(\mathcal{A}_i^r)$ as required by Definition 2.12.

**Transition Dependencies** DEC-MDPs with changing action sets and partially ordered transition dependencies feature some structure according to which agents' local action may exert influence on the local state of other agents. After having finished an operation of a job, this job is transferred to another resource, which corresponds to influencing another agent's local state by extending that agent's action set.

**Dependency Functions** The order of resources on which a job's operations must be processed in a JSSP is given by the set of strict total orders $\mathcal{T}$. These orders imply that, upon executing a local action by processing a job's next operation, the local state of maximally one further agent is influenced. Let $\alpha \in A_i$ (and so $\alpha \in \mathcal{J}$) be the job whose current operation $o_{\alpha,k}$ is processed by resource $r_i$. Then, after having finished $o_{\alpha,k}$, the action set $A_i$ of agent $i$ is adapted according to $A_i := A_i \setminus \{\alpha\}$, whereas the action set of agent $i' = \varrho(o_{\alpha,k+1})$ is extended ($A_{i'} := A_{i'} \cup \{\alpha\}$).

Therefore, we can define the dependency functions $\sigma_i : \mathcal{A}_i^r \rightarrow Ag \cup \{\emptyset\}$ (cf. Definition 2.13) for all agents $i$ (and resource $r_i$, respectively) as

$$\sigma_i(\alpha) = \begin{cases} \varrho(o_{\alpha,k+1}) & \text{if } \exists k \in \{1, \ldots, \nu_\alpha - 1\} : \varrho(o_{\alpha,k}) = i \\ \emptyset & \text{else} \end{cases} \tag{3.2}$$

where $k$ corresponds to the number of that operation within job $\alpha$ that has to be processed on resource $r_i$, i.e. $k$ such that $\varrho(o_{\alpha,k}) = i$.

**Dependency Graphs** Given the no recirculation property (Section 3.1.1) and the definition of $\sigma_i$ (Equation 3.2), the directed graph $G_\alpha$ from Definition 2.13 is indeed acyclic and contains only one directed path.

For job-shop scheduling problems with recirculation the definition of $G_\alpha$ must be slightly extended; this depicts a rather technical change and is beyond our scope. For the no recirculation case we are addressing we prove the properties of $G_\alpha$ in the following proposition.

---
[1] Recall that $\mathcal{A}_i^r = \mathcal{A}_i \setminus \{\alpha_0\}$ where $\alpha_0$ represents an idle action, cf. Definition 2.12.

## 3 Distributed Scheduling Problems

**Proposition 1.**
*Given a job-shop scheduling problem $\mathbb{J}$ without recirculation (cf. Definition 3.1) and the definition of the dependency functions $\sigma_i$ (cf. Equation 3.2), the dependency graphs $G_\alpha$ for all $\alpha \in \mathcal{A}_i^r = \mathcal{J}$ (cf. Definition 2.13) are acyclic and contain only one directed path.*

*Proof.* We show the acyclicity of $G_\alpha = (Ag, E)$ with

$$E = \{(j, \sigma_j(\alpha)) | j \in Ag, \sigma_j(\alpha) \neq \emptyset\} \quad (3.3)$$

by contradiction. Assume there is a cycle of length $c > 1$ in $G_\alpha$, consisting of nodes $v_1, \ldots, v_c \in Ag$ and directed edges $(v_1, v_2), \ldots, (v_{c-1}, v_c), (v_c, v_1) \in E$. Since $(v_x, v_{x+1}) \in E$ and, hence, $v_{x+1} = \sigma_{v_x}(\alpha)$ (for $1 \leq x \leq c-1$), and, consequently, $\sigma_{v_x}(\alpha) \neq \emptyset$, there exists a $k_x \in \{1, \ldots, \nu_\alpha - 1\}$ such that $\varrho(o_{\alpha,k_x}) = v_x$. Because also $(v_c, v_1) \in E$ and, hence, $v_1 = \sigma_{v_c}(\alpha)$ and, in particular, $\sigma_{v_c}(\alpha) \neq \emptyset$, there also exists a $k_c \in \{1, \ldots, \nu_\alpha - 1\}$ such that $\varrho(o_{\alpha,k_c}) = v_c$. So, we have $\varrho(o_{\alpha,k_1}) = v_1$ as well as $\sigma_{v_c}(\alpha) = \varrho(o_{\alpha,k_c+1}) = v_1$. By definition, $k_i < k_j$ for all $i < j$, and $k_c > k_1$. Because of the latter there are two operations within job $\alpha$ ($o_{\alpha,k_1}$ and $o_{\alpha,k_c+1}$) that both must be processed on the same resource (on $v_1$). This contradicts to the assumption of a JSSP without recirculation from above.

Next, we prove that there exists only one directed path in $G_\alpha$ for every $\alpha \in \mathcal{A}_i^r = \mathcal{J}$. Obviously, Equation 3.3 implies $|E| \leq |Ag|$ and

$$(i, j) \in E \Leftrightarrow \exists k \in \{1, \ldots, \nu_\alpha - 1\} : \varrho(o_{\alpha,k}) = i.$$

By definition of $\sigma_i$ (Equation 3.2), it also holds $j = \sigma_i(\alpha) = \varrho(o_{\alpha,k+1})$. Let $k \in \{1, \ldots, \nu_\alpha - 1\}$ and denote $i_k = \varrho(o_{\alpha,k})$. Then, it holds $(i_k, \sigma_{i_k}(\alpha)) \in E$ and, again, by definition of $\sigma_{i_k}$

$$e_k := (i_k, \sigma_{i_k}(\alpha)) = (\varrho(o_{\alpha,k}), \varrho(o_{\alpha,k+1})) \in E.$$

Thus, the set of all $e_k \in E$ (for $k \in \{1, \ldots, \nu_\alpha\}$) forms a path of length $\nu_\alpha$. □

Obviously, the ensemble of agents interacting with the DEC-MDP corresponding to a JSSP have to strive for the same goal, namely for optimizing the objective function of the scheduling problem. Consequently, a crucial precondition to enable the agents to learn to make sophisticated scheduling decisions is that the global reward function of the DEC-MDP coincides with the overall objective of scheduling. If, for example, the goal of scheduling is to minimize tardiness (due date violations), then it may be appropriate to allot negative rewards, if one or more jobs violate their deadlines. As indicated in Section 3.1.1, in this work our scheduling objective is to minimize the makespan $C_{max}$ of the resulting schedule. From scheduling theory it is known that the makespan of a schedule is minimized, if as many resources as possible are processing jobs concurrently and if as few as possible resources with queued jobs are in the system: Usually, a high utilization of the resources implies a minimal makespan (Pinedo, 2002), i.e. the minimal makespan of a non-delay schedule is achieved when the number of time steps can be minimized during which jobs are waiting for processing at the resources' queues. Therefore, the DEC-MDP's reward function can be brought into alignment with the scheduling objective, if negative rewards are incurred when many jobs, that are waiting for further processing, are in the system and, hence, the overall utilization of the resources is poor.

We will more formally define suitable global reward functions in subsequent chapters when we develop corresponding learning algorithms for DEC-MDPs with changing action sets and partially ordered transition dependencies. For the time being, we have demonstrated that JSSPs can be easily cast as sequential decision problems using the subclass of general DEC-MDPs we have identified and analyzed in Section 2.4. Accordingly, we are in the position to exploit the benchmarking character of job-shop scheduling problems in a productive manner for the purpose of evaluating the performance of the reinforcement learning algorithms for DEC-MDPs we propose in Chapters 4 and 5.

## 3.3 Related Work on Solving Job-Shop Scheduling Problems

Job-shop scheduling has received an enormous amount of attention in the research literature. Both, complexity results and solution procedures have frequently been presented. As mentioned in Section 3.2, research in production scheduling traditionally distinguishes predictive and reactive solution approaches. Assuming complete knowledge about the entire scheduling problem to be solved (thus about all jobs, their operations and belonging durations as well as about the resources and which operations must be executed on which resource), and aiming at the achievement of global coherence in the process of job dispatching, Operations Research has brought about a variety of predictive scheduling algorithms that yield optimal solutions for individual problem instances – at least up to certain problem sizes, since the computational effort scales exponentially with problem size. By contrast, reactive scheduling approaches support decentralized, local decision-making, which is beneficial when no centralized control can be instantiated (e.g. when a factory's resource does not know about the current workload at any other resource) or when quick responses to unexpected events are required.

Nearly all of the approaches that utilize ideas from research in artificial intelligence to solve scheduling problems belong to the realm of predictive scheduling. We will briefly review that body of work and give an outline of classical optimal solution methods and meta-heuristics. As our formulation of JSSPs using decentralized Markov decision processes belongs to the realm of reactive scheduling we will pay special attention to related work from that field, including, most prominently, dispatching rules and further AI-based methods.

### 3.3.1 Optimal and Near-Optimal Solution Algorithms

Classical, predictive approaches to solving job-shop scheduling problems are mostly based upon disjunctive programming, i.e. on the disjunctive graph formulation of the problem presented in Section 3.1.2. Based on this and on related graph formulations powerful algorithms have been proposed, such as branch-and-bound procedures (Carlier and Pinson, 1989; Applegate and Cook, 1991; Brucker et al., 1994) or tabu search approaches (Dell'Amico and Trubian, 1993; Nowicki and Smutnicki, 1996, 2005).

Moreover, there is a large number of local search procedures and meta-heuristics to solve job-shop scheduling problems near-optimally in a centralized manner. These include the

## 3 Distributed Scheduling Problems

shifting bottleneck heuristic (Adams et al., 1988), beam search (Ow and Morton, 1988), simulated annealing (van Laarhoven et al., 1992), greedy randomized adaptive search procedures (GRASP, Binato et al., 2001), as well as squeaky wheel optimization (Joslin and Clements, 1999).

Given the disparity of centralized solution approaches from the distributed ones we are focusing on in this work, we refer to Pinson (1995) for a more thorough overview of predictive solution methods to JSSPs and to Vaessens et al. (1996) for scheduling methods employing local search.

### 3.3.2 Dispatching Priority Rules

In contrast to these predictive methods yielding to search for a single problem's best solution, our problem interpretation as sequential decision problem utilizing decentralized Markov decision processes belongs to the class of reactive scheduling techniques. When addressing reactive scheduling and providing a partial view on each of the processing resources only, dispatching priority rules represent the most notable reference.

Generally speaking, a dispatching algorithm decides how to use a factory's resources only upon the resources' availability, eventually upon the availability of other resources, and with respect to the set of waiting jobs. In practice, dispatching rules have turned out to be highly appropriate for situations where there is a wide or changing variety of products or where advance scheduling is difficult to implement.

Most dispatching rule research has been on deciding which job a resource will work on next. Basically, the rule computes a priority value for each of the waiting jobs based on some of its parameters – such as jobs' due dates, customer priorities, shortest remaining processing times as well as any of dozens of different features characterizing a job – and selects the one which it considers to be the most urgent one. Panwalkar and Iskander (1977), Bhaskaran and Pinedo (1977), Wisner (1993), and Pinedo (2002) provide comprehensive reviews of dispatching rules and their usage in industrial practice.

Dispatching priority rules (DPRs) can be classified along a number of dimensions. Static DPRs, for example, make their decisions based solely on the waiting jobs' and the respective resource's data. By contrast, dynamic DPRs may change their behavior over time: If job deadline violations are to be minimized, the minimal slack rule, for instance, orders the waiting jobs with respect to their remaining processing times and their due dates. Hence, depending on the current time and on the closeness of the jobs' deadlines, this rule behaves differently.

Another way to classify DPRs considers whether a rule is a rather elementary or a composite one, where the latter are composed of a number of the former ones. The distinction of DPRs most relevant in the scope of this book focuses on the amount of information a rule bases its decisions on. A *local DPR* uses information only that pertain to the queue where a job is waiting or to the resource on which that rule is deployed. Contrarily, *global DPRs* may additionally have access to information regarding other resources (such as the processing time of a job on another resource) or even to the current state of other resources' waiting queues.

The following list provides a selection of well-established dispatching priority rules that we are going to utilize for comparative reasons in the subsequent chapters. We provide brief characterizations and point out that this selection covers rather simple and more complex rules, as well as those that benefit from having granted access to more information than just the local view onto their respective resource.

**Avoid Maximum Current Makespan (AMCC)** Focusing on job-shop scheduling with blocking and no-wait constraints, Mascis and Pacciarelli (2002) develop heuristic dispatching rules, among them the powerful AMCC rule which benefits from having a global view onto the entire plant, when making its dispatch decisions (global view rule). AMCC is a heuristic to avoid the maximum current $C_{max}$ based on the idea of repeatedly enlarging a consistent selection, given a general alternative graph representation of the scheduling problem (Mascis and Pacciarelli, 2002).

**First In First Out (FIFO)** This well-known rule selects the job which has been waiting for the longest time at the respective resource. The FIFO rule requires local view only.

**Longest Processing Time (LPT)** This rule iterates over all waiting jobs and executes that job whose next operation's processing time is longest. To make this decision, again, only a local view is required.

**Random Dispatch Rule (RND)** A random dispatcher always selects randomly one out of the currently waiting jobs.

**Shortest Processing Time (SPT)** This rule iterates over all waiting jobs and executes that job whose next operation's processing time is shortest. The SPT rule is the counterpart to the LPT rule.

**Shortest Queue for Next Operation (SQNO)** This dispatching rule is allowed to retrieve information regarding the situation on other resources (i.e. it is a global rule). Let resource $r_i$ be controlled by the SQNO rule. Then, for each job $j$ out of the set of waiting jobs this rule determines on which resource job $j$ has to be processed after having been processed on $r_i$. Then, the current status of the waiting queues of those potential successor resources is retrieved. Finally, the job is executed whose successor resource has currently the fewest jobs waiting.

DPRs are helpful, when attempting to find reasonably good schedules with regard to one specific objective (such as makespan). They are easy to deploy and require minimal computational effort. For large-scale or even real-life applications, however, DPRs are of limited use only: Just sorting the jobs with respect to one or a few of their parameters may in general not lead to satisfying solutions. Composite rules, as mentioned above, depict an emending extension for yielding a higher degree of generality, but their use and their composition is a knowledge-intensive task that requires a fair amount of prior knowledge about the scheduling problem at hand. Having that in mind, some of the learning algorithms we are going to present in subsequent chapters can be regarded as an approach to make agents learn highly complex composite dispatching priority rules that are adaptively customized.

### 3.3.3 Artificial Intelligence-Based Approaches

First of all, we stress that nearly all work on solving scheduling problems using approaches enhanced by AI methods assume full knowledge about the problem and, hence, perform predictive scheduling. Many of these approaches depict intelligent search methods: Local search procedures employ the idea that a given solution, i.e. a given schedule, may be improved by making small changes. A neighborhood between possible solutions is assumed and solutions are changed over and again which brings about better and better schedules. For example, there exists a substantial body of work that employs methods and ideas from evolutionary computing and genetic algorithms (e.g. Bean, 1994, Ombuki and Ventresca, 2004, or González et al., 2008). Distributed AI-based approaches to solve job-shop scheduling problems are rare. Wu et al. (2005) point out that decentralized methods for resource allocation typically assume self-interested agents and that market mechanisms (e.g. auctions) can be used to achieve the desirable collective behavior among agents. While the focus of this line of research is on the design of multi-agent systems to resemble financial markets and on coalition formation, our intention, when using JSSPs as application domain, is to study the learning capabilities of the agents.

**Reinforcement Learning for Job-Shop Scheduling**

Zhang and Dietterich (1995) were the first to apply a reinforcement learning approach for a special scheduling problem: They developed a repair-based scheduler that is trained using the temporal difference reinforcement learning algorithm and that starts with a critical-path schedule and incrementally repairs constraint violations. Mahadevan et al. (1997) have presented an average-reward reinforcement learning algorithm for the optimization of transfer lines in production manufacturing which resembles a simplifying specialization of a scheduling problem. They show that the adaptive resources are able to effectively learn when they have to request maintenance, and that introducing a hierarchical decomposition of the learning task is beneficial for obtaining superior results (Wang and Mahadevan, 1999). Another repair-based approach relying on an intelligent computing algorithm is suggested by Zeng and Sycara (1995) who make use of case-based reasoning and a simplified reinforcement learning algorithm to achieve adaptation to changing optimization criteria.

Using our reactive approach to scheduling, the finally resulting schedule is not calculated beforehand, viz before execution time. Insofar, our reinforcement learning approach to job-shop scheduling, interpreting the problem as a sequential decision problem and using decentralized Markov decision processes, is rather different from these pieces of work mentioned. A reactive (closed-loop) perspective is also adopted by Schneider et al. (1998) who employ approximate dynamic programming algorithms to solve scheduling problems. However, they assume a single learning agent that fully observes the state. Similarly, Aydin and Öztemel (2000) developed an extended version of Q learning, which they entitle Q-III learning and embed into an agent-based system which performs scheduling in a centralized way.

Independently learning agents for a reactive scheduling setting were also investigated by Csaji and Monostori (2004). They interpret JSSPs as a market-based production control

## 3.3 Related Work on Solving Job-Shop Scheduling Problems

system, attach agents to resources as well as to jobs, allow them to interact with each other using biddings and contracts, and to optimize their bidding behavior using temporal difference reinforcement learning. In later work, these authors turned to centralized solution approaches for job-shop scheduling problems using a combination of Q learning, rollout algorithms, and support vector regression for value function approximation (Csaji and Monostori, 2006) plus a technique for parallelizing the learning algorithm (Csaji and Monostori, 2008).

While the references mentioned so far are barely or only loosely related to our approach, in using JSSPs as challenging application domain for investigating the performance of cooperative learning multi-agent systems, we have drawn a lot of inspiration from the work by Riedmiller and Riedmiller (1999) who employed neural reinforcement learning in conjunction with multi-layer perceptrons for Q function approximation to learn local dispatching policies. The investigations we present in Chapter 5 are highly related to their work and depict a direct extension of their approach.

Before, however, we are going to explore value function-based reinforcement learning approaches for cooperative multi-agent systems and for the application domain of job-shop scheduling, we analyze the use of policy search-based reinforcement learning techniques in the next chapter.

# 4 Policy Search-Based Solution Approaches

In Chapter 2 we have seen that the jump from one to many agents interacting with the environment brings about a significant increase in complexity, when aiming at the acquisition of a joint policy that yields global welfare. This kind of problem aggravation is mainly caused by the fact that each single agent is unaware about other agents' local states, their beliefs, and the policies they are pursuing.

In Section 2.4, we treaded a path of counteracting that rise in complexity by identifying a specific subclass of general distributed decision problems, viz the class of decentralized DEC-MDPs with changing action sets and partially ordered transition dependencies, which is provably easier to solve (NP- instead of NEXP-hard). While this is a positive result (since NP$\subsetneq$NEXP), solving NP-hard problems is far from being easy: Except for the case that NP=P, which is a hitherto unanswered question, there exists no algorithm that is capable of solving NP problems in time bounded polynomially in the problem's size.

Consequently, in this as well as in the next chapter we are going to investigate alternative approaches to tackling decentralized decision problems. Instead of attempting to find an optimal solution, i.e. an optimal joint policy, for a given multi-agent problem, we strive for acquiring approximate and potentially near-optimal solutions in feasible time using reinforcement learning. While we advocate Chapter 5 to the value function-based approach to reinforcement learning, in the chapter at hand we develop two different policy search-based reinforcement learning methods for cooperative multi-agent systems, analyze their theoretical properties, and investigate them empirically.

After some foundations and motivation for the use of policy search reinforcement learning (Section 4.1), we propose a direct policy search technique, dubbed joint equilibrium policy search (JEPS, Section 4.2), and a gradient-descent policy search approach (GDPS, Section 4.3) for the subclass of DEC-MDPs we are addressing. The performance of both of these methods in terms of quickly acquiring high-quality joint policies will be analyzed for numerous intricate job-shop scheduling benchmarks that are interpreted as DEC-MDPs with changing action sets as described in Section 3.2.2. We finish this chapter with a discussion of the advantages and drawbacks of policy search reinforcement learning, leading us to the alternative value function-based approach that will, as mentioned, move into our focus in the subsequent chapter.

## 4.1 Foundations

According to Sutton and Barto (1998), reinforcement learning is a problem description rather than a specific solution method. The policy search-based approach to the reinforce-

## 4 Policy Search-Based Solution Approaches

ment learning problem draws quite some of its motivation from a simplicity argument: The goal of learning is to solve the learning problem by finding the best policy of action, irrespective of the deeper structure of the experience gathered during interacting with the environment. Thus, if it is possible for the learning process to directly yield solutions without performing an intermediate system identification process (e.g. by estimating the transition or reward model), then robust and high-quality learning results can be obtained even when the underlying system is too complex to estimate (Strens and Moore, 2001).

In this spirit and with regard to the actor-critic architecture introduced in Section 2.1.3, policy search methods correspond to actor-focused techniques which basically rely on an explicit representation of an actor, i.e. on an explicit representation of the policy.

Policy search represents an attractive approach to reinforcement learning problems for various reasons:

1. As outlined in Section 2.1.4, the complexity of the search through the space of possible policies can be heavily reduced, if the search is restricted to a relevant subspace which can be defined through the exploitation of possibly available problem knowledge.

2. Besides this, it is important to stress that policy search reinforcement learning focuses on the evaluation of policies as a whole, assessing their performance over, typically, larger sequences of action choices. This is one of the reasons, why policy search approaches have been found useful for learning under partial observability (Meuleau et al., 1999). Logically, this merit also applies to multi-agent reinforcement learning within DEC-MDPs where each agent has only its local and, hence, incomplete perception of the world state (Baird and Moore, 1999).

3. By definition, policy search algorithms are model-free techniques, not requiring knowledge about the transition and reward functions of the underlying Markov decision process. While model-based methods presume to possess or estimate a model of the environment and compute or infer a policy with the help of this model, policy search algorithms are facilitated to attempt for finding a good policy directly.

4. Policy search methods have sometimes been reported to outperform traditional value function-based temporal difference reinforcement learning algorithms for several tasks (Taylor et al., 2006; Stanley and Miikkulainen, 2002).

### 4.1.1 Policy Performance

Policy search methods search directly in the space $\mathbb{P}$ of policies without learning value functions. This can be a highly effective approach, particularly if a fair amount of problem knowledge regarding the learning task at hand is available. The exploitation of background knowledge as a mean to guide machine learning algorithms and to restrict search processes is well-known and frequently applied approach (Gabel and Stahl, 2004). Concerning policy search reinforcement learning, the incorporation of task knowledge may take shape as parameterizing a policy using a (small) vector $\theta$ of real-valued parameters: By defining the domains of these parameters as well as how the parameter vector influences action

## 4.1 Foundations

choices, and moreover interpreting the search process as a search over those parameters, a tremendous reduction of the search complexity can be achieved. For decentralized Markov decision processes with changing action sets and partially ordered transition dependencies, additional prior knowledge may enhance the search, for example, by exploiting the fact that each agent may execute each action $\alpha \in \mathcal{A}_i^r$ only once (cf. Lemma 1).

Central to policy optimization using policy search-based reinforcement learning is the notion of the quality or *performance* $J(\pi_\theta)$ of a policy $\pi_\theta$ that is defined through its parameters $\theta$.

**Definition 4.1** (Policy Performance).
*Given a distribution over a set $S_0 \subset S$ of starting states, the* performance *of a policy $\pi_\theta$ is defined as the expected value of the return $R_0$, which is defined as the discounted sum of immediate rewards $r$, that is to be expected when starting from a state $s_0 \in S_0$ and pursuing $\pi_\theta$ thereafter until reaching a final state after $D$ decision stages:*

$$J(\pi_\theta) = \mathbb{E}[R_0|s_0 \in S_0, \pi_\theta] = \mathbb{E}[\sum_{k=0}^{D}\gamma^k r(k)|\pi_\theta] = \lim_{N\to\infty} \frac{1}{N}\sum_{l=1}^{N} R(l) \quad (4.1)$$

*where $R(l)$ refers to the return obtained during the lth episode.*

From Equation 4.1 it is obvious, that $J(\pi_\theta)$ is closely related to the definition of the value $V^\pi(s)$ of a state according to Equation 2.2, if we consider $\mathbb{E}[V^\pi(s)|s \in S_0]$. Moreover, for problems with a single starting state, i.e. $S_0 = \{s_0\}$, it holds $J(\pi_\theta) = V^\pi(s_0)$. Given Definition 4.1 it follows immediately, that the goal of a policy search approach is to improve $J(\pi_\theta)$ by adapting $\theta$ in a purposive and efficient manner.

### 4.1.2 Multi-Agent Policy Search Reinforcement Learning

The core idea of policy search-based reinforcement learning is to directly adapt the policy to be learned with respect to its performance, while the key point of cooperative multi-agent reinforcement learning is to have independent agents that try to improve their local policies with respect to a common goal. Algorithm 4.1 provides a straightforward implementation of a procedure that is tailored for policy search reinforcement learning and that lets a single agent interact with the environment (in our case, a DEC-MDP) and improve its policy independently. Note that this algorithm is to be executed in parallel by each agent involved; we here describe it from a single agent's perspective only.

Until some external stop signal indicates the end of the entire learning process, agent $i$ alternates between fully observing its local state, choosing actions, and obtaining global immediate rewards. On the occasion of having finished a single episode, as indicated by having entered the terminal state $s^f$, the agent calls a policy update algorithm (line 10) whose task is to purposively process the experience collected during the recent episode. In the following two subsections we develop and analyze different variants of such update algorithms. Thus, Algorithm 4.1 realizes a rather generic procedure for performing policy search-based reinforcement learning using decentralized control. Basically, it realizes the interaction of a single agent (agent $i$) with the DEC-MDP with changing action sets at hand and delegates the task of learning to the respective policy update methods.

## 4 Policy Search-Based Solution Approaches

**Input:** policy $\pi_i$ initialized by a randomly chosen real-valued parameters $\theta^i$
1: $d \leftarrow 0$, $h_i \leftarrow [\,]$
2: **while** *not stop* **do**
3:     observe $s_i(d)$
4:     **if** $s_i(d) \neq \emptyset$ **or** $s_i(d) = s^f$ **then**
5:        **if** $d > 0$ **then**
6:           **receive** global immediate reward $r(d-1)$ //r(s(d-1),a(d-1),s(d))
7:           **append** $[s_i(d-1), \alpha(d-1), r(d-1)]$ to $h_i$
8:        **endif**
9:        **if** $s_i(d) = s^f$ **then**
10:           call `PolicyUpdate`$(h_i)$
11:           $d \leftarrow 0$, $h_i \leftarrow [\,]$
12:     **else**
13:        **select** $\alpha(d) \in s_i(d)$ with probability given by $\pi_i$
14:        **execute** $\alpha(d)$
15:        $s_{\sigma_i(\alpha(d))} \leftarrow s_{\sigma_i(\alpha(d))} \cup \{\alpha(d)\}$ //influence local state of agent $\sigma_i(\alpha(d))$
16:        $s_i(d) \leftarrow s_i(d) \setminus \{\alpha(d)\}$
17:        $d \leftarrow d + 1$
18:     **endif**
19: **endif**

**Algorithm 4.1:** Decentralized Policy Search from the Perspective of Agent $i$

We note that variable $d$ in Algorithm 4.1 does not necessarily have to correspond to time steps, but merely represents a counter of decision steps experienced by agent $i$. Thus, this algorithm can also handle environments with temporally extended actions, i.e. where the execution of a local action $\alpha$ lasts longer than one time step. For this to happen, the execution of $\alpha$ in line 14 would correspond to a *blocking* function call and the global reward to be received (line 6) must be a collection of time step-based rewards accrued during the execution of $\alpha$.

An important data structure utilized by Algorithm 4.1 is that of an experience sequence $h$ that is realized as a simple list. It corresponds to the processing of a single episode starting from some initial state and ending upon having reached the terminal state $s^f$ where no more actions are available for any of the agents. Because we will use the notion of an experience sequence repeatedly below, we provide a formal definition.

**Definition 4.2** (Experience Sequence).
*For agent $i$ interacting with a decentralized Markov decision process with changing action sets and partially ordered transition dependencies, an experience sequence $h_i$ over $D$ decision points is defined as*

$$h_i = [s_i(0), a_i(0), r(0), s_i(1), a_i(1), r(1), \ldots, s_i(D-1), a_i(D-1), r(D-1), s^f] \quad (4.2)$$

*where, for all $d \in \{0, \ldots, D-1\}$, $s_i(d) \in S_i$ are the local states $i$ passes through, $a_i(d) \in s_i \subset \mathcal{A}_i^r$ are the local actions $i$ executes, and $r(d) \in \mathbb{R}$ are the global immediate rewards received.*

*Accordingly, the experience sequence h of the ensemble of agents is specified by a collection of individual sequences: $h = \langle h_1, \ldots, h_m \rangle$.*

Moreover, we let $h_i^d$ denote the prefix of $h_i$ truncated after $s(d)$ for some $d < D$. To denote a specific component within an experience sequence $h_i$, we write $a(d, h_i)$ when referring to the $d$th action in that sequence, i.e. $a(d, h_i)$ equals $a_i(d)$ in Equation 4.2. Accordingly, $s(d, h_i)$ denotes the $d$th state within $h_i$ and $\bar{s}(d, h_i)$ the sequence $(s_i(0), \ldots, s_i(d))$ of the first $d+1$ states within $h_i$.

## 4.2 Joint Equilibrium Policy Search

As discussed in Chapter 2, we consider teams of cooperative agents that all seek to optimize a global reward and we assume that the corresponding multi-agent system can be modelled using DEC-MDPs with changing action sets and partially ordered transition dependencies. Therefore, it is taken for granted that there exists at least one sequence of actions that maximizes the expected reward for all agents. From an agent coordination point of view (as adopted frequently in the game theoretic literature), a joint policy that yields maximal global reward, is also denoted as a coordination equilibrium[1] or *joint equilibrium*. Choosing actions according to that type of equilibrium, the collective of agents will yield a maximal return $R$, collecting maximal summed rewards as they reach the final state.

Establishing inter-agent coordination in multi-agent systems depicts a challenging task. Agents that are disallowed to exchange coordinative messages must both determine where equilibria are located in the joint policy space and also find out which equilibria are strived for by other agents. The general problem of equilibrium selection (Myerson, 1991) can be addressed in several ways. For example, communication between agents might be allowed, or one could impose conventions or rules that restrict the agents' behavior such that coordination is assured (Boutilier, 1999).

In this section, we advocate the idea that coordinated action choice and, hence, the attainment of an optimal joint policy (i.e. a joint equilibrium) can be learned through repeated interaction between the agents and the DEC-MDP, i.e. by means of reinforcement learning. Our goal is to develop a policy search-based learning algorithm that enables the agents approach a joint equilibrium – dubbed Joint Equilibrium Policy Search (JEPS, Gabel and Riedmiller, 2008c) –, where maximal payoff is earned by the agents with increasing frequency by allowing them to adjust their probabilities of executing actions appropriately.

### 4.2.1 Learning Joint Policies

Fulda and Ventura (2004) proposed an equilibrium selection algorithm for reinforcement learning agents, called incremental policy learning (IPL), that is capable of learning to play an optimal equilibrium in deterministic environments and assuming that a heuristic

---
[1] A coordination equilibrium is a special case of an optimal equilibrium. While an optimal equilibrium, which is defined as a pareto-optimal Nash equilibrium, does not necessarily maximize the reward for all agents, a coordination equilibrium does so (Myerson, 1991).

## 4 Policy Search-Based Solution Approaches

is available which tells whether an optimal joint action has been executed by the agents, i.e. whether a joint equilibrium was attained, or not. IPL's greatest disadvantage is that it is restricted to single-stage games, i.e. to stateless environments (also called $m$-player cooperative repeated games), where the agents repeatedly choose their actions, obtain rewards, eventually adapt their policies, and start over again. Consequently, the interesting case of sequential optimality is not addressed by incremental policy learning.

Here, we present the JEPS algorithm which borrows some elements of IPL and, most importantly, extends it (a) towards scenarios with multiple states at which actions can be executed and (b) towards a compact and efficient representation of the agents' policies. JEPS relies on stochastic agent-specific policies parameterized by probability distributions defined for every state as well as on a heuristic that tells whether a joint equilibrium could be obtained. To combat the tremendous memory requirements for storing policies brought about, when making the step from single-stage games to sequential decision problems, in the next section we also suggest an extended version where each agent employs a global policy parameterization which yields substantial savings in terms of computation time and memory requirements and which renders the approach applicable to larger-scale problems.

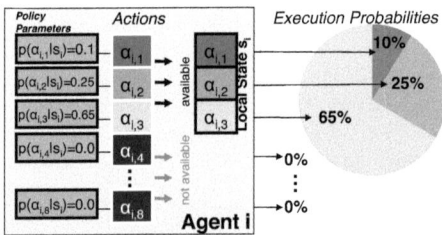

Figure 4.1: Joint Equilibrium Policy Search: In its basic version, each JEPS agent stores action probability vectors for each state it can encounter.

As denoted, JEPS is a purely policy-search based algorithm (i.e. no value functions are employed), where all agents' policies are stochastic and are dependent on state-specific probability vectors denoting the probabilities with which each action is executed. This is visualized in Figure 4.1: Agent $i$ finds itself in state $s_i = \{\alpha_{i,1}, \alpha_{i,2}, \alpha_{i,3}\}$ and chooses each available action with a state-dependent probability $p(\alpha_j | s_i)$ for all $\alpha_j \in s_i$; obviously, agent $i$ executes $\alpha_{i,3}$ with highest probability. Concretizing the definition of a policy (Definition 2.9), we formalize a JEPS agent's stochastic local policy as follows:

**Definition 4.3** (JEPS Policy with Local Parameterization).
*Let $s_i \in \mathcal{P}(\mathcal{A}_i)$ be the current state of agent $i$, where $s_i = A_i(s_i) = \{\alpha_1, \ldots, \alpha_{|s_i|}\}$ corresponds to the set of actions agent $i$ can currently execute. Let $\theta_L^i(s_i) = \{p(\alpha_1|s_i), \ldots, p(\alpha_{|s_i|}|s_i)\}$ be a probability distribution over all actions from $s_i$, thus $0 \leq p(\alpha_j | s_i) \leq 1$ and $\sum_j p(\alpha_j | s_i) = 1$.*
*Then, for JEPS agent $i$'s policy of action $\pi_{\theta_L^i} : S_i \times \mathcal{A}_i^r \to [0,1]$ it holds $s_i \times \alpha \mapsto p(\alpha | s_i)$. Accordingly, the joint policy is defined as $\pi = \langle \pi_{\theta_L^1}, \ldots, \pi_{\theta_L^m} \rangle$.*

## 4.2 Joint Equilibrium Policy Search

Note that, for the time being, we consider reactive policies only (cf. Definition 2.9), implying that JEPS agents regard only their current local state, when stochastically choosing their actions, and ignore their state history. In so doing, JEPS agents never remain idle, if there is at least one action available, i.e. $s_i \neq \emptyset$. Hence, they never execute the idle action $\alpha_0$ which is why $\pi_{\theta_L^i}$ is defined over $S_i \times \mathcal{A}_i^r$ (and not over $\mathcal{A}_i$).

We assume that all action probability vectors $\theta_L^i(s_i)$ are randomly initialized and that the set of agents repeatedly interacts with the DEC-MDP until the final state $s^f$ has been reached (also called the processing of a single episode). Then, the return $R$ (more precisely, $R_0$) which is the discounted sum $\sum_{t=0}^{T} \gamma^t r(t)$ of time step specific immediate global rewards as specified in Equation 2.1 can be determined by all agents. Note that the cooperative nature of the multi-agent system is reflected by the fact that all agents receive the same return. Finally, the system is reset to a starting state and starts over.

JEPS borrows from Fulda and Ventura (2004) in that it employs a binary heuristic $H(r)$ that is capable of telling whether a joint equilibrium has been attained. If so, it returns true, otherwise false. The existence of such a heuristic represents a rather strong assumption. However, it allows us to deduce some nice theoretical properties of the JEPS learning algorithm. For the purpose of empirical evaluation of the algorithm, we utilize a rather straightforward approximative implementation of $H$ that returns true only, if the current episode's return equals or exceeds the maximal return $R_{max}$ obtained so far, i.e. $H(R) = 1 \Leftrightarrow R \geq R_{max}$. This idea has been exploited in a different context already by the Rmax algorithm (Brafman and Tennenholtz, 2003) and by optimistic assumption Q learning (Lauer and Riedmiller, 2000).

The joint equilibrium policy search algorithm is presented in Algorithm 4.2. It can be easily plugged in as the policy update procedure PolicyUpdate($h_i$) in line 10 of Algorithm 4.1 (where the latter realizes episode-based interaction with the DEC-MDP). After having finished a single episode and only if having found that $H(R) = 1$, each agent starts updating its action probabilities for all states it has encountered during that episode. Here, the probabilities of all actions that were executed (and thus contributed to achieving maximal return, i.e. representing a joint equilibrium) are increased, while the probabilities for executing any of the actions despised is decreased (lines 5 and 6 in Algorithm 4.2). Note, that this update scheme preserves that $\sum_j p(\alpha_j|s_i) = 1$ for all $s_i$. While the updates to the action probabilities made by the JEPS algorithm are calculated in a similar manner as in IPL (Fulda and Ventura, 2004), the improvements are that JEPS stores a single action probability vector for each local state it possibly encounters, that it is capable of recognizing and distinguishing between multiple states $s_i$, and that it can handle sequential decision problems (not just single-stage games). Moreover, in the next section we will use this basic version of JEPS as a point of departure and develop an extension that renders this algorithm applicable to larger-sized problem.

JEPS extends the mentioned learning approach for single-stage games in a purposive manner to problems with multiple states. Consequently, the policy update mechanism is guaranteed to converge[2] to a joint equilibrium as long as the heuristic $H$ is correct in the sense that it tells a true joint equilibrium. This follows immediately from the convergence

---
[2]Here, convergence means that for all states $s_i$ there is an $\alpha \in s_i$ such that $p(\alpha|s_i) \rightarrow 1$ in the course of learning.

## 4 Policy Search-Based Solution Approaches

---

**Input:** learning rate $\gamma \in (0,1]$, experience sequence of current episode
$h_i = [s_i(0), a_i(0), r(0), s_i(1), \ldots, s_i(D-1), a_r(D-1), r(D-1), s^f]$
where $D = |\mathcal{A}_i^r|$ denotes the episode's length (number of actions executed)
1: $R \leftarrow \sum_{d=0}^{D-1} r(d)$  //no discounting
2: **if** $H(R) = 1$ **then**
3:    **for** $d = 0$ to $d < D$ **do**
4:      **for all** $\alpha \in s_i(d)$ **do**
5:        **if** $\alpha = a_i(d)$ **then** $p(\alpha|s_i(d)) \leftarrow p(\alpha|s_i(d)) + \gamma(1 - p(\alpha|s_i(d)))$
6:        **else** $p(\alpha|s_i(d)) \leftarrow (1-\gamma)p(\alpha|s_i(d))$
7: $R_{max} \leftarrow \max\{R, R_{max}\}$

**Algorithm 4.2:** JEPS Policy Updates by Agent $i$ Using Local Action Parameters

---

proof for single-stage games, since each of JEPS' states together with its belonging action probability vector can be regarded as an individual single-stage game considered by Fulda and Ventura (2004).

When intending to apply the version of JEPS presented to practical problems, two considerable problems arise. First, with a growing number of actions $|\mathcal{A}_i|$ available to the agents, the size of the state space grows exponentially, since states correspond to sets of available actions and, hence, in the worst case it holds $|S_i| = |\mathcal{P}(\mathcal{A}_i)| = 2^{|\mathcal{A}_i|}$. Accordingly, storing action probability vectors for all states (separately for each of the agents) quickly becomes intractable as the problem size grows. Additionally, the large number of action probability vectors also increases the learning time needed until convergence to a nearly deterministic policy is achieved.

To tackle these problems, in the next section, we suggest a compact policy representation in combination with an alternative policy update mechanism that clearly reduces the computational complexity and memory requirements while still allowing for convergence to a joint equilibrium.

### 4.2.2 Global Action Parameterization

Knowing the properties of DEC-MDPs with changing action sets and partially ordered transition dependencies (Definition 2.13) and given the problems mentioned before, a crucial observation is that each agent has to be capable of learning a *total order* in which it executes all actions from $\mathcal{A}_i^r$.

That is why, the basic idea for a version of JEPS that employs *global* action parameters (to which we refer as JEPS$_G$) is that, for each of the agents, we attach a single (global) parameter to each action in $\mathcal{A}_i^r$ from which then its probability of execution is induced.

**Definition 4.4** (JEPS$_G$ Policy with Global Action Parameterization).
Let $\theta_G^i = \{p_G(\alpha_k) | \alpha_k \in \mathcal{A}_i^r\}$ be a probability distribution over the set $\mathcal{A}_i^r$ of local actions agent $i$ can execute, and let $s_i = A_i(s_i) = \{\alpha_1, \ldots, \alpha_{|s_i|}\} \in \mathcal{P}(\mathcal{A}_i^r)$ be its current state. Then, for agent $i$'s local policy of action $\pi_{\theta_G^i} : S_i \times \mathcal{A}_i^r \to [0,1]$ it holds $s_i \times \alpha \mapsto Pr(\alpha|s_i)$

## 4.2 Joint Equilibrium Policy Search

where the probability $Pr(\alpha|s_i)$ is calculated as

$$Pr(\alpha|s_i) = \begin{cases} \frac{p_G(\alpha)}{\sum_{\alpha_k \in s_i} p_G(\alpha_k)} & \text{if } \alpha \in s_i \\ 0 & \text{else} \end{cases},$$

and, again, the joint policy $\pi$ is the concatenation of local policies $\langle \pi_{\theta_G^1}, \ldots, \pi_{\theta_G^m} \rangle$.

Using this kind of policy representation each agent must store only $|\mathcal{A}_i^r|$ parameters which represents an enormous saving in terms of memory requirements compared to the JEPS version with local action probabilities. Whereas in Figure 4.1 a parameter vector was attached explicitly to each state, enabling an action probability dependency on $s_i$, now only a single global parameter vector $\theta_G^i$ is to be considered (Figure 4.2). While both figures visualize the same state $s_i = \{\alpha_{i,1}, \alpha_{i,2}, \alpha_{i,3}\}$ and, moreover, identical stochastic action choices are realized in both cases, the respective policy parameters $p(\alpha_j|s_i)$ and $p_G(\alpha_j)$ differ.

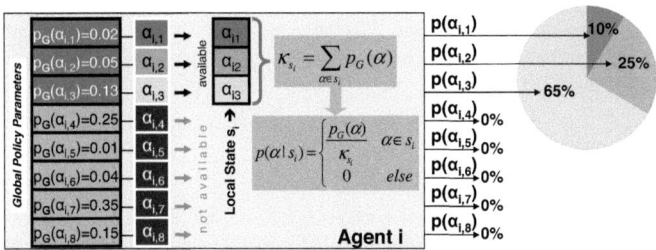

Figure 4.2: Joint Equilibrium Policy Search: In its extended version, each JEPS agent stores a single global policy parameter vector $\theta_G^i = \{p_G(\alpha_{i,1}), \ldots, p_G(\alpha_{i,|\mathcal{A}_i^r|})\}$, only. From this, action execution probabilities are inferred, depending on the agent's current state $s_i$ using $\pi_{\theta_G^i}$ as specified in Definition 4.4.

Based on the policy representation with global parameters according to Definition 4.4, we suggest a learning algorithm that, for each agent, performs the parameter updates directly on the global parameter vector $\theta_G^i$. Algorithm 4.3 extends the basic JEPS updating algorithm (Algorithm 4.2): Its distinguishing property is that all positive updates, i.e. updates for action choices corresponding to a joint equilibrium indicated by $H$ (line 5), are performed relative to a state-specific baseline $\kappa_{s_i(d)}$ that is defined as

$$\kappa_{s_i(d)} := \sum_{\alpha_k \in s_i(d)} p_G(\alpha_k).$$

By this, it is possible to relate the local situation of agent $i$, i.e. its current local state, to the set of global action parameters, and it is also ensured that $\theta_G^i$ stays a proper probability distribution with $\sum_{\alpha_k \in s_i(d)} p_G(\alpha_k) = 1$.

Next, we analyze the convergence properties of the JEPS$_G$ update algorithm under the assumption that $H$ is a perfect heuristic, meaning that it is capable of truly telling whether the action sequence recently executed depicts a joint equilibrium.

4 Policy Search-Based Solution Approaches

---

**Input:** learning rate $\gamma \in (0, 1]$, experience sequence of current episode
$h_i = [s_i(0), a_i(0), r(0), s_i(1), \ldots, s_i(D-1), a_r(D-1), r(D-1), s^f]$
where $D = |\mathcal{A}_i^r|$ denotes the episode's length (number of actions executed)
1: $R \leftarrow \sum_{d=0}^{D-1} r(d)$ //no discounting
2: **if** $H(R) = 1$ **then**
3:     **for** $d = 0$ **to** $d < D$ **do**
4:         **forall** $\alpha \in s_i(d)$ **do**
5:             **if** $\alpha = a_i(d)$ **then** $p_G(\alpha) \leftarrow p_G(\alpha) + \gamma(\sum_{\alpha_k \in s_i(d)} p_G(\alpha_k) - p_G(\alpha))$
6:             **else** $p_G(\alpha) \leftarrow (1 - \gamma) p_G(\alpha)$
7: $R_{max} \leftarrow \max\{R, R_{max}\}$

**Algorithm 4.3:** Policy Updates by JEPS$_G$ Agent $i$ Using Global Action Parameters

### 4.2.3 Theoretical Properties

For the JEPS$_G$ algorithm (Algorithm 4.3), we can show that for every agent and each local state $s_i$ the probability of executing an action $\alpha \in s_i$ that does *not* support yielding a joint equilibrium is declining, if it exceeds some threshold.

**Lemma 4.** *Let $\alpha \in s_i$ and $p_G(\alpha) > \frac{\kappa_{s_i}}{2}$. If the execution of $\alpha$ in state $s_i$ does not yield a joint equilibrium, then $\Delta p_G(\alpha) < 0$, where $\Delta p_G$ represents the difference of $p_G(\alpha)$ after and prior to the call to Algorithm 4.3.*

*Proof.* If the current episode did not correspond to an equilibrium, no updates are performed. Consider the case when an equilibrium has been reached and focus on the smallest value of $d$ for which it holds $\alpha \in s_i(d)$ for an arbitrary $\alpha \in \mathcal{A}_i^r$. Let $d + v$ ($v \geq 1$) be the stage at which $\alpha$ has finally been selected for execution. Then, the value of $p_G(\alpha)$ will have been decremented $v$ times according to line 6 (denote the result of this calculation as $p_G^-(\alpha)$) and been increased a single time at $s_i(d+v)$. Thus,

$$p_G'(\alpha) := p_G(\alpha) + \Delta p_G(\alpha) = p_G^-(\alpha) + \gamma(\kappa_{s_i(d+v)} - p_G^-(\alpha))$$
$$= (1-\gamma)^{v+1} p_G(\alpha) + \gamma \sum_{\alpha_k \in s_i(d+v)} p_G^-(\alpha_k).$$

For the sum on the right-hand side there exist values $v_k \geq 0$ for all $\alpha_k \in s_i(d+v)$ such that $p_G^-(\alpha_k) = (1-\gamma)^{v_k} p_G(\alpha_k)$. Since we are looking for the circumstances under which $p_G'(\alpha) < p_G(\alpha)$, i.e. $\Delta p_G(\alpha) < 0$, we finally arrive at

$$\Delta p_G(\alpha) < 0 \Leftrightarrow p_G(\alpha) > \frac{\gamma \sum_{\alpha_k \in s_i(d+v)} (1-\gamma)^{v_k} p_G(\alpha_k)}{1 - (1-\gamma)^{v+1}} =: \delta(\gamma).$$

The term $\delta(\gamma)$ attains its maximal value for $v = 1$ and $v_k = 0$ for all $k$. Then,

$$\delta(\gamma) = \frac{1-\gamma}{2-\gamma} \sum_{\alpha_k \in s_i(d+v)} p_G(\alpha_k).$$

Maximizing subject to $\gamma$ ($\gamma \to 0$), we obtain $\delta = \frac{\kappa_{s_i(d+v)}}{2}$. And because by definition $\kappa_{s_i(d)} > \kappa_{s_i(d+v)}$ for all $v \geq 1$, we finally see that for $p_G(\alpha) > \frac{\kappa_{s_i(d)}}{2}$ it holds $\Delta p_G(\alpha) < 0$. □

## 4.2 Joint Equilibrium Policy Search

Lemma 4 shows that probability updates cannot enforce convergence to suboptimal action choices. Unfortunately, still there may be the case of two or more joint equilibria with identical global reward between which the agent may oscillate. However, we can show that for any state $s_i$ there is a critical action probability value such that upon exceeding that value one joint equilibrium starts dominating another one.

**Lemma 5.** *If $\alpha \in s_i(d)$ is an action within a joint equilibrium episode, then there exists a value $p^\star$ such that, if $p_G(\alpha) > p^\star$, then $p_G(\alpha)$ is more likely to increase over time than to decrease.*

*Proof.* The critical case of $p_G(\alpha)$ decreasing can occur, if there is a $\beta \in s_i(d)$ such that still a joint equilibrium can be obtained when $\beta$ is executed in $s_i$. If $\alpha$ is executed, then $p_G(\alpha)$ is increased (line 5), whereas $p_G(\beta)$ is decreased (line 5) at least one time and later increased at $d+v > d$ when $\beta$ is finally executed. If $\beta$ is selected in $s_i$, the situation is the other way round ($p_G(\alpha)$ decreased $v$ times according to line 6, if it is selected $v$ decision time points later). Consequently, with a probability of $\frac{p_G(\alpha)}{\kappa_{s_i(d)}}$ it holds

$$p_G^\alpha(\alpha) := p_G(\alpha) + \Delta p_G(\alpha) = p_G(\alpha) + \gamma(\kappa_{s_i(d)} - p_G(\alpha))$$

and with a probability of $\frac{p_G(\beta)}{\kappa_{s_i(d)}}$ it holds

$$p_G^\beta(\alpha) := p_G^-(\alpha) + \gamma(\kappa_{s_i(d+v)} - p_G^-(\alpha))$$
$$= (1-\gamma)^v p_G(\alpha) + \gamma(\kappa_{s_i(d+v)} - (1-\gamma)^v p_G(\alpha)).$$

Since we look for the conditions under which $\Delta p_G(\alpha) = p_G'(\alpha) - p_G(\alpha) > 0$, we can express this inequation using a weighted average as

$$\frac{p_G(\alpha)p_G^\alpha(\alpha) + p_G(\beta)p_G^\beta(\alpha)}{\kappa_{s_i(d)}(p_G(\alpha)+p_G(\alpha))} - p_G(\alpha) > 0.$$

After a number of algebraic reformulations, this simplifies to

$$\frac{\kappa_{s_i(d)}}{p_G(\beta)} + \frac{\kappa_{s_i(d+v)}}{p_G(\alpha)} > \frac{1+\gamma-(1-\gamma^{v+1})}{\gamma}.$$

The right-hand side of this inequation attains its maximum for $v \to \infty$ which becomes $1 + \frac{1}{\gamma}$. For the left-hand side, we know that $\kappa_{s_i(d)} \geq p_G(\alpha) + p_G(\beta)$ and $\kappa_{s_i(d+v)} \geq p_G(\alpha)$. Assuming the worst case (both equalities) here, too, we arrive at

$$\frac{p_G(\alpha)+p_G\beta}{p_G(\beta)} + \frac{p_G(\alpha)}{p_G(\alpha)} > 1 + \frac{1}{\gamma} \text{ and thus } \frac{p_G(\alpha)}{p_G(\beta)} > \frac{1-\gamma}{\gamma}.$$

Consequently, if for a state $s_i$ one joint equilibrium action $\alpha \in s_i$ dominates all other actions by a share of at least $p^\star := \frac{1-\gamma}{\gamma}$, then $\Delta p_G(\alpha)$ tends to be positive. $\square$

If for some action $\alpha$ within an equilibrium episode the probability of execution exceeds some critical value, then $p_G(\alpha)$ tends to be increasing continually. Since updates are not just made for single actions, but for all actions taken during an equilibrial episode, this argument transfers to the remaining actions from $\mathcal{A}_i^r$ as well.

As a consequence, with continued positive updates all $p_G(\alpha_k)$ converge such that for all states there is a dominant action $\alpha_{s_i}^\star$,

$$\forall s_i \in \mathcal{A}_i^r \exists \alpha_{s_i}^\star \in s_i : \frac{p_G(\alpha_{s_i}^\star)}{\kappa_{s_i}} \to 1, \tag{4.3}$$

which means that the policy the agent pursues approaches a deterministic one. We summarize this by the following theorem.

# 4 Policy Search-Based Solution Approaches

**Theorem 2.** *Using the $JEPS_G$ update algorithm, the local policies of the agents, that are interacting with the DEC-MDP with changing action sets and partially ordered transition dependencies, in the limit converge to deterministic policies that are optimal with respect to the equilibrium heuristic H.*

*Proof.* Follows directly from Lemmas 4 and 5. Note, however, that convergence is taking place with respect to the definition of $H$. If $H$ is imperfect and incapable of correctly identifying a joint equilibrium, then the algorithm is still guaranteed to converge, but a suboptimal policy will be attained. □

## 4.2.4 Discussion

Of course, the time required for convergence to occur may be high. Setting the learning rate $\gamma$ to a higher value, learning can be speeded up. In fact, if a perfect heuristic $H$ is available which correctly detects joint equilibria, then $\gamma$ can be safely set to 1.0 and still Equation 4.3 holds. Unfortunately, in practice, a fully accurate heuristic cannot always expected to be known. On the one hand, the stochastic nature of the JEPS policies and update algorithm is supposed to handle minor fluctuations in $H$'s accuracy well, mainly resulting in increased learning and convergence times. On the other hand, when using an $R_{max}$-based heuristic (as we will do below: $H(R) = 1 \iff R \geq R_{max}$) and the accurate value of $R_{max}$ is not given a priori, but must be estimated from data during learning, then the learning rate $\gamma$ has a significant influence on the progress and the results of learning: Setting $\gamma$ to very small values, clearly increases the learning time. Increasing the value of $\gamma$, by contrast, comes at the cost of a higher probability that learning converges prematurely to a suboptimal joint policy, i.e. missing a joint equilibrium. Insofar, adjusting $\gamma$ represents a mean to trade off learning speed and the goal of obtaining a joint policy very close to a joint equilibrium.

Returning to the point of view of a total order of action execution that is represented by the vector of global action parameters $\theta_G^i$, we observe that $JEPS_G$ may drive the parameters $p_G(\alpha)$ and $p_G(\beta)$ for some actions $\alpha$ and $\beta$ (in particular for actions whose execution is repeatedly postponed) to very small numerical values – while at the same time it may be required that the share of $p_G(\alpha)$ and $p_G(\beta)$ must be either very large or small. As a consequence, a limiting factor when implementing and using Algorithm 4.3 is given by the smallest real-valued number that can be represented on the respective hardware[3]. Accordingly, the convergence behavior of a practical implementation of $JEPS_G$ will be as follows:

a) Convergence to a joint equilibrium policy, as indicated by heuristic $H$ in conjunction with $R_{max}$, occurring with a probability of nearly one may occur. This means, after $\lambda$ learning episodes it holds for all agents $i$, for all states $s_i$, and for all $\alpha \in s_i$ that $\frac{p_G(\alpha)}{\kappa_{s_i}} > 1 - \epsilon$ for some small $\epsilon > 0$.

b) Numerical underflow problems arise[4], i.e. that there is an agent $i$ and a state $s_i$

---
[3] According to the IEEE standard for binary floating-point arithmetic (IEEE 754), when using 64 bit, the smallest number is approximately $2.2 \cdot 10^{-308}$ (*double* type).
[4] This case is more likely to occur, the larger $|\theta_G^i|$ is.

where for an $\alpha \in s_i$ it holds $p_G(\alpha) < \epsilon_{min}$, where $\epsilon_{min} \in \mathbb{R}^+$ is the smallest floating number representable on the respective hardware platform.

c) The learning time allotted to the algorithm is exceeded, i.e. $\lambda_{max}$ learning episodes have been processed without situation a) and b) having occurred.

Note that, although no convergence is achieved in cases b) and c), the algorithm does not diverge – in fact, it rather stops its learning process too early. At least, in these cases we can use the value of the presumed joint equilibrium found so far ($R_{max}$) as an indicator of the true equilibrium that eventually would have been discovered if $\lambda_{max}$ was larger or $\epsilon_{min}$ smaller.

### 4.2.5 Empirical Evaluation

In this section, we use the class of DEC-MDPs with changing action sets to model job-shop scheduling problems (JSSP), and we evaluate the performance of JEPS and $\text{JEPS}_G$ in this context using various established scheduling benchmarks. Note that, within this chapter, we primarily study the properties of the policy search approaches we are proposing and perform no comparison to alternative solution techniques. Later in this work, however, we will contrast the results our solution algorithms yield to standard scheduling methods such as dispatching priority rules.

As a proof of concept, we first apply both versions of JEPS suggested to the educational benchmark instance FT6 introduced in Section 3.1.1. In so doing, we aim at demonstrating that it is possible for the independently learning agents to achieve coordination when aiming at the acquisition of a high-quality joint policy for a difficult problem.

Given a JSSP instance, all agents process waiting jobs in a reactive manner according to Algorithm 4.1, i.e. they select jobs with respect to the probability determined by their current policy parameters, and never remain idle, if there is at least one job waiting. The policy update algorithms the agents employ are Algorithm 4.2 (JEPS) and Algorithm 4.3 ($\text{JEPS}_G$), respectively. Since minimizing makespan (i.e. processing time) is our objective, each time step's immediate global reward can be set to $r(t) = -1$. Equivalently, we can simplify the determination of the global return by letting $R = -C_{max}$, when all jobs are finished and, hence, $s^f$ has been reached. After the processing of a single scheduling episode, the system is reinitialized to the starting state where no jobs have been processed, and the agents start processing jobs again.

As depicted in Figure 3.3 on page 38, an optimal schedule for this problem has a makespan of $C_{max}^{opt} = 55$, but this one, as explained in Section 3.1.1 represents a delay schedule which requires some resources to remain idle for some time in spite of waiting jobs. Since JEPS agents are defined to learn reactive policies (cf. Definition 4.3) which correspond to the class of non-delay schedules, the joint equilibrium attainable by the agents corresponds to the best non-delay schedule, for which, in the case of the FT6 problem, it holds $C_{max}^{nd-opt} = 57$.

Knowing the value of a joint equilibrium ($R_{max} = -C_{max}^{nd-opt} = -57$) and, hence, being enabled to employ a fully accurate heuristic $H$, clearly both JEPS and $\text{JEPS}_G$ are guaranteed to converge to optimal policies (Lemmas 4 and 5). The more relevant case is,

## 4 Policy Search-Based Solution Approaches

however, when $R_{max}$ is not known a priori, but instead must be estimated during learning and, hence, an imperfect heuristic

$$H(R) = 1 \iff R \geq R_{max},$$

where $R = -C_{max}$ as the negative makespan of the current episode, is utilized. Figure 4.3 summarizes the average learning performance of JEPS and JEPS$_G$ for varying values of the learning rate $\gamma$. Each data point corresponds to 10 learning experiment repetitions; so, average and, in part, standard deviations of the expected policy performance $-J(\pi_\theta)$ in terms of makespan (which corresponds to the expectation $\mathbb{E}[-R]$ of the global return given the current policy) as well as of the development of $-R_{max}$ are plotted.

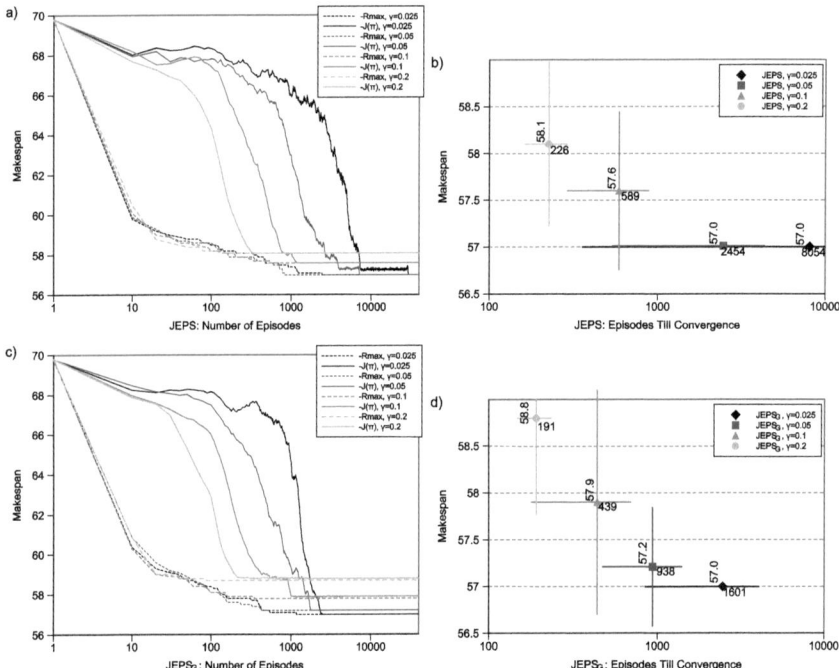

Figure 4.3: Learning Performance of JEPS (top row) and JEPS$_G$ (bottom row) for the FT6 benchmark and for growing values of the learning rate $\gamma \in \{0.025, 0.05, 0.1, 0.2\}$. Solid curves denote the expected joint policy performance $-J(\pi)$, dashed curves show the value of $-R_{max}$. The charts in the right column visualize how much interaction with the environment is on average necessary until the stochastic local policies have converged to a deterministic one; horizontal and vertical lines indicate the belonging standard deviations.

## 4.2 Joint Equilibrium Policy Search

Considering parts a) and b) of Figure 4.3, i.e. JEPS in its basic version, the most important point to note is that for smaller learning rates ($\gamma = 0.025/0.05$), the agents consistently acquire an optimal policy. This empirically confirms the effectiveness of the JEPS approach for bringing about inter-agent coordination and yielding a joint equilibrium. Increasing $\gamma$ has a significant impact on the speed of the learning progress (note the log scale abscissa). While with $\gamma = 0.025$ convergence to the joint equilibrium is attained after 8054 learning episodes on average, doubling the learning rate yields convergence after 2454 episodes on average.

With a further increase of the learning rate (e.g. to $\gamma = 0.1$ or $0.2$) the trade-off made becomes apparent: Now, the corresponding solid curve (denoting the performance $-J(\pi)$ of the agents' stochastic joint policy) in Figure 4.3a) approaches the dashed one (denoting the maximal global reward $R_{max}$ obtained so far and, thus, corresponding to the value the agents presume the joint equilibrium has) much faster. More importantly, these curves converge even before $R_{max}$ has adopted the value of the true joint equilibrium ($C_{max}^{nd-opt} = 57$), which indicates that the agents' local stochastic policies have approached (nearly-)deterministic, but sub-optimal ones. In other words, the increase of the learning rate and the corresponding acceleration of the learning process comes at the cost of risking premature convergence.

The bottom row of Figure 4.3 corresponds to the version of joint equilibrium policy search that utilizes a global action parameterization according to Section 4.2.2, i.e. to JEPS$_G$. A first observation to be made, when comparing the top and the bottom row of Figure 4.3, is that JEPS$_G$ brings about a significant learning speed-up which, seemingly, also comes at the cost of convergence to slightly worse joint policies.

The dependency of the learning results on the learning rate $\gamma$ is similar to the trade-off described above for basic JEPS, which might give rise to the conclusion that the switch from JEPS to JEPS$_G$ corresponds merely to an increase of $\gamma$. This conclusion, however, is incorrect: The crucial difference between both versions of JEPS lies in the way the agents' local policies are represented. JEPS$_G$ employs far less policy parameters using a global parameterization (one parameter per potential action) and, therefore, the occurrence of a learning speed-up (traded off against slightly impaired performance) is logical as fewer policy parameters have to be adjusted. As a consequence, JEPS$_G$ requires substantially less memory or disk space for storing its policies: Summing the storage requirements of all JEPS/JEPS$_G$ agents when learning for the FT6 problem, we see that they need to store 0.5 kilobyte and 33.9 kilobyte, respectively, for saving their policies. This difference plays a decisive role, when intending to apply the joint equilibrium policy search approach to larger scale problems.

Before seeking results for such larger benchmarks, we want to reveal the inner workings of a single JEPS$_G$ agent, when learning for the FT6 benchmark. Figure 4.4a) contrasts the learning progress (top) for a single learning experiment (no average over multiple repetitions) with the development of the local stochastic policy of a single agent (bottom). More precisely, the bottom part visualizes the development of the global policy parameter vector $\theta_G^2$ of the agent attached to resource $r_2$ (agent 2). For reasons of readability, the local policies of the other agents are not drawn. As FT6 is a job-shop scheduling problem with 6 jobs and without recirculation, it holds $|A_i^r| = 6$ and the global policy parameter vector of agent 2 can be written as $\theta_G^2 = (p_G(\alpha_1), \ldots, p_G(\alpha_6))$ where $\alpha_j$ can be equated

## 4 Policy Search-Based Solution Approaches

with a certain job $j \in \mathcal{J}$.

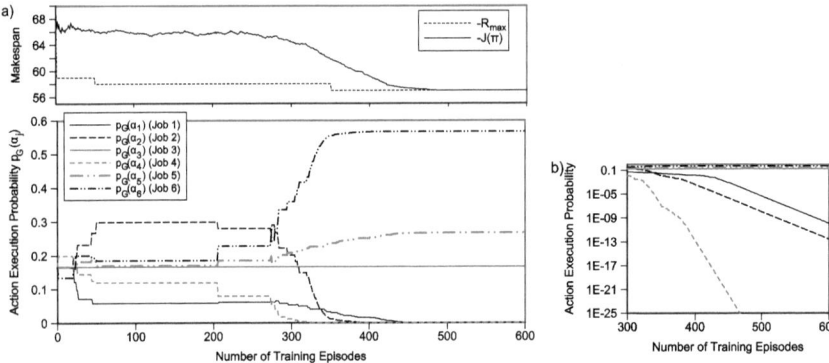

Figure 4.4: Policy Development within a Single Agent Using JEPS$_G$: Part a) of this figure visualizes how the policy parameters of agent 2, i.e. the vector $\theta_L^2 = (p_G(\alpha_1), \ldots, p_G(\alpha_6))$, develops during a single learning process. Additionally, the concurrent progress of the joint policy's performance is drawn atop. Part b) represents a zoom into the bottom right part of the chart in part a) using a log scale ordinate.

After having been initialized equally, i.e. $p_G(\alpha_j) = \frac{1}{6}$ for all $j \in \mathcal{J}$, agent 2 chooses jobs with equal probability and, thus, realizes a purely random dispatcher. In the course of learning, all $p_G(\alpha_j)$ are increased and decreased according to Algorithm 4.3, such that some actions start to dominate others. Note that the curves for $p_G(\alpha_j)$ shown are also heavily influenced by the policies pursued by the other agents whose policies are not visualized.

Figure 4.4b) magnifies the bottom right part of part a): While in a) it seems that $p_G(\alpha_1)$, $p_G(\alpha_2)$, and $p_G(\alpha_4)$ are converging to zero, the magnification in part b) (using a log scale ordinate) shows that the probability values attached to those three actions or jobs are of different orders of magnitude. Thus, for instance, in learning episode 450 it holds that approximately, as can be read from the chart, $p_G(\alpha_2) = 10^{-6}$ and $p_G(\alpha_4) = 10^{-21}$. If agent 2's current local state was $s_1 = \{\alpha_2, \alpha_4\}$, then according to Definition 4.4 the probabilities of executing either $\alpha_2$ or $\alpha_4$ are

$$\pi_2(s_2, \alpha_2) = Pr(\alpha_2|s_2) = \frac{p_G(\alpha_2)}{\sum_{\alpha \in s_2} p_G(\alpha)} = \frac{10^{-6}}{10^{-6} + 10^{-21}} \approx 1.0$$

and $\pi_2(s_2, \alpha_4) \approx 0.0$, respectively, which indicates that $\pi_2$ has indeed converged to a nearly deterministic policy.

**Benchmark Results**

Figure 4.5 illustrates the learning progress averaged over 15 JSSPs involving 10 jobs and 10 machines using JEPS as well as JEPS$_G$. Again, solid curves show the average

## 4.2 Joint Equilibrium Policy Search

expected performance (in terms of makespan $C_{max}$, i.e. negative reward) of the stochastic joint policies subject to the number of training episodes. Dashed curves indicate the development of the value of the supposed joint equilibrium $-R_{max}$, as utilized by the heuristic $H$. Here, we allowed the agents to maximally process $\lambda_{max} = 250k$ episodes, however, in most cases convergence could be achieved much faster. For settling the learning rate $\gamma$ we performed a line search and, taking the insights from the experiments around the FT6 problem instance into account, found $\gamma = 0.1$ to be the most suitable and compromising value, when dealing with larger-scale problems. On the one hand, choosing smaller learning rates can yield superior performance. However, when restricting the agents to $\lambda_{max} = 250k$ episodes, the probability of not reaching convergence within that time increases rapidly. On the other hand, larger values of $\gamma$ clearly increase learning speed, but enforce premature convergence too often. For consistency, we used the same learning rate during all experiments (for JEPS and JEPS$_G$ likewise).

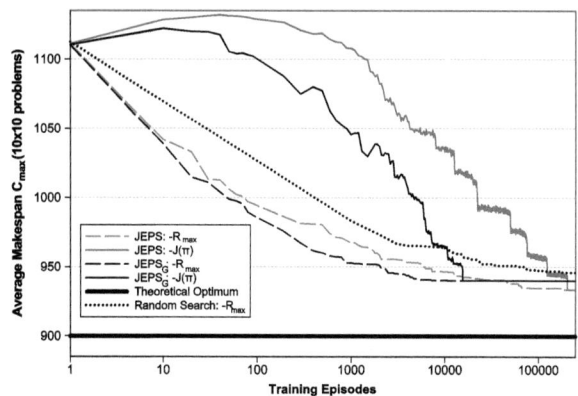

Figure 4.5: Learning Progress for JEPS and JEPS$_G$ on 10x10 Problems

Apparently, the $-R_{max}$ and $-J(\pi_\theta)$ curves approach each other much faster for the JEPS$_G$ variant of the algorithm than for JEPS with local policy parameterization. For the 15 scenarios considered, JEPS$_G$ converges at the latest after about 11k episodes. By contrast, JEPS needs much longer to yield convergence, but achieves finding slightly superior values of $R_{max}$, i.e. on average the learned joint policy comes closer to the true joint equilibrium (indicated by the average theoretical optimum for the scenarios considered).

Additionally, the plot in Figure 4.5 contains a curve for a random search (resembling a hill-climbing approach): Here, all agents steadily pursue purely random policies, and the best schedule (best $R_{max}$) is remembered. As to be expected, joint equilibrium policy represents a clearly more intelligent policy search method yielding superior policies.

The limitation of the basic form of JEPS becomes obvious when having a look at the sizes of the policies that must be kept in memory by the agents (see the rightmost columns in the JEPS and JEPS$_G$ part of Table 4.1, measured in bytes per policy). Since the number of policy parameters grows exponentially with $n$, the application of JEPS for $m \times n$

4 Policy Search-Based Solution Approaches

| Size | | Theor. | JEPS | | | | | Pol. | JEPS$_G$ | | | | | | Pol. |
|---|---|---|---|---|---|---|---|---|---|---|---|---|---|---|---|
| $m \times n$ | #Prbl | Optim. | #a | $-R_{max}$ | Err$_{R_{max}}$ | $J(\pi_\theta)$ | Err$_{J(\pi)}$ | Size | #a | #b | #c | $-R_{max}$ | Err$_{R_{max}}$ | $E[-R]$ | Err$_{J(\pi)}$ | Size |
| $5 \times 10$ | 5 | 620.2 | 5 | 631.8 | 1.9% | 631.8 | 1.9% | 1029k | 4 | 0 | 1 | 635.4 | 2.5% | 644.2 | 3.9% | 0.6k |
| $5 \times 15$ | 5 | 917.6 | 5 | 917.6 | 0.0% | 917.6 | 0.0% | 18M | 5 | 0 | 0 | 917.6 | 0.0% | 917.6 | 0.0% | 1.1k |
| $5 \times 20$ | 6 | 1179.2 | 0 | - | - | - | - | $\infty$ | 5 | 1 | 0 | 1188.3 | 0.8% | 1196.5 | 1.5% | 1.5k |
| $10 \times 10_a$ | 3 | 1035.7 | 3 | 1071.0 | 3.4% | 1071.0 | 3.4% | 3.5M | 3 | 1 | 0 | 1076.7 | 3.9% | 1076.7 | 3.9% | 1.2k |
| $10 \times 10_b$ | 5 | 864.2 | 5 | 902.4 | 4.4% | 902.4 | 4.4% | 973k | 5 | 1 | 0 | 894.2 | 3.5% | 894.2 | 3.5% | 1.1k |
| $10 \times 10_c$ | 9 | 898.2 | 8 | 935.3 | 4.1% | 937.4 | 4.4% | 6.4M | 8 | 1 | 0 | 952.4 | 6.0% | 953.6 | 6.2% | 1.2k |
| $10 \times 15$ | 5 | 983.4 | 0 | - | - | - | - | $\infty$ | 2 | 1 | 2 | 1032.4 | 5.0% | 1142.4 | 16.2% | 2.1k |
| $15 \times 15$ | 5 | 1263.2 | 0 | - | - | - | - | $\infty$ | 3 | 1 | 1 | 1341.2 | 6.1% | 1375.8 | 8.9% | 3.0k |
| $15 \times 20$ | 3 | 676.0 | 0 | - | - | - | - | $\infty$ | 0 | 0 | 3 | 732.0 | 8.3% | 819.7 | 21.2% | 4.1k |
| Average | 46 | 946.5 | | | | | | | | | | 983.3 | 3.9%$_{\pm 3.3}$ | 1007.0 | 6.6%$_{\pm 7.3}$ | |

Table 4.1: Learning results for scheduling benchmarks of varying size, opposed for JEPS and JEPS$_G$. All entries are averaged over the number of benchmark problems considered (#Prbl), #a, #b, and #c correspond to the convergence possibilities listed in Section 4.2.4. The last column in each part shows the average size of a policy measured in bytes. Err columns denote the relative remaining error (%) of the makespan ($-R_{max}$ and $J(\pi_\theta)$, respectively) achieved by the joint policy compared to the theoretical optimum and, thus, indicate to what extent reaching the true joint equilibrium was missed. Indices a, b, c stand for problem sets provided by different authors.

problems with larger values of $n$ is infeasible due to excessive memory requirements. On the contrary, the average policy sizes of JEPS$_G$ agents are negligible. Here, instead the underflow problem (cf. Section 4.2.4) may occur for larger values of $n$. However, using JEPS$_G$, policies of high quality can be learned even for larger-sized problem instances.

The experiments stress that the presented multi-agent policy search method, JEPS, is effective in learning joint equilibria, or near-optimal approximations thereof, for decentralized Markov decision processes with changing action sets. Using the variant of the learning algorithm that employs a highly compacted policy representation, JEPS$_G$, it is possible to apply this learning approach to even larger problem instances without impairing performance. We will critically discuss the results obtained in a comprehensive manner in Section 4.4 below.

Obviously, a limiting factor of the JEPS approach is its necessity for a heuristic that indicates whether a joint equilibrium has been acquired by the ensemble of agents. Therefore, an interesting direction for future research may be the investigation of more sophisticated versions of this heuristic. In the scope of this work, however, we instead pursue the idea of employing alternative state of the art mechanisms for policy search-based reinforcement learning. So, in the following section we develop a multi-agent gradient-descent method for updating the policy parameters of the agents interacting with the DEC-MDP.

## 4.3 Gradient-Descent Policy Search

In this section, we are continuing to consider teams of cooperative agents that aim at maximizing the global reward in a decentralized Markov decision process with changing action sets and partially ordered transition dependencies. In particular, further on we utilize simple and independent agents that employ probabilistic local policies of action.

## 4.3 Gradient-Descent Policy Search

By contrast to the ideas presented before, the learning approach to be presented subsequently employs *policy gradient* (PG) reinforcement learning (Williams, 1992; Sutton et al., 2000) as a special type of policy search-based reinforcement learning to optimize the agents' policies. Policy gradient algorithms have established themselves as the most frequently used and investigated policy search technique and, hence, as the main alternative reinforcement learning approach besides value function-based methods. Omitting the need to enumerate states and being well applicable to multi-agent settings, policy gradient methods represent a natural option for solving decentralized MDPs with changing action sets and, thus, for tackling job-shop scheduling problems that are modelled using that framework.

The basic idea of policy gradient reinforcement learning algorithms is to estimate the gradient of the expected return of the process. In terms of the application domain we are targeting, i.e. when addressing scheduling tasks with stochastic dispatching policies, where for example an objective function such as the makespan $C_{max}$ shall be optimized, this translates to an estimate of the gradient of the makespan of the resulting schedule, which is derived with respect to a set of real-valued policy parameters. These parameters make up the agents' stochastic policies and determine their dispatching behavior. To this end, we will suggest a compact representation of the agents' local policies that can also directly be mapped to a complete selection of a disjunctive graph for the problem at hand. Following the gradient by adjusting the policy parameters' values (and assuming the correctness of the gradient estimate), it is guaranteed that the expected return of the policy is improved, i.e. that schedules that are better in terms of makespan are created with higher probability.

### 4.3.1 Gradient-Descent Policy Learning

As explained in Section 4.1.1, the general idea of policy optimization in reinforcement learning is to optimize the policy parameter vector $\theta$ such that the policy performance $J(\pi_\theta)$ defined as the sum of immediate global rewards (Equation 4.1) is maximized. When employing $m$ independently acting and learning agents, each one strives for optimizing its own parameter set $\theta^i$ optimizing its corresponding local policy $\pi_{\theta^i}$.

In this section, we introduce the concept of gradient-descent policy learning for one single agent, i.e. we assume a single entity controlling action choices and, in so doing, can disregard the agent-specific indices $i$ (e.g. an experience sequence then is the history of states, actions, and rewards of the action, and no longer a collection of sequences $\langle h_1, \ldots, h_m \rangle$). Thereafter (Section 4.3.2), we generalize these ideas to the multi-agent case.

**Single-Agent Policy Gradient Estimation**

Assuming a single agent interacting with its environment (MDP), this central authority collects an experience sequence (adapted from Definition 4.2)

$$h = [s(0), a(0), r(0), s(1), \ldots, s(D-1), a(D-1), r(D-1), s(D)]$$

## 4 Policy Search-Based Solution Approaches

of length $D$ using its policy $\pi_\theta$ which is parameterized by parameter vector $\theta = (\theta_1, \ldots, \theta_u)$ ($u \geq 1$ denotes the number of parameters used). Policy gradient methods follow the steepest descent on the expected return. This requires that the policy performance $J(\pi_\theta)$ must be differentiable with respect to each component $\theta_k$ of the parameter vector $\theta$. It holds

$$\begin{aligned}\nabla_{\theta_k} J(\pi_\theta) &= \nabla_{\theta_k} \mathbb{E}\left[\sum_{d=0}^{D-1} \gamma^k r(k) | \pi_\theta\right] \\ &= \nabla_{\theta_k} \sum_{h \in \mathcal{H}} Pr(h|\theta) R(h)\end{aligned} \quad (4.4)$$

where $\mathcal{H}$ denotes the space of all possible experience sequences. $R(h)$ corresponds to the return collected in one specific episode (experience sequence) that is denoted by $h$ and that arose using current policy parameters $\theta$. Exploiting the properties of the log likelihood, Equation 4.4 can be written as

$$\begin{aligned}\nabla_{\theta_k} J(\pi_\theta) &= \sum_{h \in \mathcal{H}} R(h) \frac{\nabla_{\theta_k} Pr(h|\theta)}{Pr(h|\theta)} Pr(h|\theta) \\ &= \mathbb{E}\left[R(h) \nabla_{\theta_k} \ln Pr(h|\theta) | \pi_\theta\right].\end{aligned} \quad (4.5)$$

The term $Pr(h|\theta)$ needs some more profound consideration. It denotes the probability that an experience sequence $h$ is created given that the agent chooses its actions according to the policy defined through parameters $\theta$. This probability can be defined recursively: Let $\mathcal{H}^D$ denote the space of sequences of length $D$. Given a shortened experience sequence $h^{D-1} \in \mathcal{H}^{D-1}$ and assuming knowledge of $Pr(h^{D-1}|\theta)$, the probability of $h^D$ can be computed by multiplying $Pr(h^{D-1}|\theta)$ with (a) the probability of executing action $a(D-1)$ depending on $h^{D-1}$ and policy $\pi_\theta$, (b) the probability of receiving reward $r(D-1)$ given $s(D-1)$, $a(D-1)$ and $s(D)$, and (c) the probability of entering $s(D)$ given $s(D-1)$ and $a(D-1)$. Thus,

$$\begin{aligned}Pr(h^D|\theta) &= Pr(h^{D-1}|\theta) \cdot Pr(a(D-1)|h^{D-1}, \pi_\theta) \\ &\quad \cdot Pr(r(D-1)|s(D-1), a(D-1), s(D)) \cdot Pr(s(D)|s(D-1), a(D-1)) \\ &= Pr(h^{D-1}|\theta) \cdot \pi_\theta(\bar{s}(D-1, h^{D-1}), a(D-1)) \\ &\quad \cdot r(s(D-1), a(D-1), s(D)) \cdot p(s(D-1), a(D-1), s(D)),\end{aligned}$$

where functions $r$ and $p$ are the reward and transition function of the underlying MDP, and based on this recursive formulation, we can state the following auxiliary lemma.

**Lemma 6.** *Given an experience sequence $h^D$ of length $D$ and a policy $\pi_\theta$ that parameterizes the single agent's actions through parameters $\theta = (\theta_1, \ldots, \theta_u)$, it holds for all $\theta_k$ ($1 \leq k \leq u$)*

$$\nabla_{\theta_k} \ln Pr(h^D|\theta) = \sum_{d=0}^{D-1} \nabla_{\theta_k} \ln \pi_\theta(\bar{s}(d, h^D), a(d, h^D)) \quad (4.6)$$

*where $\bar{s}(d, h^D)$ denotes the sequence of the first $d+1$ states from $h^D$ (cf. Definition 4.2).*

## 4.3 Gradient-Descent Policy Search

*Proof.* By induction over $D$.
*Induction Base Case:* $D = 0$. The set $\mathcal{H}^0$ contains only one single element $h = [s(0)]$ which is why $Pr(h|\theta) = 1$ and $\nabla_{\theta_k} \ln Pr(h|\theta) = 0$ for all $j$. The right-hand side of Equation 4.6 is 0 as it represents an empty sum. Thus, the base case holds.
*Induction Assumption:* For all experience sequences $h^D \in \mathcal{H}^D$ of length $D$ Equation 4.6 holds.
*Induction Hypothesis:* For all experience sequences $h \in \mathcal{H}^{D+1}$ of length $D+1$ it holds

$$\nabla_{\theta_k} \ln Pr(h^{D+1}|\theta) = \sum_{d=0}^{D} \nabla_{\theta_k} \ln \pi_\theta(\bar{s}(d, h^{D+1}), a(d, h^{D+1})).$$

*Induction Step:* Let $h^{D+1} = [s(0), a(0), r(0), s(1), \ldots, s(D), a(D), r(D), s(D+1)] \in \mathcal{H}^{D+1}$ be an experience sequence of length $D+1$ and $h^D \in \mathcal{H}^D$ its prefix of length $D$. Then, by the recursive definition of $Pr(h|\theta)$ we have

$$\begin{aligned}
&\nabla_{\theta_k} \ln Pr(h^{D+1}|\theta) \\
&= \nabla_{\theta_k} \ln \left( Pr(h^D|\theta) \cdot Pr(a(D)|h^D, \pi_\theta) \right. \quad (4.7) \\
&\quad \left. \cdot Pr(r(D)|s(D), a(D), s(D+1)) \cdot Pr(s(D+1)|s(D), a(D)) \right) \\
&= \nabla_{\theta_k} \ln Pr(h^D|\theta) + \nabla_{\theta_k} \ln \pi_\theta(\bar{s}(D, h^D), a(D)) \\
&\quad + \nabla_{\theta_k} \ln r(s(D), a(D), s(D+1)) + \nabla_{\theta_k} \ln p(s(D), a(D), s(D+1)).
\end{aligned}$$

The third and fourth term of this sum evaluate to zero as the state transition and reward probabilities do not depend on $\theta_k$. Using the induction assumption, we obtain

$$\begin{aligned}
\nabla_{\theta_k} \ln Pr(h^{D+1}|\theta) &= \sum_{d=0}^{D-1} \nabla_{\theta_k} \ln \pi_\theta(\bar{s}(d, h^D), a(d, h^D)) + \nabla_{\theta_k} \ln \pi_\theta(\bar{s}(D, h^D), a(D)) \\
&= \sum_{d=0}^{D} \nabla_{\theta_k} \ln \pi_\theta(\bar{s}(d, h^{D+1}), a(d, h^{D+1})).
\end{aligned}$$

$\square$

Lemma 6 allows us to determine the log derivative of $Pr(h|\theta)$ with respect to any policy parameter without the need for an explicit representation of that distribution. The only requirement that must be fulfilled is that the policy $\pi_\theta$ must be differentiable with respect to any $\theta_k$. Rewriting Equation 4.5, we can express the gradient of a policy's performance as

$$\begin{aligned}
\nabla_{\theta_k} J(\pi_\theta) &= \mathbb{E}\left[ R(h) \sum_{d=0}^{D_h - 1} \nabla_{\theta_k} \ln \pi_\theta(\bar{s}(d, h), a(d, h)) \right] \\
&= \sum_{h \in \mathcal{H}} R(h) Pr(h|\theta) \left( \sum_{d=0}^{D_h - 1} \nabla_{\theta_k} \ln \pi_\theta(\bar{s}(d, h), a(d, h)) \right), \quad (4.8)
\end{aligned}$$

where $D_h$ denotes the length of a specific sequence $h$.

# 4 Policy Search-Based Solution Approaches

It must be emphasized that an exact computation of the gradient $\nabla_\theta J(\pi_\theta)$ becomes quickly intractable as the problem size grows. Therefore, throughout this chapter, we revert to determining Monte-Carlo estimates of the gradient, similar to related work (Williams, 1992; Sutton et al., 2000; Peshkin et al., 2000), generated from a samples set $E$ of experience sequences. Consequently, when applying Equation 4.8, the outer sum does not run over $h \in \mathcal{H}$, but over $h \in E$ instead.

**Updating the Policy**

An update to the agents' policy parameters $\theta = (\theta_1, \ldots, \theta_u)$ uses for all $k \in \{1, \ldots, u\}$ the standard rule

$$\theta_k \leftarrow \theta_k + \beta_b \nabla_{\theta_k} J(\pi_\theta) \qquad (4.9)$$

where $\beta_b \in \mathbb{R}^+$ denotes a learning rate.

If $b \in \mathbb{N}$ counts the number of policy updates made and $\sum_b \beta_b = \infty$, $\sum_b \beta_b^2 = const$, then the learning process is guaranteed to converge to a local optimum, at least. The policy gradient update scheme realized resembles the episodic Reinforce gradient estimator (Williams, 1992). For various applications, the fact that this algorithm estimates the gradient for a dedicated recurrent state, is problematic. Hence, other algorithms, such as GPOMDP (Baxter and Bartlett, 1999) or the natural actor critic (NAC, Peters et al., 2005), were suggested that are intended to overcome the need of identifying a specific recurrent state. Meanwhile, they come at the cost of introducing a bias to the gradient estimate and trading this off against reducing variance. Because, for DEC-MDPs with changing action sets and partially ordered transition dependencies which will return into the center of our interest subsequently, a recurrent state (starting state) is naturally available, we keep with doing the gradient calculation using the likelihood ratio method described.

## 4.3.2 Independent Agents and Decentralized Policy Gradient

The line of arguments given in the previous section assumed a single agent executing solitary actions. We now return to the consideration of $m$-agent factored DEC-MDP environments where the actions can be broken up into $m$ partial, or local actions.

As specified in Definition 2.9, the joint policy $\pi$ is defined as the tuple of $m$ local policies, i.e. $\pi = \langle \pi_1, \ldots, \pi_m \rangle$. We assume that the policy $\pi_i$ of each agent $i$ is defined through a small set of parameters $\theta^i = (\theta^i_1, \ldots, \theta^i_{u_i})$ where all $\theta^i_k \in \mathbb{R}$. These parameter vectors form the basis for defining probabilistic agent-specific policies of action.

Accordingly, the parameter vector for the joint policy is made up of the concatenation of all local policies' parameters: $\theta = (\theta^1, \ldots, \theta^m)$. For clarity of notation, in the remainder of this chapter we will denote local policies by $\pi_{\theta^i}$ (instead of $\pi_i$) to stress their dependency on their parameters $\theta^i$.

Our goal retains to perform gradient descent-based policy search under these conditions where, in analogy to the single agent case, we also estimate the gradient of policy performance using Monte-Carlo methods. In what follows, we distinguish between two different approaches to action execution and gradient-descent policy search-based learning.

## 4.3 Gradient-Descent Policy Search

**a) Joint Control and Learning** This corresponds to a central authority that takes actions and performs learning updates. Insofar, it resembles the single agent case from Section 4.3.1 to some extent. However, since we are addressing $m$-agent factored DEC-MDPs we assume that any action must be split into $m$ independent components. Therefore, this approach explicitly considers joint policies $\pi_\theta = \langle \pi_{\theta^1}, \ldots, \pi_{\theta^m} \rangle$ and executes joint actions $a = (a_1, \ldots, a_m)$, though each partial policy $\pi_{\theta^i}$ is represented by its own set of parameters $\theta^i$.

Under these assumptions the gradient of policy performance can be expressed[5] as

$$\nabla_\theta J(\pi_\theta) = \sum_{h \in \mathcal{H}} R(h) Pr(h|\theta) \left( \sum_{d=0}^{D_h - 1} \nabla_\theta \ln \pi_\theta(\overline{s}(d,h), a(d,h)) \right) \quad (4.10)$$

where $\pi_\theta$ is composed as the product of $\pi_{\theta^i}$ (for $i = 1, \ldots, m$)

$$\pi_\theta(\overline{s}, a) = \prod_{i=1}^{m} \pi_{\theta^i}(\overline{s}_i, a_i) \quad (4.11)$$

and where $a = (a_1, \ldots, a_m)$ and $h = \langle h_1, \ldots, h_m \rangle$ denote joint actions and joint experience sequences, respectively (cf. Definitions 2.5 and 4.2).

**b) Decentralized Control and Learning** While we have mentioned the former approach for reference, the fully decentralized approach is the one that we consistently pursue in this book: We have $m$ independent agents that select their actions independently using their local policies $\pi_{\theta^i}$ that are specified through parameters $\theta^i = (\theta^i_1, \ldots, \theta^i_{u_i})$. Furthermore, we equip each agent with the same policy gradient algorithm to update its local policy.

Under these assumptions the gradient of policy performance can be expressed as

$$\nabla_{\theta^i} J(\pi_\theta) = \sum_{h_i \in \mathcal{H}_i} R(h_i) Pr(h_i|\theta) \left( \sum_{d=0}^{D_{h_i} - 1} \nabla_{\theta^i} \ln \pi_{\theta^i}(\overline{s}_i(d, h_i), a(d, h_i)) \right) \quad (4.12)$$

with the distinctive feature that each agent $i$ calculates its individual gradient $\nabla_{\theta^i} J(\pi_\theta)$ based on local information stored in agent-specific experience sequences $h_i$.

Needless to say, that the factorization of action choice and execution we assume results in the fact that any of the two approaches outlined can represent only a subset of policies that a central non-factored controller (corresponding to, for example, the single agent case) can implement. Therefore, when subsequently speaking about learning updates made to policies we have to keep in mind that a factored learning approach can at best yield the best set of local policies from the restricted class of factored policies.

One may wonder how decentralized policy gradient learning (approach b)) relates to updates that are performed by a central learning authority (approach a)). As it turns out,

---
[5]Recall that $s(d, h)$ and $a(d, h)$ access the $d$th state and action of sequence $h$.

## 4 Policy Search-Based Solution Approaches

both approaches produce identical results: As shown by Peshkin et al. (2000), gradient-descent policy search performed by independent agents (distributed gradient-descent) is identical to joint gradient descent, i.e. to learning updates made by a central authority, as long as factored policies $\pi_\theta = \langle \pi_{\theta_1}, \ldots, \pi_{\theta_m} \rangle$ are considered. We adapt their finding to our problem settings and prove the following theorem.

**Theorem 3.** *Given a factored DEC-MDP controlled by $m$ local policies $\pi_{\theta^1}, \ldots, \pi_{\theta^m}$ that are parameterized by parameter vectors $\theta^1, \ldots, \theta^m$, we denote the joint policy realized by $\pi = \langle \pi_{\theta^1}, \ldots, \pi_{\theta^m} \rangle$ and by $\theta = (\theta^1, \ldots, \theta^m)$ the concatenation of those parameters. Then, the gradient of policy performance $G_C = \nabla_\theta J(\pi_\theta)$ (Equation 4.10) is equal to the vector of gradients $G_D = (\nabla_{\theta^1} J(\pi_\theta), \ldots, \nabla_{\theta^m} J(\pi_\theta))$ where each $\nabla_{\theta^i} J(\pi_\theta)$ (for $1 \leq i \leq m$, Equation 4.12) is determined by an independent agent $i$.*

*Proof.* For the case of centralized control and learning we can write
$$\theta = (\theta^1_1, \ldots, \theta^1_{u_1}, \ldots \ldots, \theta^m_1, \ldots, \theta^m_{u_m})$$
Accordingly, for each component $\nabla_{\theta^i_k}$ of $G_C$ ($1 \leq i \leq m$, $1 \leq k \leq u_i$) there exists a corresponding entry within the $i$th component of $G_D$, i.e. within $\nabla_{\theta^i}$. Let $i \in \{1, \ldots, m\}$ and $k \in \{1, \ldots, u_i\}$. Substituting Equation 4.11 into Equation 4.10 yields

$$\nabla_{\theta^i_k} J(\pi_\theta) = \sum_{h \in \mathcal{H}} R(h) Pr(h|\theta) \left( \sum_{d=0}^{D_h-1} \nabla_{\theta^i_k} \ln \prod_{j=1}^m \pi_{\theta^j}(\overline{s}_j(d,h), a_j(d,h)) \right)$$

$$= \sum_{h \in \mathcal{H}} R(h) Pr(h|\theta) \left( \sum_{d=0}^{D_h-1} \sum_{j=1}^m \nabla_{\theta^i_k} \ln \pi_{\theta^j}(\overline{s}_j(d,h), a_j(d,h)) \right).$$

Because, however, the action choice probabilities of one agent do not depend on the policy parameters of any other agent, it holds

$$\nabla_{\theta^i_k} \ln \pi_{\theta^j}(\overline{s}_j(d,h), a_j(d,h)) = 0$$

for all $i \neq j$ and for all $k$, and the previous expression simplifies to

$$\nabla_{\theta^i_k} J(\pi_\theta) = \sum_{h \in \mathcal{H}} R(h) Pr(h|\theta) \left( \sum_{d=0}^{D_h-1} \nabla_{\theta^i_k} \ln \pi_{\theta^i}(\overline{s}_i(d,h), a_i(d,h)) \right),$$

and, since $\overline{s}_i(d,h) = \overline{s}_i(d,h_i)$ and $a_i(d,h) = a_i(d,h_i)$,

$$\nabla_{\theta^i_k} J(\pi_\theta) = \sum_{h \in \mathcal{H}} R(h) Pr(h|\theta) \left( \sum_{d=0}^{D_h-1} \nabla_{\theta^i_k} \ln \pi_{\theta^i}(\overline{s}_i(d,h_i), a_i(d,h_i)) \right).$$

Because we consider cooperative agents that receive the same global immediate rewards, the return of an episode $R(h)$ equals the return of agent-specific experience sequences $R(h_i)$. Finally, we note that
$\sum_{h \in \mathcal{H}} Pr(h|\theta) f(h_i) = \sum_{\langle h_1 \ldots h_m \rangle \in \mathcal{H}} Pr(\langle h_1 \ldots h_m \rangle | \theta) f(h_i) = \sum_{h_i \in \mathcal{H}_i} Pr(h_i|\theta) f(h_i)$
for each function $f$. Thus, we obtain

$$\nabla_{\theta^i_k} J(\pi_\theta) = \sum_{h_i \in \mathcal{H}_i} R(h_i) Pr(h_i|\theta) \left( \sum_{d=0}^{D_{h_i}-1} \nabla_{\theta^i_k} \ln \pi_{\theta^i}(\overline{s}_i(d,h_i), a_i(d,h_i)) \right)$$

which is equal to the definition of the gradient $G_D$ determined in a decentralized manner (Equation 4.12). Hence, both gradients are identical. □

Theorem 3 tells that the decentralization of action execution among independent agents has no effect on the policy gradient estimates. Independent agents that are not aware of their teammates' actions and only receive local state information determine the same gradient as a centralized learning algorithm would do. An important requirement to be fulfilled, however, is that all agents perform simultaneous learning, i.e. update their policies at the same time. In the next section, we present an algorithmic realization of the decentralized gradient-descent policy search method derived using independent agents that synchronize their learning by means of episode endings.

### 4.3.3 Policy Gradient under Changing Action Sets

In this section, we tailor the policy search-based reinforcement learning approach using gradient-descent outlined above for DEC-MDPs with changing action sets. We repeat that, for this class of decentralized decision problems the agents' local states are fully described by the set of available actions and, hence, the local state spaces $S_i$ correspond to the power set over all local actions $\mathcal{P}(\mathcal{A}_i^r)$.

**Compact Policy Representation**

We assume that the policy of each agent $i$ is compactly represented by a small set of parameters $\theta^i = (\theta_1^i, \ldots, \theta_n^i)$ where all $\theta_j^i \in \mathbb{R}$. In particular, we presume that there is exactly one parameter for each action from $\mathcal{A}_i^r$ (e.g. for each job the agent can execute when focussing on job-shop scheduling problems). As a shortcut, we refer to the parameter belonging to $\alpha \in \mathcal{A}_i^r$ by $\theta_\alpha^i$. Accordingly, for a $m \times n$ job-shop scheduling problem (with no recirculation and $m$ operations in each job), we have $m$ agents with $n$ policy parameters, thus a total of $mn$ parameters to fully describe the agents' joint policy.

The parameter vectors mentioned form the basis for defining probabilistic agent-specific policies of action.

**Definition 4.5** (Gibbs Policy).
*Let $s_i \subseteq \mathcal{A}_i^r$ be the current state of agent $i$ where, as explained before, $s_i$ is the set containing all actions currently available for agent $i$. The probability of action $Pr(\alpha|s_i, \theta^i) = \pi_{\theta^i}(s_i, \alpha)$ for policy $\pi_{\theta^i}$ is for all actions $\alpha \in \mathcal{A}_i^r$ defined according to the Gibbs distribution,*

$$\pi_{\theta^i}(s_i, \alpha) = \begin{cases} \frac{e^{-\theta_\alpha^i}}{\sum_{x \in s_i} e^{-\theta_x^i}} & \text{if } \alpha \in s_i \\ 0 & \text{else} \end{cases}$$

*so that actions that are currently not available have zero probability of being executed. Again, the joint policy $\pi$ is the concatenation of local policies $\langle \pi_{\theta^i}, \ldots, \pi_{\theta^i} \rangle$.*

With respect to scheduling, the probabilistic action selection scheme according to Definition 4.5 represents a stochastic and reactive scheduling policy that, when applied, yields

## 4 Policy Search-Based Solution Approaches

the creation of non-delay schedules. Every time $s_i \neq \emptyset$, an action $\alpha \in \mathcal{A}_i^r$ is being executed, i.e. a resource never remains idle when jobs are waiting for further processing. As a consequence, all stochastic policies (for any values of $\theta^i$) reach the terminal state $s^f = (s_1, \ldots, s_m)$ where all jobs have been finished and, hence, for all $i$ it holds that $s_i = \emptyset$. Note that in a later chapter (Chapter 6), we relax the restriction of acting purely reactively in order to be able to create schedules from beyond the class of non-delay schedules, too.

As pointed out in Section 4.3.1, a crucial precondition for applying a gradient-descent approach to policy optimization is that an agent's policy $\pi_{\theta^i}$ must be differentiable with respect to any component of the parameter vector $\theta^i$. For the compact policy representation using $|\mathcal{A}_i^r|$ parameters as proposed in Definition 4.5 (Gibbs policy) this naturally holds true. For all $\theta_\alpha^i$ ($1 \leq i \leq m$, $\alpha \in \mathcal{A}_i^r$), $s_i \subset \mathcal{A}_i^r$, and $a_i \in \mathcal{A}_i^r$ it holds

$$\nabla_{\theta_\alpha^i} \ln \pi_{\theta^i}(s_i, a_i) = \begin{cases} 1 - \pi_{\theta^i}(s_i, a_i) & \text{if } a_i = \alpha \\ -\pi_{\theta^i}(s_i, a_i) & \text{else.} \end{cases} \quad (4.13)$$

Consequently, given a set $E$ of experience sequences for agent $i$, the gradient $\nabla_{\theta^i} J(\pi_\theta)$ of the policy's performance can be calculated for each parameter $\theta_\alpha^i$ from $\theta^i = (\theta_1^i, \ldots, \theta_{|\mathcal{A}_i^r|}^i)$ as

$$\nabla_{\theta_\alpha^i} J(\pi_\theta) = \frac{1}{|E|} \sum_{h_i \in E} \left( R(h_i) \sum_{d=0}^{D_{h_i}-1} \nabla_{\theta_\alpha^i} \ln \pi_{\theta^i}(s_i(d, h_i), a(d, h_i)) \right).$$

Note, that $\pi_{\theta^i}$ is a reactive policy considering not the sequence $\bar{s}_i(d, h_i)$ of local states, but only the most recent observation, which is why in this way search can be performed only in the limited class of reactive local policies. Moreover, the gradient is not calculated analytically, but sampled in a Monte-Carlo manner by interacting with the environment and, hence, determined from a finite set of experience sequences $E \subset \mathcal{H}_i$ as noted before.

Finally, we employ the average performance

$$\bar{J}_E(\pi_\theta) = \frac{1}{|E|} \sum_{h_i \in E} R(h_i)$$

as a simple baseline to reduce the variance of the gradient estimate (Greensmith et al., 2004). Thus, the component for parameter $\theta_\alpha^i$ of the policy gradient estimate becomes

$$g_\alpha^E := \nabla_{\theta_\alpha^i} J(\pi_\theta) = \frac{1}{|E|} \sum_{h_i \in E} \left( (R(h_i) - \bar{J}_E(\pi_\theta)) \sum_{d=0}^{D_{h_i}-1} \nabla_{\theta_\alpha^i} \ln \pi_{\theta^i}(s_i(d, h_i), a_i(d, h_i)) \right) \quad (4.14)$$

where $\nabla_{\theta_\alpha^i} \ln \pi_{\theta^i}(\cdot)$ is determined according to Equation 4.13.

**Gradient-Descent Policy Update Algorithm**

The considerations on gradient-descent policy search (GDPS) made so far in this section lead to the formulation of Algorithm 4.4. This algorithm is meant to be plugged in the generic decentralized policy search reinforcement learning algorithm specified in Section

## 4.3 Gradient-Descent Policy Search

4.1 (Algorithm 4.1) taking the role of the policy update mechanism to be called there in line 10. The GDPS update scheme employs an experience sequence store $E$ as a global variable (which, of course, is empty initially) and repeatedly adds the respective current experience sequence to that set.

---

**Input:** learning rate $\beta \in (0,1]$, experience sequence of current episode
$h_i = [s_i(0), a_i(0), r(0), s_i(1), \ldots, s_i(D-1), a_r(D-1), r(D-1), s^f]$
where $D = |\mathcal{A}_i^r|$ denotes the episode's length (number of actions executed)

**Static Variables:** experience sequence storage $E$ (initially empty), policy $\pi_{\theta^i}$ determined by parameters $\theta^i = (\theta_1^i, \ldots, \theta_{|\mathcal{A}_i^r|}^i)$

1: $E \leftarrow E \cup \{h\}$
2: **if** $H(E, h) = 1$ **then**
3:    **for all** $e \in E$ **do**
4:       $R(e) = \sum_{d=0}^{D-1} r(d)$ //no discounting
5:    $\overline{J}_E(\pi_\theta) \leftarrow \frac{1}{|E|} \sum_{e \in E} R(e)$ //baseline
6:    **for all** $\alpha \in \mathcal{A}_i^r$ **do**
7:       $g_\alpha^E \leftarrow \frac{1}{|E|} \sum_{h_i \in E} \left( (R(h_i) - \overline{J}_E(\pi_\theta)) \sum_{d=0}^{D_{h_i}-1} \nabla_{\theta_\alpha^i} \ln \pi_{\theta^i}(s_i(d, h_i), a_i(d, h_i)) \right)$
8:       $\theta_\alpha^i \leftarrow \theta_\alpha^i + \beta g_\alpha^E$
9:    $E \leftarrow \emptyset$

**Algorithm 4.4:**
GDPS Policy Updates by Agent $i$ Using the Gibbs Policy and Parameterization

---

In order to signify the relatedness between GDPS and the JEPS algorithms presented in Section 4.2, we likewise provided GDPS with a heuristic $H$ (line 2) that decides whether an update to the policy's parameters should be performed or whether further experience sequences ought to be collected. An obvious implementation of $H$ might focus on the convergence of the gradient estimation process, determine both the gradient for $E$ as well as $E \setminus \{h\}$, i.e. calculate $g_\alpha^E$ and $g_\alpha^{E \setminus \{h\}}$, and return true, if $|g_\alpha^E - g_\alpha^{E \setminus \{h\}}|$ falls below some threshold. Such an implementation would be data-efficient insofar as each agent could individually determine when it has a stable estimate of the gradient and, subsequently, adapt its policy. Unfortunately, then the requirement of all agents performing gradient descent-based policy updates in parallel (as formulated in Section 4.3.2 and required for Theorem 3) would be violated.

At the cost of necessitating coordinative communication between the agents, this problem might be circumvented, if each agent broadcasts, when it has calculated a stable gradient estimate, and all agents actually do their updates upon having received a corresponding message from any other agent.

In what follows, however, we rely on a built-in synchronization of the policy learning updates realized through episode endings encountered. We define a global constant $e$ that determines after how many experience sequences each agent within the collective of agents must compute an estimate of the gradient and perform its policy update, i.e. we let

$$H(E, h) \Leftrightarrow |E| \geq e.$$

4 Policy Search-Based Solution Approaches

Since each agent is notified about an episode's end ($s^f$ has been reached), in this way a natural synchronization of learning is established and policy updates are made in parallel (line 3-8). After that, the experience sequence store $E$ is emptied such that all agent start sampling new experience sequences using their updated local policies.

### 4.3.4 Discussion

The GDPS learning algorithm allows for model-free learning in decentralized Markov decision processes where the learning agents have only a partial view of the global system state. In developing the algorithm, we have exploited the properties of DEC-MDPs with changing action sets and partially ordered transition dependencies – since each action can be executed only once by each learner, a single parameter per action is sufficient for representing local policies.

Gradient-descent algorithms are guaranteed to at least converge to a local optimum in policy space (Arrow and Hurwicz, 1960). Since a Nash equilibrium also represents a local optimum when doing decentralized gradient-descent for a factored controller (Peshkin et al., 2000), it is clear that any Nash equilibrium is a possible point of convergence for GDPS as well. Unfortunately, the reverse is not true: There may be additional local optima in policy space to which GDPS may converge and which are, in general, of lower value than Nash equilibria. We have visualized this situation in Figure 4.6 for a fictional 2-agent example with an extremely unevenly shaped policy performance function $J$. Both agents are parameterized by a single parameter only ($\theta^1$ and $\theta^2$), drawn along the $x$- and $y$-axis in Figure 4.6.

Because a Nash equilibrium denotes a joint policy where no agent can increase the policy's performance by changing its local policy single-handedly, we might say that – from a single agent's perspective[6] – a Nash equilibrium depicts a global optimum. For the toy problem at hand, these points of convergence are shown as triangles. Additionally, there are further local optima in policy space to which a policy gradient method might converge (depending on the starting point of the search process and the update step size), denoted by circles. Consider, for example, the local optimum marked with a '⋆' at $(\theta^1, \theta^2) = (180, 75)$. Here, apparently, it holds $\nabla_{\theta^1} J(\pi_\theta) = \nabla_{\theta^2} J(\pi_\theta) = 0$, which is why GDPS might be attracted by this point. However, $(\theta^1, \theta^2)$ does not represent a Nash equilibrium, because a unilateral change of $\theta^1$ from 180 to a value larger than 470 by agent 1 would increase $J(\pi_\theta)$.

Note that Figure 4.6 also highlights the well-known fact that several Nash equilibria of different value may exist. The one with the highest value (the joint equilibrium, or coordination equilibrium, cf. Section 4.2[7]) is visualized with a black triangle. On the whole, even if GDPS does not provide guarantees for yielding the optimal joint policy, we will show that near-optimal joint policies of high value can be acquired within little learning time.

Speaking about learning time, the rate of convergence is, of course, strongly influenced by the learning rate $\beta$ as well as by the heuristic $H$ that determines after how much

---
[6]More precisely, from *any* single agent's perspective simultaneously.
[7]The case of two joint equilibria with identical value is considered in depth in Section 4.2.3 (cf. Lemma 5).

## 4.3 Gradient-Descent Policy Search

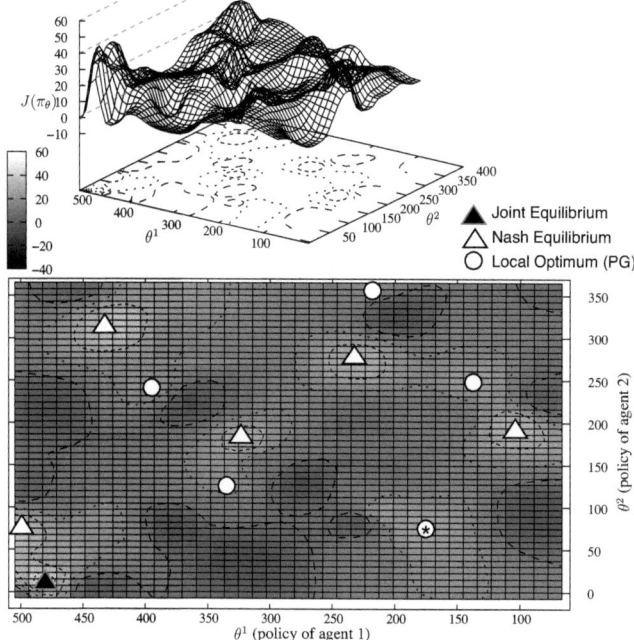

Figure 4.6: Visualization of Possibilities of Convergence and Optimality of GDPS: The 3D plot (top) shows an exemplary policy performance function $J(\pi_\theta)$ subject to the factored policies realized by 2 agents. Each agent's policy is determined by a single parameter, $\theta^1$ and $\theta^2$, respectively, that are drawn along the $x$- and $y$-axis. The bottom chart provides a gray map representation including surface lines of the same function $J(\pi_\theta)$. Here, all possible points of convergence for the GDPS learning algorithm are sketched by triangles and circles.

interaction with the environment learning updates to the policies are made by the agents. Concerning the former we note that, during our empirical experiments (next section), we always used a constant learning rate. Although policy gradient theory actually requires a diminishing learning rate (as described in Section 4.3.1), we found that not decreasing $\beta$ during ongoing learning brings about excellent and convergent results and allows us to omit the introduction of additional parameters controlling the concrete rate of decay of the learning rate.

As denoted above, we employ an implementation of $H$ that initiates policy updates after having sampled a fixed number $e$ of experience sequences by interacting with the DEC-MDP. Clearly, too large a value of $e$ slows down learning in that sampling additional sequences does not help in improving the gradient estimate, if agent $i$ can reliably assessed $\nabla_{\theta^i} J(\pi_\theta)$ using $e' < e$ sequences already. By contrast, too small values of $e$ yield immature,

## 4 Policy Search-Based Solution Approaches

high-variance gradient estimates and, hence, are likely to require a larger total number of policy updates. Hence, it must be kept in mind that, in an extreme case, poor gradient estimates with high variance in conjunction with a constant learning rate might also prevent the learning process from converging to a local optimum. To this end, an adaptive method, as the one suggested in Section 4.3.1 which relies on inter-agent communication, might clearly enhance learning performance. In the next section, we empirically analyze the influence of the values of $\beta$ and $e$ on the learning progress and convergence time.

An alternative approach to reduce the variance of the gradient estimate is to use a gradient calculation based on the policy gradient theorem (Sutton et al., 2000; Peters et al., 2005). Here, the simple observation that in many environments future actions do not depend on past rewards can result in a significant decrease of the variance of the gradient estimate determined in a Monte-Carlo manner. The analogon to the distributed likelihood ratio gradient estimation by Equation 4.12 becomes

$$\nabla_{\theta^i} J(\pi_\theta) = \sum_{h_i \in \mathcal{H}} Pr(h|\theta) \left( \sum_{d=0}^{D_{h_i}-1} (\gamma^d r(d,h) - b(d)) \left( \sum_{k=0}^{d} \nabla_{\theta^i} \ln \pi_{\theta^i}(\overline{s}_i(k,h_i), a(k,h_i)) \right) \right)$$

where $b(d)$ represents some time step-specific baseline. For the type of problems we are addressing, however, the precondition of the action choices being independent of past rewards is not fulfilled. In $m$-agent factored DEC-MDPs with changing action sets and partially ordered transition dependencies the execution of (joint) actions determines the immediate global rewards and, also, which actions will be available by which agents further on. In turn, also future action probabilities are influenced which is why past rewards and future actions are not independent. For these reasons, we use the likelihood ration gradient estimate with the average return $\overline{J}_E(\pi_\theta)$ over $E$ as baseline (Equation 4.14).

Given the sensitivity of policy gradient learning techniques with respect to local optima, an important question is how the parameters of the agents' policies are initialized. Obviously, the type and value of the optimum towards which the learning process converges depends on where in the policy space the search is started. As pointed out in Section 4.1, this gives rise to the possibility of exploiting possibly available task knowledge to initialize $\theta$ such that the search process starts in a "good" region of the joint policy space. In what follows, however, we will not examine this option, instead assume that no prior knowledge is available and, accordingly, initialize all agents' local policies equally by setting all $\theta^i_j = 0$ which gives rise to policies that initially realize purely random action choices.

### 4.3.5 Empirical Evaluation

In analogy to to the empirical evaluation presented in Section 4.2.5, we employ the class of factored $m$-agent DEC-MDPs with changing action sets and partially ordered transition dependencies to model job-shop scheduling problems, and evaluate the learning behavior of the GDPS algorithm using different scheduling benchmark problems.

For JSSPs, the notion of an experience sequence translates to a (simulated) scheduling and execution of all jobs' operations until all jobs have entirely been processed, and the expected return corresponds to the general objective of scheduling. Since our goal is to

## 4.3 Gradient-Descent Policy Search

minimize $C_{max}(\pi_\theta)$, i.e. we aim at creating schedules of minimal length, the expected return can be expressed by providing the learning agents with $R(h) = -C_{max}$ when an episode ends, or equivalently, by providing the agents with immediate global rewards of $-1$ per time step. Furthermore, since a finite horizon is guaranteed and, thus, no discounting is necessary, the goal of policy optimization using policy gradient reinforcement learning for scheduling problems means to optimize $\theta = (\theta^1, \ldots, \theta^m)$ such that $J(\pi_\theta) = \mathbb{E}\left[-C_{max}(\pi_\theta)\right]$ is maximized.

Again, we begin our investigations by applying GDPS to the educational benchmark problem FT6 (cf. Section 3.1.1), before using it for larger-scale problems. To start with, we provide an illustration that interprets stochastic joint policies as stochastic schedules using the notion of disjunctive graphs (cf. Section 3.1.2).

### Illustration: Probabilistic Disjunctive Graphs

As outlined in Section 3.1.2, disjunctive graphs $G = (V, C, D)$ are frequently used to represent schedules for job-shop scheduling problems. The set $V$ of vertices represents the set of all operations, the set $C$ of conjunctions represents the precedence constraints between consecutive operations of the same job, and the set $D$ is meant to represent the different orders in which operations on the same machine might be processed. Fixing the directions of all disjunctions in $D$, while assuring that $G$ remains acyclic, corresponds to finding a feasible schedule for the JSSP at hand.

By attaching action choice probabilities to the jobs' operations as described above, we implicitly determine probabilistic directions for the disjunctive arcs defined by $\pi$. When we sample from the joint distribution of probabilistic disjunctive arcs, we obtain a set $\mathcal{S}$ of fixed disjunctions (a complete selection). Additionally, the selection $\mathcal{S}$ is also consistent, i.e. graph $G(\mathcal{S}) = (V, C \cup \mathcal{S})$ is acyclic, if we do the sampling by interacting with the DEC-MDP (corresponding to the scheduling problem at hand): Then, at each decision point, an agent decides probabilistically to process an operation of one of the waiting jobs and in so doing assigns an orientation to up to $n$ disjunctive arcs. This way of sampling a selection of orientations for the disjunctive arcs corresponds to a scheduling episode and depicts an experience sequence.

We call the schedule that arises when each agent always picks those jobs with the highest action probabilities the *maximum likelihood schedule* (MLS) of a joint policy $\pi_\theta$.

**Definition 4.6** (Maximum Likelihood Schedule).
*The set of agents following their local policies $\pi_{\theta^i}$ generates the* maximum likelihood schedule $\mu$, *when each agent $i$ picks jobs according to a local policy $\hat{\pi} : S_i \times \mathcal{A}_i^r$ that is defined on top of the Gibbs policy $\pi_{\theta^i}$ (Definition 4.5) according to*

$$\hat{\pi}_{\theta^i}(s_i, a_i) = \arg\max_{\alpha \in \mathcal{A}_i^r} \pi_{\theta^i}(s_i, \alpha) \quad (4.15)$$

*for all $s_i \in S_i$ and $a_i \in \mathcal{A}_i^r$.*

Figure 4.7 visualizes a small JSSP with probabilistic directions of its disjunctive arcs implicitly defined through the policy parameter vectors $\theta^i$. The corresponding maximum likelihood schedule is also shown. Generally, the spread of selections that can be sampled

4 Policy Search-Based Solution Approaches

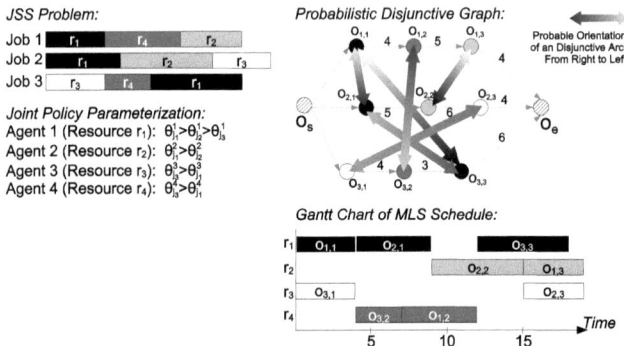

Figure 4.7: Example of a Probabilistic Disjunctive Graph: A small JSSP is considered and, for a fictional policy parameterization, a corresponding probabilistic disjunctive graphs is drawn. The orientations of the disjunctive arcs are stochastic with darker shades of gray indicating more probable and lighter ones indicating less probable orientations. The resulting maximum likelihood schedule resulting from that policy is, obviously, not an optimal one.

varies depending highly on the agents' policy parameters and the corresponding action probabilities. Finally, the goal of adapting policy parameters is, of course, to find parameters such that the corresponding MLS is of high quality (low makespan). To which extent the GDPS algorithm succeeds in reaching that goal shall be discussed next.

**Evaluation on the FT6 Benchmark**

Given an $m \times n$ job-shop scheduling problem, we let all agents initialize their policies by $\theta^i_\alpha = 0$ for all agents $i \in \{1, \ldots, m\}$ and all actions $\alpha \in \mathcal{A}^r_i$ such that, initially, the agents dispatch all waiting jobs with equal probability. Hence, such a purely random policy, to which we refer as $\pi_{\theta_{init}}$ subsequently, represents a baseline for learning. It yields the creation of schedules with an average makespan of $68.43 \pm 6.6$, i.e. $-J(\pi_{\theta_{init}}) = \mathbb{E}[C_{max}|\pi_{\theta_{init}}] = 68.43$, whereas we know that an optimal reactive policy[8] would create non-delay schedules of length $C^{nd-opt}_{max} = 57$. The corresponding distribution of created schedules using an ensemble of reactive and randomly dispatching agents is visualized in Figure 4.8. Clearly, the goal of learning is to alter that histogram such that the peak of frequency is to be found at small makespan values, preferably with 100% at $C^{nd-opt}_{max} = 57$.

Pursuing the goal of minimizing maximum makespan, we focus on the following evaluation criteria.

- We are mainly interested in the expected value of the joint policy's performance, i.e. in $J(\pi_\theta) = \mathbb{E}[-C_{max}|\pi_\theta]$.

---

[8] As in Section 4.2, we here focus on learning purely reactive policies, while in Chapter 6 we will consider delay schedules as well.

## 4.3 Gradient-Descent Policy Search

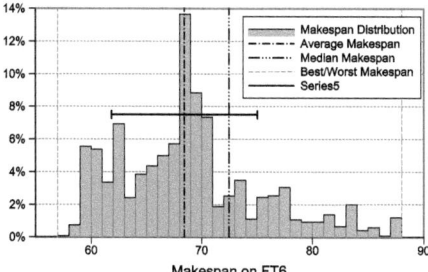

Figure 4.8: Makespan Histogram for FT6: Using independent agents that dispatch waiting jobs reactively in a purely random manner, schedules with an average makespan of $68.43 \pm 6.6$ are created.

- Moreover, we also consider the makespan $C_{max}^{best}$ of the best schedule that, during ongoing learning, has been produced occasionally by the set of probabilistic policies executed by the agents.
  This value corresponds to the value of $R_{max}$ as utilized in the context of joint equilibrium policy search (Section 4.2).

- Furthermore, the makespan $C_{max}(\mu)$ of the maximum likelihood schedule $\mu$ (Definition 4.6), and its development over time, is also of importance. As pointed out, this value arises when at all decision points all of the agents select actions that, given their stochastic local policies, have highest probabilities of execution.

- Our final concern is the convergence behavior and speed of the algorithm. As shown in Section 4.3.2, GDPS is guaranteed to converge to a local optimum in policy space at least. To this end, we distinguish between two different notions of convergence.

  **Policy Convergence** The standard interpretation of convergence requires that the stochastic local policies of the agents have approached deterministic ones. This refers to the case where for all agents' policies and for all states $s_i$ there is an $\alpha \in s_i$ such that $\pi_{\theta^i}(s_i, \alpha) > 1 - \varepsilon$ for some small $\varepsilon > 0$. If this happens after $b^\star \in \mathbb{N}$ policy updates and each update involved a gradient estimation based on $e$ sampled experience sequences, then we say that the policy has converged after $\lambda^\star = b^\star \cdot e$ episodes of interaction with the DEC-MDP. Under this notion of convergence, of course, it holds $-J(\pi_\theta) \approx C_{max}(\mu)$.

  **MLS Convergence** The second notion of convergence refers to the maximum likelihood schedule $\mu$. It is present, if there is a $\hat{b} \in \mathbb{N}$ such that for all $b > \hat{b}$ it holds $C_{max}(\mu_b) = C_{max}(\mu_{\hat{b}})$, where $\mu_b$ denotes the MLS after the $b$th policy update. If convergence of the maximum likelihood schedule appears after $\hat{\lambda} = \hat{b} \cdot e$ experience sequences, then it of course holds $\hat{b} \leq b^\star$ (policy convergence represents a stronger definition of GDPS' convergence behavior than MLS convergence does). To this end, the best case arises, if it holds $C_{max}(\mu) = C_{max}^{best}$ from the

$\hat{b}$th policy update on. However, it may also happen that $C_{max}(\mu)$ converges to another local optimum of a value worse than $C_{max}^{best}$ ($C_{max}^{best} \lesssim C_{max}(\mu)$).

For the FT6 benchmark we primarily focus on policy convergence, while during later experiments we will also regard MLS convergence.

Figure 4.9 summarizes a number of parameter studies with respect to policy convergence for the FT6 benchmark. Part a) shows the final performance of the policy learned using GDPS. Here, the ensemble of agents was allowed to interact with the DEC-MDP for an unlimited time – until policy convergence occurred, i.e. until $\pi_\theta$ had converged to a quasi-deterministic policy such that, when sampling experience sequences with that policy, it holds

$$Pr(R(h) \neq -C_{max}(\mu)|\pi_\theta) < 0.01 \qquad (4.16)$$

where $R(h) = -C_{max}$ is the makespan of a single episode and $\mu$ denotes the maximum likelihood schedule.

The chart reveals that, for different settings of the learning rate $\beta$ and the number $e$ of experience sequences sampled during gradient estimation, GDPS may converge to different local optima: Each data point corresponds to the average final policy performance over 10 repetitions of the entire learning experiment (corresponding standard deviations are plotted as well).

We repeat that, for the FT6 problem, an optimal schedule realized by a reactive factored controller has a makespan of 57. It is interesting to see that during most of the experimental repetitions it indeed held $C_{max}^{best} = 57$, indicating that the team of agents occasionally created the optimal solution. However, given the starting point of learning in policy space (all agents pursuing a random policy), the true gradient $\nabla J(\pi_{\theta_{init}})$ actually points to a local optimum with $C_{max} = 59$. This implies that, when starting the policy search at $\theta = 0$ and allowing the agents either to obtain a sufficiently accurate estimate of the true gradient (e.g. by setting $e$ to a very large value) or to make only tiny steps into the direction of the steepest descent, then GDPS yields a local optimum with $-J(\pi_\theta) = 59$ which is worse than the global one.

Figure 4.9a) highlights that more variance in the gradient estimation by performing less Monte-Carlo samples results in a larger standard deviation of the outcome of the learning process: In some experiment repetitions $-J(\pi_\theta) \approx C_{max}(\mu) = 57$ can be attained, while at times even another local optimum with $-J(\pi_\theta) > 59$ is entered. For a reliable estimation of the true gradient in the context of the FT6 problem, at least $e = 50$ experience sequences are necessary before making a policy update.

Part b) of Figure 4.9 shows the actual learning times required for policy convergence to be achieved. Note that in this part of the figure not the number $b^\star$ of policy updates till convergence are plotted, but the number $\lambda^\star = b^\star \cdot e$ of experience sequences sampled by interacting with the environment. Naturally, the time for convergence grows both with $e$ as well as with the inverse $1/\beta$ of the learning rate. Again, each bar denotes the average over 10 experiment repetitions.

Finally, part c) of Figure 4.9 focuses not on policy, but on MLS convergence, i.e. on the point $\hat{b}$ in the learning process after which the performance of the deterministic policy $\hat{\pi}$ (cf. Equation 4.15) changes no further and the corresponding maximum likelihood schedule

## 4.3 Gradient-Descent Policy Search

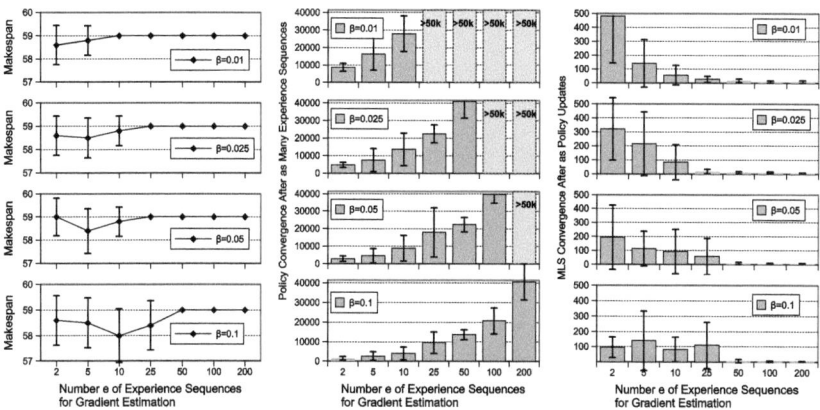

Figure 4.9: Learning Performance of GDPS for the FT6 Benchmark: The figure shows a) final policy values, b) numbers of experience sequences needed to achieve policy convergence, and c) numbers of policy updates undergone until MLS convergence occurred. In each part, variations with respect to the learning rate $\beta$ and the number $e$ of episodes for gradient estimation are investigated.

remains the same. Furthermore, this chart does not plot the total number $\hat{\lambda} = \hat{b} \cdot e$ of experience sequences experienced, but the number of policy updates $\hat{b}$ performed. In so doing, it emphasizes the fact that, when using a reliable, low-variance estimate of the gradient based on 50 or more experience sequences, only a small number $\hat{b}$ of policy updates (clearly less than 100) is necessary until MLS converge can be achieved. This even holds for small values of the learning rate $\beta$. We stress, however, that MLS convergence typically occurs significantly faster than policy convergence: For the experiments considered here, achieving policy convergence required the learners to sample approximately between 3 and 50 times as many experience sequences as necessary for MLS convergence.

Starting from purely random dispatching policies, the policy search process for FT6 performed by GDPS may converge to different optima in policy space. We can conclude this from the fact that, at least for certain parameter settings, the standard deviation of the final policy performance (Figure 4.9a)) is larger than zero. This characteristic is depicted from a single agent's (agent 2) point of view in Figure 4.10.

Part a) of Figure 4.10 consists of two charts. It opposes the development of the policy performance $J(\pi_\theta)$ and the makespan $C_{max}(\mu)$ of the maximum likelihood schedule (top chart) with the development of the policy parameter vector $\theta^2 = (\theta^2_{\alpha_1}, \ldots, \theta^2_{\alpha_2})$ that agent 2 uses (bottom chart). The important point here is that a highly accurate determination of $\nabla J(\pi_\theta)$ has been made: Policy updates are not performed until the ensemble of agents has sampled $e = 1000$ experience sequences ($\beta = 0.1$). We observe that the curves of $C_{max}(\mu)$ and $-J(\pi_\theta)$ approach one another which indicates that the joint policy converges. Policy convergence according to Equation 4.16 occurs after 243000 experience sequences. By then,

## 4 Policy Search-Based Solution Approaches

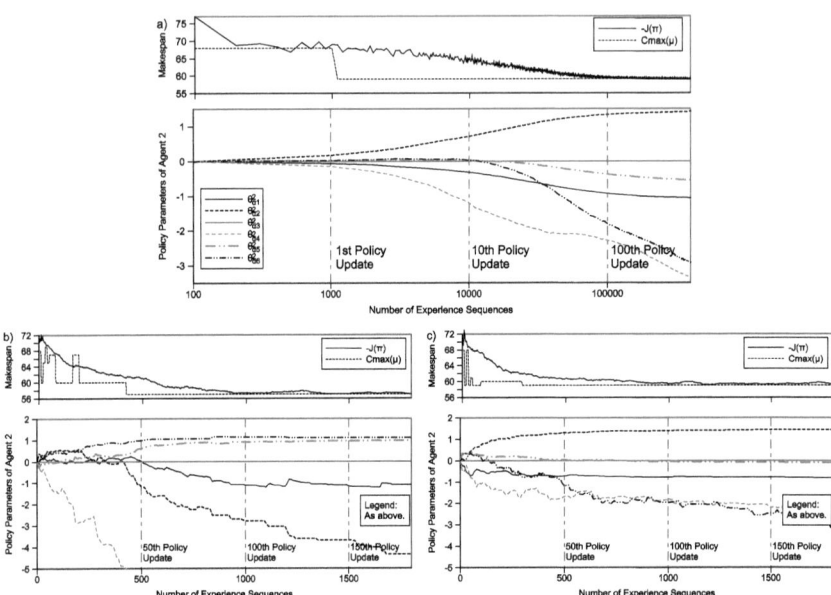

Figure 4.10: GDPS Learning Process from Agent 2's Perspective: While in a) gradient descent is performed based on highly accurate gradient estimates ($e = 1000$), the two bottom parts visualize the learning progress for two different experiment runs using larger-variance gradient estimations (based on $e = 10$). In each part of this figure, the upper diagram presents the development of joint policy performance and MLS makespan, whereas the lower chart draws the development of agent 2's policy parameter vector $\theta^2 = (\theta^2_{\alpha_1}, \ldots, \theta^2_{\alpha_6})$.

$b^\star = 243$ policy updates were made, and the makespan of the resulting converged policy is $-J(\pi_\theta) \approx C_{max}(\mu) = 59$. The bottom part of Figure 4.10a) plots the corresponding development of agent 2's policy parameters $\theta^2$ over time.

By contrast, Figures 4.10b) and 4.10c) visualize the progress of two runs of the same learning experiment using identical parameters except for a coarser estimation of the gradient by setting $e = 10$ instead of $e = 1000$. Apparently, both runs yield different outcomes, i.e. converge to different local optima (with value 57 and 59, respectively). This is caused by noisy gradient estimates following which can bring the joint policy from one valley of the policy performance function to another one. Note that the development of policy parameters in the run visualized in Figure 4.10c) is very similar to the one seen when following the true gradient (part a)). Accordingly, in both cases the joint policy is driven towards a local optimum of identical value (presumably the same one).

A final remark concerns the development of the maximum likelihood schedule in Figure 4.10a): Due to the highly accurate estimation of the gradient, the value of $C_{max}(\mu)$ falls to

## 4.3 Gradient-Descent Policy Search

its final value of 59 already after the first policy update (after 1000 experience sequences) which indicates that here a large step into the direction of the steepest descent has been made. Hence, for this example and thanks to a comparatively large learning rate $\beta = 0.1$ we have MLS convergence already after $\hat{b} = 1$ updates or, equivalently, after $\hat{e} = 1000$ experience sequences. The achieving of MLS convergence can also be observed in parts b) and c) of that figure: Here, the MLS has converged after $\hat{b} = 45$ and $\hat{b} = 30$ policy updates, respectively (after $\hat{e} = 450$ and 300 sequences).

So far, we have seen that GDPS depicts an effective method for making a team of cooperative scheduling agents learn a joint policy that represents a local optimum in policy space. For the FT6 benchmark, expected policy performance (measured in terms of negative makespan) can be increased from $J(\pi_{\theta_{init}}) = -68.8$ to $-59$, when following the direction of the steepest descent of a low-variance gradient estimate. Thus, a local optimum in the vicinity of the joint equilibrium (with $-C_{max}^{nd-opt} = -57$) is achieved. While FT6 is an interesting educational problem for studying the properties of an algorithm, subsequently we will apply GDPS to a variety of larger-scale scheduling benchmarks.

**Benchmark Results**

Figure 4.11 illustrates the learning progress of GDPS when applied to the same set of 15 job-shop scheduling problems used for the evaluation of the JEPS algorithms in Section 4.2.5, each problem instance involving each 10 jobs and 10 machines. For this series of experiments we aimed at using low-variance gradient estimates by letting $e = 100$ and $\beta = 0.01$, thus taking rather small steps into the direction of the steepest descent of policy performance. In analogy to the investigations for the FT6 benchmark, all agents initially deployed purely random, reactive policies, selecting each action with equal probability at each decision step.

Learning with gradient descent policy search brings about quick improvements of the joint policy. The solid black curve denotes the development of the policy's performance $-J(\pi_\theta)$ which is equal to $-\mathbb{E}[R(h)|\pi_\theta] = \mathbb{E}[C_{max}(\pi_\theta)]$ (cf. Section 4.3.5). Interestingly, this curve converges to the value $C_{max}(\mu)$ of the maximum likelihood schedule $\mu$ (drawn in gray), which indicates that the learning process has converged: After approximately 137700 experience sequences policy convergence has occurred. Since $e = 100$, this corresponds to an average of $b^\star = 1377$ policy updates.

The fact that in general not the globally optimal joint policy, viz the joint equilibrium, is learned, but a Nash equilibrium or a local optimum of lower value (i.e. of higher makespan) can be concluded from the gap between the development of $-J(\pi_\theta)$ and the average theoretical optimum ($C_{max}^{opt} = 899.8$) for the 15 job-shop scheduling scenarios considered[9].

Moreover, the fact that in general not a Nash equilibrium is attained, but in many cases a local optimum of worse value (cf. the explanations in Section 4.3.4) can be inferred from the progress of $-J(\pi_\theta)$ when compared to the development of $C_{max}^{best}$. The latter denotes the average (over 15 problems) of the best schedules occasionally created by the stochastic policies executed by the agents. Since the former does obviously not converge towards the

---

[9]Note, however, that GDPS in its current form, i.e. taking purely reactive scheduling decisions, can create *non-delay* schedules only. Hence, the upper limit for its learning performance is $C_{max}^{nd-opt}$. Though the exact average value of $C_{max}^{nd-opt}$ for the 15 problems considered is not known, it holds $C_{max}^{nd-opt} \gtrsim C_{max}^{opt}$.

## 4 Policy Search-Based Solution Approaches

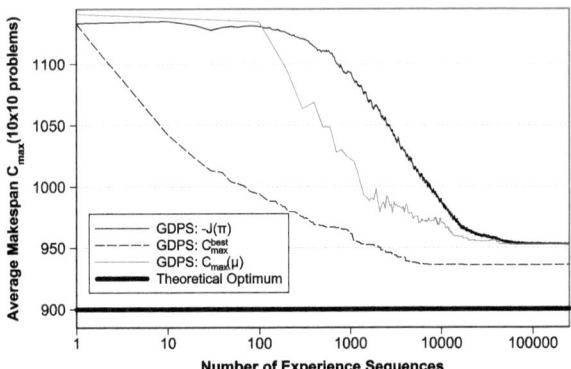

Figure 4.11: Gradient-Descent Policy Search Applied to a Selection of 10x10 Job-Shop Scheduling Problems: Reactive independent agents are improving their policies using gradient-descent. Starting with a random policy, a gradient descent-based update is made after any 100 experience sequences. All curves are averaged over 15 different benchmark problems. MLS convergence is obtained after 1377 policy updates on average.

latter, the collective of agents is heading towards a local optimum in policy space in most cases.

Table 4.2 summarizes the learning results for different JSSP benchmarks averaged over problems of different $m \times n$ sizes. The initial policy $\pi_{\theta_{init}}$ (random job execution) yields relative errors in the range of 20-30%. Speaking about relative errors, we refer to the amount of processing time some suboptimal policy needs beyond the theoretical optimum $C_{max}^{opt}$ of the makespan. Hence, the relative error of the initial policy is computed as the average of $Err_{init} = 100\%(C_{max}(\pi_{init})/C_{max}^{opt} - 1)$ over the benchmark instance under consideration.

Starting from this baseline, the agents were allowed to improve their scheduling policies in the described manner (again, $\beta = 0.01$) and achieved substantial improvements in doing so. The table lists the makespan $C_{max}^{best}$ for the best intermediate schedule found plus corresponding relative errors $Err_{best} = 100\%(C_{max}^{best}/C_{max}^{opt} - 1)$, the makespan $C_{max}(\mu)$ of the maximum likelihood schedules with belonging relative errors $Err_\mu = 100\%(C_{max}^{\mu}/C_{max}^{opt} - 1)$, as well as expected policy performance $-J(\pi_\theta)$ with belonging error $Err_{\lambda_{max}}$ after $\lambda_{max} = 250k$ sequences of interaction with the DEC-MDP and, hence, maximally $b_{max} = 2500$ policy updates, because we relied on $e = 100$ experience sequences for a single determination of the gradient again.

Note that policy convergence was not obtained within that learning time for all scenarios considered – especially for the larger-sized ones where more agents with larger policy parameter vectors are involved. However, MLS convergence could be achieved for all problems considered; the corresponding number $\hat{b}$ of policy updates for this to happen are

| Size $m \times n$ | #Prbl | Theor.Opt. $C^{opt}_{max}$ | Initial Policy $-J(\pi_{\theta_{init}})$ | $\text{Err}_{init}$ | $C^{best}_{max}$ | $\text{Err}_{best}$ | GDPS $C_{max}(\mu)$ | $\text{Err}_\mu$ | $\hat{b}$ | $-J(\pi_\theta)$ | $\text{Err}_{\lambda_{max}}$ |
|---|---|---|---|---|---|---|---|---|---|---|---|
| 5 × 10 | 5 | 620.2 | 765.4 | 23.4% | 631.8 | 1.9% | 640.4 | 3.3% | 229 | 640.7 | 3.3% |
| 5 × 15 | 5 | 917.6 | 1052.4 | 14.7% | 917.6 | 0.0% | 918.4 | 0.1% | 69 | 918.4 | 0.1% |
| 5 × 20 | 6 | 1179.2 | 1358.4 | 15.2% | 1181.3 | 0.2% | 1181.7 | 0.2% | 226 | 1182.1 | 0.2% |
| 10 × 10 | 17 | 912.5 | 1158.0 | 26.9% | 951.2 | 4.2% | 968.5 | 6.1% | 158 | 968.6 | 6.1% |
| 10 × 15 | 5 | 983.4 | 1285.3 | 30.7% | 1029.0 | 4.6% | 1041.6 | 5.9% | 948 | 1042.8 | 6.0% |
| 15 × 15 | 5 | 1263.2 | 1640.8 | 29.9% | 1338.6 | 6.0% | 1367.2 | 8.2% | 159 | 1368.6 | 8.3% |
| 15 × 20 | 3 | 676.0 | 878.0 | 29.9% | 713.0 | 5.4% | 729.0 | 7.8% | 678 | 733.9 | 8.6% |
| Average | 46 | 946.5 | 1178.0 | 24.5% | 977.9 | 3.4%$_{\pm 2.8}$ | 990.9 | 4.7%$_{\pm 3.5}$ | 285 | 991.6 | 4.8%$_{\pm 3.6}$ |
| 10 × 20 | 5 | 1236.2 | 1608.2 | 30.1% | 1272.0 | 2.9% | 1284.6 | 3.9% | 556 | 1288.7 | 4.2% |
| 10 × 30 | 5 | 1792.4 | 2118.6 | 18.2% | 1792.4 | 0.0% | 1792.8 | 0.0% | 1634 | 1800.2 | 0.4% |
| Average | 56 | 1050.3 | 1300.4 | 23.8% | 1076.9 | 3.1%$_{\pm 2.8}$ | 1088.7 | 4.3%$_{\pm 3.6}$ | 429 | 1090.3 | 4.4%$_{\pm 3.5}$ |

Table 4.2: Benchmark Result Overview for GDPS: Learning results for scheduling benchmarks of varying size achieved using GDPS. All entries are averaged over #Prbl. Err columns denote the relative remaining error (%) of the makespan achieved by the joint policy compared to the theoretical optimum and, thus, indicates to what extent the globally best schedule could be approximated. The row of averages in the middle is provided for better comparison with the results achieved using JEPS$_G$ (Section 4.2.5).

given in the table's third to the last column.

## 4.4 Discussion

This chapter has been advocated to the policy search-based approach to reinforcement learning. Our main contribution lies in the development and careful analysis of two different multi-agent policy search RL algorithms that are tailored to decentralized Markov decision processes with changing action sets and feature a number of nice theoretical properties. The remainder of this chapter addresses related work on policy search reinforcement learning and discusses the advantages and limitations of the methods proposed.

### 4.4.1 Related Work

Joint equilibrium policy search, as presented in Section 4.2, is a novel multi-agent reinforcement learning algorithm. It features some relatedness to the multi-agent policy search technique "incremental policy learning" (Fulda and Ventura, 2004). While the latter, however, is limited to single-stage games, i.e. to stateless environments, JEPS consistently addresses sequential decision problems. In estimating the value of the joint equilibrium, JEPS follows a straightforward approach of remembering the best global return obtained so far which is related to the Rmax algorithm (Brafman and Tennenholtz, 2003) as well as to optimistic assumption Q learning (Lauer and Riedmiller, 2000).

The utilization of policy gradient methods in the context of distributed problem solving is not new. Building upon the statistical gradient-following policy learning scheme by Williams (1992), Peshkin et al. (2000) show that, when employing distributed control of factored actions, it is possible to find at least local optima in the space of the agents' policies. While these authors evaluate their gradient-descent learning algorithm for a simulated soccer game, another prominent application domain targeted by several authors using PG approaches is the task of network routing (Tao et al., 2001; Peshkin and Savova, 2002), which had previously been examined with the value function-based Q-Routing algorithm (Boyan and Littman, 1994). In contrast to these pieces of work, the application of gradient-descent policy search to distributed problems modelled as decentralized MDPs with changing action sets, and in particular for job-shop scheduling problems, as pursued in this work, is new.

Yagan and Tham (2007) study policy gradient methods for reinforcement learning agents in the DEC-POMDP framework (Bernstein et al., 2002), as we do. In order to establish coordination, they define a neighborhood of locally interacting agents which are allowed to fully exchange their local policies. By contrast, JEPS is explicitly geared towards learning joint (coordination) equilibria and GDPS, in the form proposed, regards inter-agent dependencies only implicitly. However, in Chapter 6 we will propose a mechanism for resolving transition dependencies allowing agents to dedicatedly notify a single agent about a dependent action they have just taken and, in so doing, improve coordination. With regard to inter-agent communication, the idea of exploiting locality of interaction in distributed systems to optimize a global objective function had already been adopted in the context of dynamic constraint optimization and satisfaction problems (e.g. Modi et al., 2005). Moreover, job-shop scheduling problems have also been interpreted and solved as constraint optimization problems (e.g. Liu and Sycara, 1995) with the goal of finding an optimal solution through applying a sequence of distributed repair operations. In fact, such an approach bears some resemblance to the repair-based reinforcement learning approach to job-shop scheduling by Zhang and Dietterich (1995), but it is less related to our work since we interpret the scheduling task as a sequential decision problem. By contrast, of higher relevance to the GDPS approach is the work by Aberdeen and Buffet (2007) on PG methods for planning problems. Here, also a factorization of the global policy is made and independently learning agents are employed for various temporal planning tasks.

### 4.4.2 Advantages and Limitations of JEPS and GDPS

Policy search methods have established as a reasonable alternative to value function-based reinforcement learning methods. While the latter aim at estimating state-action values and, hence, consume an amount of memory that is proportional to the state space size, the former focus on the evaluation and direct optimization of the actor, i.e. the policy, as a whole.

In developing JEPS and GDPS, we have created two multi-agent policy search RL algorithms, that successfully tackle the fundamental problem of decentralized learning. Both algorithms exploit characteristics of DEC-MDPs with changing action sets and partially ordered transition dependencies on their behalf. For instance, in parameterizing the agents' policies it suffices to utilize only one single parameter per local action, which gives rise to a compact policy representation: Each agent needs only a few parameters to represent its policy[10] and, in so doing, severely restricts its space of representable policies.

All policies considered are stochastic ones which is of special advantage for partially observable domains for which it is well-known that the best deterministic policy can be arbitrarily worse than the best stochastic one. Although each local state can be fully observed in the class of DEC-MDPs we are concerned with, the global system state is hidden from any agent and, hence, can be observed in part only.

The empirical evaluation of JEPS as well as of GDPS has shown that both algorithms are well suited to acquire good approximate solutions, i.e. to learn joint policies of high quality. Applied to job-shop scheduling problems, for many problem instances indeed optimal solutions are found, for others near-optimal schedules with small relative errors with respect to the optimum. While JEPS in its basic version featured some problems (mainly due to too excessive memory requirements) when applied to larger-scale problems, $JEPS_G$ and GDPS performed well in learning factored policies using independent agents and achieved comparable performance: On an identical problem set they reduced the relative error from an initial value (random policy) of about 24% to 6.6% ± 7.3 and 4.8% ± 3.6, respectively, which represents quite a successful result given the intricacy of the problems considered.

A highly appealing characteristic of the policy search procedures presented is that they adhere to a number of interesting theoretical properties. On the one hand, for $JEPS_G$ we have proved that it converges with probability one to the joint equilibrium indicated by the heuristic function it employs. On the other hand, GDPS is guaranteed to acquire a local optimum in the space of factored multi-agent policies and, in fact, performs the same policy updates that a centralized gradient descent learner would carry out.

A limitation of the suggested methods in their current form is that we enabled them to realizing reactive policies only, implying that each agent never executes its idle action, if other actions are available. In terms of scheduling problems, this means that at best non-delay schedules can be created and the optimal solution, which may be represented by a delay schedule (cf. Section 3.1.1), is possibly missed. In order to counteract this confinement, in Chapter 6 we analyze two approaches that let the agents interacting with the DEC-MDP reason about their inter-agent dependencies and allow them to behave not purely reactively. These ideas can be easily integrated into the policy search reinforcement learning methodology pursued in this chapter and can be expected to expedite the performance of JEPS and GDPS.

Another limitation of JEPS is that it requires a deterministic environment, at least for the proposed version that relies on an accurate and deterministic determination of the maximal return. On the one hand, noisy immediate rewards render the current approach infeasible, as no longer a fixed value of the maximal return exists. On the other hand, if rewards are deterministic and only state transitions are probabilistic and, moreover, we assume the existence of a heuristic function that is capable of noticing correctly whether a joint equilibrium has been reached, JEPS is applicable for such a DEC-MDP. Although, in the context of this book, all experimental evaluations focus on deterministic job-shop scheduling problems, GDPS is well utilizable for stochastic ones as well and has been shown

---

[10]With the exception of the basic version of JEPS which employs a local, state-specific action parameterization.

## 4 Policy Search-Based Solution Approaches

to bring about good results in the presence of probabilistic durations of job operations (Gabel and Riedmiller, 2008b).

A vulnerability of both of our policy search methods is their dependency on learning-specific parameters. We have seen that JEPS may converge prematurely depending on its learning rate and, by contrast, a practical implementation of $JEPS_G$ can run into numerical underflow problems when computing action probabilities. Likewise, the performance of GDPS is subject to the accuracy of its gradient estimates – increasing which requires the agents to do more interaction with the environment – and subject to its learning rate. To this end, an adaptive method that modifies the learning rate as learning continues might bring about some relief; a successful combination of policy gradient reinforcement learning with the Rprop technique for realizing an adaptive learning rate has been suggested by (Riedmiller et al., 2007b). Apart from these points, GDPS is guaranteed to find local optima in the space of factored policies and, hence, in general may attain neither a Nash equilibrium nor the optimal joint equilibrium. Additionally, the empirical results obtained in Sections 4.2.5 and 4.3.5 show that the difficulties mentioned grow with the sizes of problems tackled.

A weakness of both policy search techniques discussed is the fact that they aim at distributed learning of a joint policy for one specific problem. The acquired policy is, in general, of little use, if the task or the environment changes. Stated differently, the generalization capabilities of both JEPS and GDPS are poor. In terms of our application domain of scheduling one may say that the presented policy search-based reinforcement learning algorithms are capable of finding very good schedules for individual problem instances, but that they do not support the reuse of the learned policies for different, though similar, scheduling problems. Therefore, in the following chapter, where value function-based reinforcement learning approaches move into the center of our interest, we will focus on the issue of generalization in more detail.

# 5 Value Function-Based Solution Approaches

In the previous chapter, we have focused on policy search-based reinforcement learning approaches to tackle complex multi-agent problems. In spite of the mentioned intricacy of the class of problems considered, we could show that reactive and independently learning agents can be enabled to acquire near-optimal policies. The ability to learn from experience on a trial and error basis and with strongly limited state information denotes a challenge in itself, especially when compared to analytical solution methods that aim at finding a globally optimal policy in a centralized manner and with full information about the state of the world.

Another striking aspect, that goes beyond the idea of learning a solution instead of designing it, is however, to which extent the acquired joint policy is appropriate for different and similar problems, i.e. the question how well does it perform in previously unseen situations. The chapter at hand addresses the value function-based approach to reinforcement learning and, besides exploring the ability to perform distributed learning, focuses also on the mentioned issue of generalization performance.

We start by providing some foundations on value function-based RL in general, on the idea of batch-mode reinforcement learning, and on distributed approximative value functions. The main contribution of this chapter lies in Section 5.3 where we develop OA-NFQ, a data-efficient multi-agent RL algorithm for DEC-MDPs with changing action sets that is based on learning agent-specific local value functions. Thereafter, we empirically evaluate all algorithms presented in the context of distributed job-shop scheduling problems. We finish this chapter with a discussion and point to related work.

## 5.1 Foundations

As pointed out, in reinforcement learning the purpose of the learning agent is formalized in terms of a reward signal conveyed by the environment. More precisely, the agent's goal is to maximize the immediate rewards it perceives in the long run, which is denoted as the return $R_t = \sum_{k=0}^{\infty} \gamma^t r(t+k)$. We have introduced the value $V^\pi(s)$ of a state $s$ under policy $\pi$ as the expected return, when taking actions determined by $\pi$ starting from $s$. Similarly, by $Q^\pi(s,a)$, which is defined as the expected return starting from state $s$ by taking action $a$ and following $\pi$ thereafter, we denote the value of the state-action pair $(s,a)$. These types of values, i.e. state values as well as state-action values, and the corresponding value functions ($V$ and $Q$) represent the central concept of value function-based reinforcement learning approaches. Besides, they take the role of the critic, when adopting the actor-critic view on reinforcement learning systems as done in Section 2.1.3. And, as outlined

## 5 Value Function-Based Solution Approaches

in Section 2.1.5, learning optimal value functions constitutes the ultimate goal of the RL approaches we will be pursuing now.

### 5.1.1 The Issue of Generalization

In the previous chapter, we investigated actor-oriented policy search RL methods for multi-agent problems. In so doing, we exploited some properties of DEC-MDPs with changing sets, pre-eminently the fact that each agent can execute each action only once. This allowed us to make the agents learn, under certain convergence guarantees, high-quality policies which basically determine action execution orders: From the point of view of solving complex (at least NP-hard) optimization tasks, such as job-shop scheduling problems, the algorithms derived and empirical results obtained are convincing, especially when taking into account that a decentralized form of learning is taking place.

A natural question to ask then is, what happens if properties of the learning problem considered are changed. For example, for some agent some action may be removed from $\mathcal{A}_i^r$ or the order of an action's execution over the agents as determined by dependency function $\sigma_i$ is changed. Clearly, under such conditions the performance of the joint policies learned by the policy search-based approaches explored in Chapter 4 will be impaired. In order for the knowledge acquired during learning to be of more general applicability it is no longer sufficient to describe local states $s_i$ as sets of actions ($s_i = \{\alpha_1, \ldots, \alpha_{|s_i|}\}$) and actions merely by some index or label (e.g. label 'x' to denote some action $\alpha_x$ from $\mathcal{A}_i^r$) which uniquely identifies it within an agent's action set.

What is necessary instead, is a characterization of the properties of individual actions and, correspondingly, of sets of local actions (that is local states). Such a characterization ought to be rich enough to reflect similarities and dissimilarities between actions with respect to the effects their execution has. Hereby, it should rather represent properties of typical problem classes instead of single problem instances, such that acquired knowledge is general and valid for similar problems as well. Moreover, it should be comprehensive in describing an agent's local situation and, hence, comprise features that exhibit some relation to the goal of learning.

Finally, we consider it important that the local policies which the agents learn independently are modest regarding their computational requirements: When it comes to their application to new, previously unseen problem instances, we demand them to be executable under real-time conditions, which means that we do not allot them arbitrary amounts of computation time. In terms of the job-shop scheduling application domain, hence, quick and reactive dispatching decisions must be taken by the agents, as opposed to the NP-hard complexity of predictive (centralized) scheduling techniques (cf. Section 3.3.1).

Although feature engineering, i.e. the accurate definition of appropriate state and action features, is not our primary concern, we provide some more details on that topic, with special regard to JSSPs, in Section 5.4.1. Regardless of the specific feature definition, what we intend to do here has crucial implications: When addressing potentially the entire space of different, though similar problem instances of DEC-MDPs with changing action sets instead of a single one, we likewise create an exponential increase in the size of the state (and action) spaces the agents have to consider. Let us illustrate this issue with the help

## 5.1 Foundations

of an example from the job-shop scheduling domain.

**Example** Consider the FT6 example that we introduced in Section 3.1 (Figure 3.1). Interpreting this problem as a decentralized Markov decision process as proposed in Section 3.2.2, we face 6 agents each of which can execute $|\mathcal{A}_i^r| = 6$ actions (corresponding to the operations of the 6 jobs involved). Since $S_i = \mathcal{P}(\mathcal{A}_i^r)$, this gives rise to $|S_i| = 2^6 = 64$ local states for every agent $i$ and to an upper limit of $|S| \leq (2^6)^6 = 2^{36}$ for the joint state space. The latter inequation is strict, because the dependency graphs $G_\alpha$ of the problem which dictate that each action $\alpha$ can be available for maximally one agent at a time. Hence, it is easy to verify that

$$|S| \leq \sum_{k=1}^{6} \binom{6}{6-k} \cdot 6^k = 117648$$

is a tighter estimation of the joint state space's size[1]. Therefore, for this single particular instance it is easily possible to store all local states per agent or even (when adopting a centralized perspective) all joint states in a table, when intending to represent a value function.

If $\mathcal{O}$ denotes the set of all operations in the FT6 problem (cf. Definition 3.1), then it obviously holds

$$\max\{\delta(o)|o \in \mathcal{O}\} = 10, \tag{5.1}$$

i.e. the operations requiring most processing time need 10 time steps to be processed. Let us now consider the class of all job-shop scheduling problems definable that involve both six jobs and resources without recirculation. Additionally, let us assume that each scheduling problem instance $\mathbb{J}_{6\times 6}$ we regard adheres to Equation 5.1 as well. Then, this class of problems comprises $10^{36}$ possible scheduling problems. Needless to say, that some kind of value function approximation mechanism is necessary already, if the learning agents shall cover (with their value functions to be learned) a small fraction of the resulting $64 \cdot 10^{36}$ possible local states. This argument is magnified in particular, if we address larger, more realistic problems that involve more than only six jobs or resources.

In the context of this work, we will employ multi-layer perceptron (MLP) neural networks to represent value functions. On the one hand, feed-forward neural networks are known to be capable of approximating arbitrarily closely any function $f : D \to \mathbb{R}$ that is continuous on a bounded set $D$ (Hornick et al., 1989). On the other hand, we aim at exploiting the notoriously good generalization capabilities of neural networks and, hence, aim at yielding general dispatching policies, i.e. policies which are not just tuned for the situations encountered during training, but which are general enough to be applied to unknown situations, too.

### 5.1.2 Batch-Mode Reinforcement Learning

In Section 2.1.5, we have briefly outlined value iteration and Q learning as two basic reinforcement learning algorithms. The associated updates to the state and state-action

---
[1]Note that, when assuming reactive agent behavior, which yields non-delay schedules, in fact only a fraction of those states can be reached.

## 5 Value Function-Based Solution Approaches

value function according to Equation 2.4 and 2.5, respectively, are meant to be performed after each single state transition experienced. This works well when reasonably small state or state-action spaces have to be considered such that the value function can be stored in tabular form. Interesting reinforcement learning problems, including the ones we are addressing, typically have very large or even continuous state or state-action spaces which is why the use of value function approximation mechanisms, as depicted in Section 5.1.1, is required.

In contrast to classic online reinforcement learning where updates to the value function are made after each transition, *batch-mode* reinforcement learning methods store and reuse their experience which takes the shape of transition four-tuples. These tuples of experience consist each of a state, and action taken in that state, the immediate reward received, as well as the successor state entered. After having collected a batch, i.e. a larger number of transition tuples, the computational update to the value function is performed.

Batch-mode reinforcement learning has recently been successfully applied to various challenging real-world applications (Riedmiller et al., 2007a; Csaji and Monostori, 2008; Deisenroth et al., 2008). Its popularity in general, and its particular advantages for the work at hand can be attributed to various reasons:

- The reuse of stored experience renders batch-more reinforcement learning algorithms particularly data-efficient. This is of importance for real-world and, more generally, for learning tasks where the amount of interaction with the environment shall be limited.

- When learning value functions in combination with a function approximator, the availability of a batch of training data instead of single training patterns can be favorable in different respects. On the one hand, there seems to be no substantial gain, if a function approximator approximates the value function in a local way, like radial basis function networks or instance- and case-based methods. However, even in that case batch-mode training can yield improvements in terms of learning speed and performance (Gabel and Riedmiller, 2006a). On the other hand, many powerful function approximation schemes approximate the target function in a global way (e.g. support vector regression, Gaussian processes, or multi-layer perceptrons). Here, changing the function value at one point with respect to a single training pattern may result in hard to predict changes at other points in the space over which the function is spanned. To this end, it is of crucial importance for the successful application of MLP nets as value function approximators in the context of reinforcement learning, that they are used embedded in a batch-mode RL algorithm where updates are performed based on a whole set of training patterns simultaneously.

- Apart from the batch-mode update that is beneficial when training global function approximators in general, another advantage is that specifically for the training of MLP neural networks, advanced batch training methods, such as the Rprop training algorithm (Riedmiller and Braun, 1993), exist which have been shown to be more powerful and parameter-insensitive than the gradient-descent method used commonly.

## 5.1 Foundations

- Our main focus is on multi-agent reinforcement learning. Assuming independently learning agents, we can conjecture that single transition tuples some agent experiences are strongly affected by the actions taken concurrently by other agents. This dependency of single transitions on external factors, i.e. on other agents' policies, gives rise to another argument for batch training: While a single transition tuple contains probably too little information for doing a reliable update, a rather comprehensive batch of experience may contain sufficient information to apply value function-based RL also in a multi-agent context. We will investigate this issue in depth in Section 5.3.

Figure 5.1 sketches the general batch-mode reinforcement learning framework. It basically consists of three main steps that are interconnected by two loops. The step of sampling experience (outer loop) realizes interaction with the environment and creates a set of transition tuples (data). The second step utilizes dynamic programming methods to generate a set of training patterns which are, subsequently and iteratively (inner loop), employed by some batch mode supervised learning algorithm that outputs an approximated function represented by the training patterns.

Note that most of the practical realizations of batch-mode reinforcement learning algorithms work in alternating batch mode. This means that the outer loop can be iterated an arbitrary number of times, involving corresponding data samplings and successive training phases realized by the inner loop.

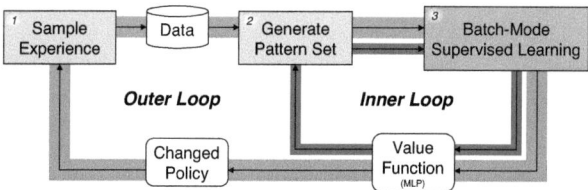

Figure 5.1: The Batch-Mode Reinforcement Learning Framework: In alternating batch mode, the stages of interaction with the environment (outer loop) and value function learning (inner loop) are interweaved.

The individual components shown in Figure 5.1 may be implemented differently, e.g. data may be sampled using a greedy or an exploring policy and for the task of fitting a function approximator to the training patterns, in principle, any of a dozen supervised learning algorithms can be utilized.

**Fitted Q Iteration**

As far as the inner loop is concerned, i.e. the alternating generation of a training pattern set and training using a supervised learning algorithm, *fitted Q iteration* is a prominent model-free batch-mode RL algorithm (Ernst et al., 2006), which we are going to extend and enhance for the use within multi-agent learning problems.

# 5 Value Function-Based Solution Approaches

Fitted Q iteration, when embedded into the inner loop of Figure 5.1, aims at computing an approximation of the optimal policy (more specifically, of the optimal value function from which the policy is induced) from a set of transition four-tuples. The set of four-tuples $\mathbb{T} = \{(s^k, a^k, r^k, s'^k) | k = 1, \ldots, |\mathbb{T}|\}$ may be collected in any arbitrary manner and corresponds to single "experience units" made up of states $s^k$, the respective actions $a^k$ taken, the immediate rewards $r^k$ received, as well as the successor states $s'^k$ entered. The basic algorithm takes $\mathbb{T}$, as well as a regression algorithm as input, and after having initialized $Q$ and a counter $q$ to zero, repeatedly processes the following three steps until some stop criterion becomes true:

1. increment $q$

2. build up a training set $\mathbb{F}$ for the regression algorithm according to:

$$\mathbb{F} := \{(in^k, out^k) | k = 1, \ldots, |\mathbb{T}|\}$$

where $in^k = (s^k, a^k)$ and

$$out^k = r^k + \gamma \max_{\alpha \in A(s^k)} Q^{q-1}(s'^k, \alpha) \tag{5.2}$$

3. use the regression algorithm and the training set $\mathbb{F}$ to induce a new approximation $Q^q : S \times A \to \mathbb{R}$

Subsequently, we will review and utilize *neural fitted Q iteration* (NFQ, Riedmiller, 2005), a realization of fitted Q iteration where multi-layer neural networks are used to represent the Q function. NFQ is an effective and efficient RL method for training a Q value function and it has been shown to require reasonably few interaction with the environment to generate policies of high quality. Beyond that, we will develop an extension of NFQ to be used in the scope of this work in the next sections.

## 5.2 Distributed and Approximated Value Functions

While in the preceding foundational section we emphasized the appeal of learning general policies, the potential of value functions represented by neural networks in regard to the former, as well as amenities of batch-mode reinforcement learning methods, we shall now again concentrate more specifically on the multi-agent aspect.

### 5.2.1 Independent Value Function Learners

The decentralized Markov decision processes of our interest are populated with independent agents. For the time being, we assume them to be independent of one another both in terms of acting as well as learning (in Chapter 6 we generalize this by addressing specific inter-agent dependencies). Our approach is to define a value function for each agent that it successively computes and improves, and that it uses to choose its local actions.

## 5.2 Distributed and Approximated Value Functions

Since this approach enforces a distributed decision-making by independent agents, the learning deployed (no matter whether it works online or in batch mode) must be implemented within each learning agent. Because, as pointed out before, we perform model-free learning, the value functions to be considered are agent-specific state-action value functions (Q functions $Q_i : S_i \times \mathcal{A}_i^r$) whose Q values $Q_i(s_i, a_i)$ estimate the expected return when executing some action $a_i$ in state $s_i$. Hence, input to a neural net, which is utilized to represent that function, are the features describing the situation of the agents as well as features describing available actions. The output $Q_i(s_i, a_i)$ allows an agent to decide for the action that promises largest return.

Thus, when focusing on JSSPs, the neural network's output is meant to directly reflect the priority value of the job corresponding to action $a_i$ depending on the current state $s_i$. Figure 5.2 sketches the arrangement of the main components just mentioned. Note that, although that figure provides an illustration for one single agent (agent 2) only, the set-up is to be used for each agent.

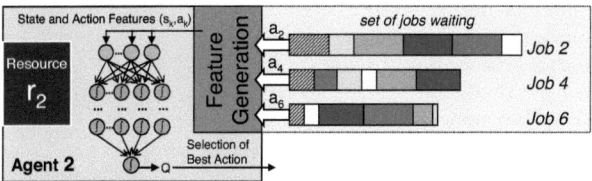

Figure 5.2: System Architecture for Value Function-Based Multi-Agent RL: Agent 2 represents its state-action value function with a neural network whose input are state and action features describing the agent's current situation. The first operation of each of the jobs 2, 4, and 6 has to be processed on resource $r_2$, hence, three actions are available.

Until the decision for one out of the actions available can be made, however, first the Q value function must be learned. Algorithm 5.1 provides pseudo-code for a value function-based batch-mode RL agent interacting with a DEC-MDP with changing action sets and partially ordered transition dependencies. Therewith, it depicts a concrete implementation of the outer loop of the general batch-mode reinforcement learning framework (Figure 5.1). Basically, this algorithm builds up a batch $\mathbb{T}$ of transition tuples and, after the completion of each episode, enables the agent to decide whether to enter the inner loop and, thus, to perform batch-mode updates to the value function: To this end, a call to a value function update procedure is made in line 11. As can be read from line 10, we provide the possibility to postpone the update and, instead, to wait for the experience set $\mathbb{T}$ to have grown even larger. This is done for practical reasons, as the update itself may be a very time-consuming procedure.

It is worth noting that the value function-based batch-mode RL algorithm features a number of commonalities with the decentralized policy search algorithm (Algorithm 4.1) specified in Section 4.1.2 on page 53: Both adopt the perspective of a single, independently learning agent, both are tailored to DEC-MDPs with changing action and, thus, to episodic tasks with a finite problem horizon. Of course, they both require the environment to be

## 5 Value Function-Based Solution Approaches

reset to some starting state after an episode's end has been reached which is indicated by the final state $s^f$. Finally, both are capable of handling temporally extended actions by interpreting $d$ not as time steps but as decision stages and by realizing action executions (line 15) as blocking function calls as delineated in Section 4.1.2.

However, both are centered around rather different data structures. While the policy search approach essentially relies on an explicit (stochastic) actor with corresponding parameters $\theta^i$ and aims at its optimization, in Algorithm 5.1 the central element is the value function $Q_i$, from which an $\varepsilon$-greedy policy can easily be inferred (line 14). Moreover, the former assesses the performance of the current policy and, therefore, has to discard all experience gathered once the policy has been changed, whereas the latter is allowed to keep and reuse transition tuples for successive value function updates.

---

**Input:** value function $Q_i$ initialized randomly, exploration rate $\varepsilon$
1:   $d \leftarrow 0$, $\mathbb{T} \leftarrow \emptyset$
2:   **while** *not stop* **do**
3:     observe $s_i(d)$
4:     **if** $s_i(d) \neq \emptyset$ or $s_i(d) = s^f$ **then**
5:       **if** $d > 0$ **then**
6:          receive immediate reward $r(d-1)$ //$r(s(d\text{-}1), a(d\text{-}1), s(d))$
7:          $\mathbb{T} \leftarrow \mathbb{T} \cup \{(s_i(d-1), \alpha(d-1), r(d-1), s_i(d))\}$
8:       **endif**
9:       **if** $s_i(d) = s^f$ **then**
10:          **if** $|\mathbb{T}|$ is large enough **then**
11:             $Q_i \leftarrow$ call `ValueFunctionUpdate`($\mathbb{T}$) //*batch-mode update*
12:             $d \leftarrow 0$ //*do not flush experience set here*
13:       **else**
14:          select $\alpha(d) \in s_i(d)$ by exploiting $Q_i$ greedily according to
$$\alpha(d) \leftarrow \arg\max_{\alpha \in s_i(d)} Q(s_i(d), \alpha)$$
or a random $\alpha \in s_i(d)$ with probability $\varepsilon$
15:          execute $\alpha(d)$
16:          $s_{\sigma_i(\alpha(d))} \leftarrow s_{\sigma_i(\alpha(d))} \cup \{\alpha(d)\}$ //*influence local state of agent* $\sigma_i(\alpha(d))$
17:          $s_i(d) \leftarrow s_i(d) \setminus \{\alpha(d)\}$
18:          $d \leftarrow d+1$
19:       **endif**
20:     **endif**

**Algorithm 5.1:** Value Function-Based Batch-Mode RL from the Perspective of Agent $i$

### 5.2.2 Neural Fitted Q Iteration

In online Q learning in conjunction with a table-based value function representation, Q updates according to Equation 2.5 can be made easily on the fly. By contrast, when faced with very large or continuous state-action spaces and when using neural networks as

## 5.2 Distributed and Approximated Value Functions

value function approximators, as we intend to do, no direct value assignment for singular state-action pairs can be realized. Instead, an error function must be introduced, which measures the deviations between (a) state-action values approximated by the function approximator (below, we denote the approximation realized by a neural network as $\tilde{Q}$) and (b) those that are defined through the Bellman equation (cf. Section 2.1.5). For example, given a single transition tuple $(s, a, r, s')$ and a current value function estimate $\tilde{Q}$ represented by an MLP, the squared Bellman error

$$\left( \tilde{Q}(s,a) - (r + \gamma \max_{b \in A(s')} \tilde{Q}(s',b)) \right)^2$$

may be employed which can be minimized using gradient descent techniques, like the backpropagation algorithm, on the neural network's connection weights.

A drawback of this type of online update is its wasteful utilization of data as each transition tuple is used only once. As a consequence, typically thousands of episodes are necessary until a policy of sufficing quality is obtained (Riedmiller, 1999). This disadvantage can be tributed, at least in part, to the global approximation character of MLPs: Weight updates for a certain state-action pair $(s, a)$ may cause unforeseen changes of the value function in very different regions of the joint state-action space.

Admittedly, the last-mentioned effect can be beneficial in terms of yielding generalization. However, recent studies on the neural fitted Q iteration (NFQ) algorithm, have shown that more stable and reliable learning results can be achieved when learning in batch-mode, while not sacrificing the excellent generalization capabilities of neural networks (Riedmiller, 2005).

As indicated, NFQ is an instance of the class of fitted Q iteration algorithms we described above, where the supervised batch-mode regression algorithm, i.e. the "fitting" part, is realized by a multi-layer perceptron neural network. Let $\mathbb{T} = \{s^k, a^k, r^k, s'^k | k = 1, \ldots, \mathbb{T}\}$ be a set of transition 4-tuples and let $\mathcal{Q}$ denote the space of Q value functions over $S \times A$ representable by MLPs. Then, for each pattern $k$, NFQ calculates target values $out^k$ as specified in the context of fitted Q iteration (cf. Equation 5.2), thereby utilizing the recent Q function estimate $Q^{(q-1)}$, and computes the next ($q$th) iterate of the state-action value function $Q^q$ by minimizing the batch error

$$\sum_{k=1}^{\mathbb{T}} (Q^q(s^k, a^k) - out^k)^2. \tag{5.3}$$

Clearly, the minimization of this expression is achieved by adapting the connection weights of the neural network representing $Q^q$ such that

$$Q^q \leftarrow \arg\min_{f \in \mathcal{Q}} \sum_{k=1}^{\mathbb{T}} (f(s^k, a^k) - out^k)^2.$$

As actual neural network training procedure, we utilize the Rprop algorithm (Riedmiller and Braun, 1993) which naturally builds on batches of training data as well and, hence, can easily be integrated into a batch-mode RL algorithm. An important merit of using

## 5 Value Function-Based Solution Approaches

Rprop, when compared against, for example, standard backpropagation, is its insensitivity with respect to learning parameters which rids us from tuning learning parameters for the supervised part of a fitted Q iteration algorithm.

NFQ is meant to be plugged in into line 11 of Algorithm 5.1, i.e. as value function update procedure. Algorithm 5.2 outlines our implementation of NFQ which slightly deviates from the one given by Riedmiller (2005) as it

- is specialized for the use by a single agent in the scope of a decentralized MDP with independently learning agents,
- makes use of the Rprop neural network training algorithm, and
- is prepared to utilize the policy screening technique to select high-quality policies while performing Q iterations (i.e. while iterating through the inner loop of a batch RL algorithm as sketched in Figure 5.1).

The third feature mentioned belongs to the different variants and extensions that can be applied to the basic NFQ algorithm. Some of these, as well as the reasons why they are needed, shall be discussed next.

---

**Input:** transition tuple set $\mathbb{T} = \{(s_i^k, a_i^k, r^k, s_i'^k) | k = 1, \ldots, |\mathbb{T}|\}$,
number of Q iterations $N \in \mathbb{N}$
1: $q \leftarrow 0$
2: **initialize** $Q_i^q \leftarrow$ random weight initialization of MLP
3: **while** $q < N$ **do**
4:     $\mathbb{F} \leftarrow \emptyset$
5:     **for** $k = 1$ **to** $|\mathbb{T}|$ **do**
6:       $in^k \leftarrow (s_i^k, a_i^k)$
7:       $out^k \leftarrow r^k + \gamma \max_{\alpha \in A(s_i^k)} Q_i^q(s_i^k, \alpha)$
8:       $\mathbb{F} \leftarrow \mathbb{F} \cup \{(in^k, out^k)\}$
9:     **end for**
10:    $Q_i^{q+1} \leftarrow$ train MLP given $\mathbb{F}$ using Rprop
11:    **perform** policy screening to evaluate $\pi_i(s_i) = \arg\max_{\alpha \in s_i} Q_i^{q+1}(s_i, \alpha)$
             and let $Q_i^{top} \leftarrow Q_i^{q+1}$ in case of an improvement
12:    $q \leftarrow q + 1$
13: **end while**
14: **return** $Q_i^{top}$

**Algorithm 5.2:** Neural Fitted Q Iteration Applied by Agent $i$

---

### 5.2.3 Heuristic NFQ Enhancements

Neural fitted Q iteration has turned out to be a very effective and highly efficient method for model-free batch-mode reinforcement learning in conjunction with neural value functions. Accordingly, it has been applied to various challenging (single-agent) problems

## 5.2 Distributed and Approximated Value Functions

(Riedmiller et al., 2007a, 2009) and, moreover, several specific heuristic enhancements have been suggested.

**Pure Offline NFQ** As an instance of the general batch-model reinforcement learning framework, NFQ is by default run in *alternating batch mode* (cf. Section 5.1.2). Alternatively, it can also be executed in a *pure offline mode*. Then, experience is sampled only once and, thereafter, the NFQ main loop (Algorithm 5.2) is entered for a single time, producing the approximation of the value function requested (Kietzmann and Riedmiller, 2009). As far as the work at hand is concerned, however, we adhere to the standard alternating batch-mode mode of operation.

Practically, we implement the criterion (line 10 in Algorithm 5.1) that decides whether to enter the inner batch-mode RL loop (cf. Figure 5.1) in a straightforward manner that returns true, if $|\mathbb{T}|$ has been increased by a constant amount of tuples since the last time the value function update procedure had been called.

**Policy Screening** A critical question concerns the convergence of the learning technique to a (near-)optimal decision policy when used in conjunction with value function approximation. In spite of a number of advantages, neural networks are known to belong to the class of "exaggerating" value function approximation mechanisms (Gordon, 1996) and as such feature the potential risk of diverging. There are, however, several methods for coping with the danger of non-convergent behavior of a value function-based reinforcement learning method and to reduce the negative effects of phenomenons like chattering and policy degradation. We will put more emphasis on a thorough discussion of that concern and of corresponding counter measures suggested in the literature in Section 5.5. For the time being we stress that, in order to be able to safely apply our learning approach to larger-scaled problems, we rely on *policy screening*, a straightforward, yet computationally intensive heuristic for selecting high-quality policies in spite of oscillations occurring during learning (suggested by Bertsekas et al., 2000): We let the policies generated undergo an additional evaluation based on simulation (by processing problems from a separate set of screening problems, which takes place in between single iterations of the NFQ learning algorithm (line 11 in Algorithm 5.2). As a result, we can determine the actual performance of the policy represented by the Q function in each iteration of the algorithm and, finally, detect and return the best value function created.

**Hint-to-Goal Heuristic** Another heuristic used frequently in conjunction with the neural fitted Q iteration algorithm is the so-called *hint-to-goal* method (Riedmiller, 2005). This technique has been shown to be particularly useful for tasks with very long episode durations and, hence, few transitions to or within the goal region. It extends the training set $\mathbb{F}$ by artificial training patterns which cover the goal region, thus have maximal target values and, in so doing, drags the neural network towards its maximal output value near the target region[2]. For the type of problems we are addressing, this heuristic is of less

---

[2] Commonly, all target values in the training set are scaled to lie within the output range of the type of output neuron employed (e.g. within $[-1, 1]$ or $[0, 1]$). Thus, the maximal output value referred to is 1.0.

# 5 Value Function-Based Solution Approaches

purpose since the nature of DEC-MDPs with changing action sets in combination with reactively acting agents guarantees that the final state is reached in any case.

**Pattern Merge Heuristic**   Working with DEC-MDPs with changing action sets and partially ordered transition dependencies, we found another heuristic improvement very helpful in improving the performance of NFQ. In the version provided in Algorithm 5.2, NFQ is defined to create a training pattern for each transition tuple $(s_i^k, a_i^k, r^k, s_i'^k) \in \mathbb{F}$, even if it holds $|s_i^k| = 1$. Since the problems we consider are DEC-MDP with changing action sets, the latter equality may hold for many local states encountered. However, given the up to here assumed reactive behavior of the agents (i.e. their disallowance to remain idle by executing the null action $\alpha_0$), it is obvious that agent $i$, if in state $s_i^k = \{\alpha\}$, executes action $\alpha$ anyway. This means that, in fact, it does not take a deliberate decision at such decision steps.

In other words, each training pattern created on the basis of a tuple $(s_i, a_i, r, s_i')$ with $|s_i| = 1$ contains no knowledge supporting the learning algorithm, since actually no decision is to be made in those states $s_i$. In fact, it features information about an immediate reward whose receipt must be tributed to a preceding decision made.

Formally, using the notion of $d$ as in Algorithm 5.1 and setting $\gamma = 1$ (no discounting), let

$$(s_i(d), a_i(d), r(d), s_i(d+1)) \text{ and } (s_i(d+1), a_i(d+1), r(d+1), s_i(d+2)) \qquad (5.4)$$

be two consecutive transition tuples with $|s_i(d+1)| = 1$. Then, the *pattern merge heuristic* replaces these two by a single transition tuple according to

$$(s_i(d), a_i(d), r(d) + r(d+1), s_i(d+2)). \qquad (5.5)$$

Apparently, this technique reduces the overall number of patterns used, when fitting the function approximator, while not discarding any information that is of relevance for the agent to decide which action to chose at stage $d$. Viewed from a pattern creation and network training point of view, the tuples in Equation 5.4 give rise to two patterns

$$((s_i(d), a_i(d)),\ r(d) + Q(s_i(d+1), a_i(d+1))) \in \mathbb{F}$$

$$\text{and } \left( (s_i(d+1), a_i(d+1)),\ r(d+1) + \max_{\alpha \in s_i(d+2)} Q(s_i(d+2), \alpha) \right) \in \mathbb{F},$$

where the target value of the first pattern directly (no max operator required) depends on the approximation available for the second. By contrast, only one pattern

$$\left( (s_i(d), a_i(d)), r(d) + r(d+1) + \max_{\alpha \in s_i(d+2)} Q(s_i(d+2), \alpha) \right) \in \mathbb{F}$$

results after having applied the pattern merge heuristic (Equation 5.5). Note that this heuristic can be applied repeatedly and, in so doing, can mask entire subsequences of experience sequences traversed in a DEC-MDP with changing action sets, namely when multiple decision steps with only one action available occur in row.

Taken together, the effective number of transitions and patterns to be considered within a single episode can be decremented and, as a consequence, learning times be reduced. We employed the pattern merge heuristic consistently during *all* experiments covered below in this chapter, viz always requiring $|s_i| \geq 2$ as condition for considering patterns for fitting the function approximator.

The heuristics listed so far do not address the issue of multiple agents learning in parallel. Therefore, in the following section we specifically target this point and develop a meaningful multi-agent extension of the neural fitted Q iteration algorithm.

## 5.3 Fitted Q Iteration with Neural Networks and Optimistic Assumption

Fitted Q iteration denotes a class of data-efficient single-agent RL algorithms. The version of neural fitted Q iteration provided in Algorithm 5.2 adopts a single agent's perspective, but disregards the possible existence of other agents and makes no attempts to enforce coordination across agents. In what follows, however, we address the problem of adequate inter-agent coordination which, as we will see, is of fundamental importance for obtaining learning results of high quality.

### 5.3.1 Optimistic Q Learning

An independently learning agent in a DEC-MDP has, in general, no chance to compute the true (optimal) Q function $Q^\star$ of the underlying process, which must be spanned over the joint state space $S$ and the joint action space $A$. On the one hand, the state space is factored ($S = S_1 \times \cdots \times S_m$) and each single agent perceives only a fraction of the global state. On the other hand, an independent learner cannot distinguish between different joint actions $a^1$ and $a^2$ within which it has executed the same local action $a_i^1 = a_i^2$, as it knows only its own contribution to the joint action.

**Average and Optimistic Projections**

Nevertheless, the local value functions $Q_i : S_i \times A_i \to \mathbb{R}$ an independent learner aims to acquire, which are "smaller" in terms of the domains over which they are defined, can be interpreted as some kind of projection: A projection $\Phi$ – from the contents of the underlying system's joint Q value function to the local $Q_i$ functions – that, for each local state[3] $\sigma_i$ and local action $\alpha_i$, determines $Q_i(\sigma_i, \alpha_i)$ by some amalgamation of the Q values of all joint state-action pairs whose $i$th components are identical to $\sigma_i$ and $\alpha_i$, respectively:

$$Q_i(\sigma_i, \alpha_i) = \Phi(\mathcal{M})$$
with $\mathcal{M} = \{Q(s,a) | s = (s_1, \ldots, s_m), s_i = \sigma_i, a = (a_1, \ldots, a_m), a_i = \alpha_i\}.$

Ideally, a learning algorithm ought to realize the projection $\Phi$ in such a manner that each agent is enabled to behave optimally. Of course, for DEC-MDPs this is too much

---
[3] We subsequently use Greek letters $\sigma_i$ and $\alpha_i$ to refer to some specific local state and action of agent $i$, which is in slight abuse of notation since in Chapter 2 we used $\sigma$ to refer to dependency functions.

## 5 Value Function-Based Solution Approaches

to demand: Restricted local state observability and inter-agent dependencies cannot be overcome easily.

However, for the class of deterministic multi-agent Markov decision processes (MMDPs, cf. Section 2.3.1), i.e. when assuming that each agent is capable of fully observing the global system state, defining a projection which still yields optimal behavior is possible: Each agent then makes assumptions concerning its teammates' behaviors and, in so doing, compresses the contents of the joint Q function by considering only those pieces of information which represent the assumed teammate behavior.

Let the joint state and action space be finite such that a corresponding value function could be represented using a simple value table and, hence, no value function approximation mechanism is used. When using Q learning in a distributed manner in an MMDP and without any further adaptations to the multi-agent setting, the individual $Q_i$ functions that are learned by independently learning agents essentially represent a weighted average of joint state-action entries that would have been stored in a global Q function, if a centralized (MDP-)perspective was adopted. Hence, after convergence of this kind of standard Q learning with its mild convergence requirements (infinite number of updates for each state-action pair and properly decaying learning rate), applied in an MMDP setting, it holds for all agents $i \in Ag$, for all global states $s \in S$, and for all local actions $\alpha_i \in A_i$

$$Q_i(s, \alpha_i) = \sum_{\substack{a=(a_1,\ldots,a_m) \\ a_i=\alpha_i}} \left( Pr(a|a_i) \cdot \left( \sum_{s' \in S} p(s,a,s') \cdot \left( r(s,a,s') + \gamma \max_{\beta \in A_i(s')} Q_i(s',\beta) \right) \right) \right)$$

(5.6)

where $Pr(a|a_i)$ denotes the probability that the joint action $a$ is executed in state $s$ when agent $i$ executes $a_i$ as its local action. Stated differently, in an MMDP with finite $S$ and $A_i$ for all $i$, the local value functions $Q_i$ represent the unique solution of the set of equations defined by 5.6.

Another more goal-oriented approach is to employ a so-called optimistic assumption regarding other agents' action choices (Lauer and Riedmiller, 2000). Here, each agent *assumes* that all other agents always act optimally, i.e. that the combination of all local actions forms an optimal joint action vector. For the MMDP setting, the optimistic assumption Q update rule is defined as

$$Q_i(s, a_i) \leftarrow \max\{ Q_i(s, a_i),\ r(s, a, s') + \gamma \max_{\alpha \in A_i(s')} Q_i(s', \alpha) \}$$

(5.7)

with current state $s$, action $a_i$, successor state $s'$. Hence, the basic idea is that the expected returns of state-action pairs are captured in the value of $Q_i$ by successively taking the maximum. This update rule (Equation 5.7) allows for learning distributed Q value functions given a deterministic environment and assuming that initially $Q_i \equiv 0$ for all $i$ and that the immediate rewards $r(s, a, s')$ are always larger or equal zero. For multi-agent systems with full global state observability granted to each agent (MMDP setting) it can be shown (see Lauer and Riedmiller (2000) for a proof) that this *optimistic assumption*-based variant of Q learning produces local state-action value functions whose best actions are the same as in centralized Q learning, i.e. for all states $s$ and local actions

## 5.3 Fitted Q Iteration with Neural Networks and Optimistic Assumption

$\alpha_i \in A_i$ it holds
$$Q_i(s, \alpha_i) = \max_{\substack{a=(a_1,\ldots,a_m) \\ a_i=\alpha_i}} Q(s, a), \tag{5.8}$$

provided that finite state-action spaces and deterministic state transitions and rewards are given. We also remark that Q learning with the optimistic update rule (Equation 5.7) within an MMDP setting yields a set of equations

$$Q_i(s, \alpha_i) = \max_{\substack{a=(a_1,\ldots,a_m) \\ a_i=\alpha_i}} \sum_{s' \in S} p(s, a, s') \cdot \left( r(s, a, s') + \gamma \max_{\beta \in A_i(s')} Q_i(s', \beta) \right)$$

whose unique solution are the local state-action value functions $Q_i$ and, as proved by Lauer and Riedmiller (2000), for all $Q_i(s, \alpha_i)$ also Equation 5.8 holds.

We emphasize that, even for MMDPs, Equation 5.8 describes only a necessary, not a sufficient condition which enables the agents to choose optimal local actions. This point is striking, if different joint actions of equal value exist, i.e. if

$$\exists s \in S, a = (a_1, \ldots, a_m) \in A(s), b = (b_1, \ldots, b_m) \in A(s) : Q(s, a) = Q(s, b)$$
and $Q(s, a) \geq Q(s, c) \; \forall c \in A(s)$.

Then it may happen, for example, that each agent, being unaware of other agents' action choices, selects its local action according to

$$\hat{a}_i = \arg\max_{\alpha \in A_i(s)} Q_i(s, \alpha),$$

but that $\hat{a} = (\hat{a}_1, \ldots, \hat{a}_m)$ is different from $a$ as well as from $b$ and, consequently,

$$Q(s, \hat{a}) \lneq \max_{c \in A(s)} Q(s, c).$$

Hence, the combination of all agents' local actions is not optimal. This difficulty of coordination among agents (for MMDPs) can be overcome by keeping a separate data structure for the local policies $\pi_i$, which is changed only, if during ongoing learning a true improvement in the local state-action values has occurred: If for some state $s \in S$ and local action $a_i \in A_i(s)$ a new value for $Q_i(s, a_i)$ is computed that strictly dominates its previous value, then $\pi_i(s)$ is adapted (Lauer and Riedmiller, 2000).

For stochastic environments, optimistic assumption-based Q learning faces difficulties because two different sources of uncertainty intermingle: Successor states and rewards are no longer just co-influenced by the other agents' behaviors, but also by the random disturbances caused by the stochastic nature of the process. Both types of stochastic perturbations must be handled differently by the learning algorithm. While fluctuations due to other agents' action choices ought to be considered in an optimistic manner (taking the maximum), noise should be taken into account with respect to its expected value (cancelling it out).

As we intend to employ the optimistic assumption subsequently, we stick to deterministic environments during the agents' learning phases. Note, however, that this requirement is no longer necessary, when greedily exploiting the learned Q functions, i.e. when applying the corresponding policies.

## 5.3.2 Optimism Under Partial State Observability

We now implement the step from systems with global state observability to systems with locally full, yet globally partial observable system states, i.e. the step from MMDPs to DEC-MDPs.

When calculating (table-based) state-action value functions $Q_i$ for agents within a DEC-MDP, these $Q_i$ functions must, for all local states $\sigma_i \in S_i$ and local actions $\alpha_i \in A_i$, adhere to the following equation

$$Q_i(\sigma_i, \alpha_i) = \sum_{\substack{s=(s_1,\ldots,s_m) \\ s_i = \sigma_i}} Pr(s|s_i) \sum_{\substack{a=(a_1,\ldots,a_m) \\ a_i = \alpha_i}} Pr(a|a_i, s_i) \sum_{\substack{s' \in S \\ s'=(s'_1,\ldots,s'_m)}} p(s, a, s') \cdot (r(s, a, s') + \gamma \max_{\beta \in A_i(s'_i)} Q_i(s'_i, \beta)). \quad (5.9)$$

Here, $Pr(s|s_i)$ denotes the probability that the system is in state $s$ when agent $i$ finds itself in local state $s_i$, $Pr(a|a_i, s_i)$ stands for the probability that the joint action $a$ is executed by the ensemble of agents while agent $i$ executes action $a_i$ in $s_i$. Needless to say, that this set of local functions $Q_i$ obtained by applying standard Q learning in a distributed fashion – which can be interpreted as an average weighted projection from the central $Q$ function to the local ones – will in general contain information, whose greedy exploitation implements suboptimal behavior.

**Definition 5.1** (Optimistic Assumption-Based Q Learning for DEC-MDPs).
*Given the global state $s = (s_1, \ldots, s_m)$, a joint action $a = (a_1, \ldots, a_m)$, and a successor state $s' = (s'_1, \ldots, s'_m)$ of a factored m-agent DEC-MDP, optimistic assumption-based Q learning performs for each agent $i \in Ag$ and each decision stage $d$ updates to the local agent-specific Q function $Q_i$ according to*

$$Q_i(s_i, a_i) \leftarrow \max\{\ Q_i(s_i, a_i),\ r(s, a, s') + \gamma \max_{\beta \in A_i(s'_i)} Q_i(s'_i, \beta)\ \}. \quad (5.10)$$

Under the assumption of initializing $Q_i \equiv 0$ for all $i$ and requiring $r(s, a, s') \geq 0$ for all $s, s' \in S$ and $a \in A$, it is easy to see that the values of all $Q_i(s_i, a_i)$ are non-decreasing.

For better differentiation, let us denote the local state-action value functions used in Equation 5.10 by $Q_i^D$ (superscript $D$ stands for the DEC-MDP setting) and the ones used in Equation 5.7 by $Q_i^M$ (here, superscript $M$ indicates the MMDP setting). Then, it is easy to verify that

$$\max_{\substack{s=(s_1,\ldots,s_m) \\ s_i = \sigma_i}} Q_i^M(s, \alpha_i) \leq Q_i^D(\sigma_i, \alpha_i) \quad (5.11)$$

for all $\sigma_i \in S_i$ and all $\alpha_i \in A_i(\sigma_i)$.

Apparently, an optimistic assumption-based Q learning agent within DEC-MDPs assumes that all other agents $j$ were in local states $s_j$ whose combination $s = (s_1, \ldots, s_m)$ is of high value, given $a_i$. In so doing, this method will in general overestimate the true value of local state-action pairs ($Q_i^D \geq Q_i^M$). This may result in sub-optimal behavior, as non-optimal local actions may be assessed with a too high value estimate. So, the crucial question is how extreme is this overestimation? Or, stated differently, are there additional assumptions we can exploit to reduce the impact of that overestimation?

## 5.3 Fitted Q Iteration with Neural Networks and Optimistic Assumption

**Discussion of the Optimistic Assumption Under Partial State Observability**

While standard Q learning applied in a DEC-MDP yields average weighted local Q values according to Equation 5.9, applying the optimistic assumption according to Definition 5.1 results in a set of equations whose unique solution are the local state-action value functions $Q_i : S_i \times A_i$ with

$$Q_i^D(\sigma_i, \alpha_i) = Q_i(\sigma_i, \alpha_i) = \max_{\substack{s=(s_1,\ldots,s_m) \\ s_i=\sigma_i}} Pr(s|s_i) \cdot \max_{\substack{a=(a_1,\ldots,a_m) \\ a_i=\alpha_i}} \left( r(s,a,s') + \gamma \max_{\beta \in A_i(s_i')} Q_i(s_i', \beta) \right)$$
(5.12)

for any $\sigma_i \in S_i$ and $\alpha_i \in A_i(\sigma_i)$. For decentralized Markov decision processes with changing action sets and partially ordered transition dependencies, the overestimation resulting from the maximum operator over states in Equation 5.11 and Equation 5.12 is limited due to several reasons.

- In the course of simultaneous learning, other agents improve their policies as well, which represents a universal argument in favor of the idea to assume that other agents behave in a beneficial way.

- Making an optimistic assumption with respect to the local states other agents are in ($\max_{s, s_i=\sigma_i}$) is meaningful in that – if all agents behaved optimally – a trajectory with joint states of high value is passed through (given a deterministic environment).

- Because local states are sets of locally available actions and since no action can be available for two different agents at the same time (due to the inter-agent dependencies formalized by the dependency graphs $G_\alpha$ given in Definition 2.13), for the global state $s = (s_1, \ldots, s_m)$ the constraint
$$\forall j \neq i \; \forall s_j : s_i \cap s_j = \emptyset$$
holds, which severely restricts the number of joint states the system can be in. Accordingly, the maximum operators mentioned are to be evaluated only over subsets of the joint state space $S$.

- When assuming reactive behavior by all agents (as we do here), local actions cannot be executed in any arbitrary order, but depending on availability. Consequently, each agent can enter states only from a fraction of the set $S_i = \mathcal{P}(A_i)$ and, hence, a fraction of the joint state space $S = S_1 \times \cdots \times S_m$ can be entered by the ensemble of agents.

For these reasons, optimistic assumption-based Q learning, when applied in the context of the special DEC-MDP settings we are interested in, is generally expected to be of superior performance when compared to the averaging made by standard Q learning (as implied by Equation 5.9), although both approaches feature identical worst case behavior. We next suggest a concrete algorithmic realization of a multi-agent reinforcement learning algorithm that combines the optimistic way of inter-agent coordination within a DEC-MDP setting with the neural batch-mode approach to reinforcement learning circumscribed in Section 5.2.2.

## 5 Value Function-Based Solution Approaches

### 5.3.3 Batch-Mode Learning of Distributed Q Values

The straightforward utilization of NFQ as learning algorithm to be employed by each of the agents interacting with a DEC-MDP corresponds to the averaging projection described by Equation 5.9, though the sums are now defined no longer over the entire state space $S$ or action space $A$, but dependent on the states visited and actions executed as stored within the transition tuple set $\mathbb{T}$.

Recall that the focus in this work is on DEC-MDPs with changing action sets and partially ordered transition dependencies, where $S_i = \mathcal{P}(\mathcal{A}_i^r)$ and the set $\mathcal{A}_i^r$ of local actions is finite. During episode-based interaction with the environment (including resets to some initial state after episode endings are reached) it thus happens that an agent encounters some state repeatedly within different episodes. Consequently, the batch of transition tuples the agent gathers may contain multiple entries for certain state-action pairs $(s_i, a_i)$. This means, there may exist $(s_i^1, a_i^1, r^1, s_i'^1), (s_i^2, a_i^2, r^2, s_i'^2) \in \mathbb{T}$ with $s_i^1 = s_i^2, a_i^1 = a_i^2$, but eventually $r^1 \neq r^2$ and $s_i'^1 \neq s_i'^2$. Since we assume a deterministic environment, the latter two inequalities are caused by variations or changes in the behavior of other agents. As a consequence, in the scope of neural fitted Q iteration two training patterns $(in^1, out^1), (in^2, out^2) \in \mathbb{F}$ with $in^1 = in^2$ but differing target values will be created, which is why the supervised learning part produces an approximation of the state-action value function that, for the state-action pair $(\sigma_i, \alpha_i) := (s_i^1, a_i^1)$, aims at minimizing the error

$$\sum_{\substack{(s_i^k, a_i^k, r^k, s_i'^k) \in \mathbb{T} \\ s_i^k = \sigma_i, a_i^k = \alpha_i}} \left( Q^q(\sigma_i, \alpha_i) - out^k \right)^2$$

with $out^k$ being calculated as specified in Algorithm 5.2. That is, a minimization of the squared difference between $Q^q(\sigma_i, \alpha_i)$ and the corresponding target values over the training set is desired. The latter are varying because at different times the local execution of some action $\alpha_i$ in local state $\sigma_i$ may have resulted in different local successor states as well as different rewards. This happens since other agents may have executed different actions simultaneously because, for example, they may have chosen explorative instead of greedy actions or because they have changed their policy.

We therefore suggest a batch-mode reinforcement learning method that adapts and combines both, NFQ and the idea of simultaneous multi-agent learning based on the optimistic assumption (Gabel and Riedmiller, 2007b). Algorithm 5.3 gives a pseudo-code realization of neural fitted Q iteration using the optimistic assumption, for short OA-NFQ.

The distinctive feature of this algorithm is that it does not create a training pattern set $\mathbb{F}$ containing one pattern per transition tuple from $\mathbb{T}$, but a reduced, optimistic training set $\mathbb{O}$ with $|\mathbb{O}| \leq |\mathbb{T}|$. As indicated, for the types of problems we are considering, for each agent the probability of reentering some state $s_i$ again during episode-based learning is larger than zero. And, if in $s_i$ a certain action $a_i \in A_i(s_i)$ is taken again, it may have incurred different rewards and resulted in arriving at a different successor state $s'$, because of different local states other agents are in and different local actions they execute. The following definition of an optimistic training pattern set takes this into account.

**Definition 5.2** (Optimistic Training Pattern Set)**.**
*Let $i \in Ag$ denote a single agent. Given a transition 4-tuple set $\mathbb{T} = \{(s_i^k, a_i^k, r^k, s_i'^k) | k =$*

## 5.3 Fitted Q Iteration with Neural Networks and Optimistic Assumption

$1, \ldots, |\mathbb{T}|\}$ and agent $i$'s current Q value function $Q_i : S_i \times \mathcal{A}_i^r \to \mathbb{R}$, the optimistic training pattern set $\mathbb{O}$ is defined as
$$\mathbb{O} = \{(in^l, out^l) | l = 1, \ldots, |\mathbb{O}|\} \text{ with } |\mathbb{O}| \le |\mathbb{T}|$$
where

1. $\forall in^l \ \exists k \in \{1, \ldots, |\mathbb{T}|\}$ with $in^l = (s_i^k, a_i^k)$,

2. $in^k \ne in^l \ \forall k \ne l$ and $k, l \in \{1, \ldots, |\mathbb{O}|\}$,

3. and $out^l = \max\limits_{\substack{(s_i^k, a_i^k, r^k, s_i'^k) \in \mathbb{T} \\ (s_i^k, a_i^k) = in^l}} \left( r^k + \gamma \max\limits_{\alpha \in A(s_i'^k)} Q_i(s_i'^k, \alpha) \right).$

Basically, the definition of the optimistic training set realizes a partitioning of the training tuple set $\mathbb{T}$ into $|\mathbb{O}|$ ($|\mathbb{O}| \le |\mathbb{T}|$) clusters with respect to identical local state-action pairs $(s_i, a_i)$ (conditions 1 and 2 in Definition 5.2). The optimistic assumption concerning the behavior of teammates manifests itself in the third condition: Here, the best joint action covered by the experience collected so far is taken into account. That means it is implicitly assumed that the other agents

- have taken optimal elementary actions that are most appropriate for the current state,

- and, hence, that they were in local states such that the execution of the joint action yielded high immediate reward,

- and, correspondingly, that the system arrived at a joint successor state of high value.

Thus, the target value $out^l$ for some state-action pair $in^l = (s_i^l, a_i^l)$ is the maximal sum of the immediate reward and discounted expected rewards over all tuples $(s_i^k, a_i^k, \cdot, \cdot) \in \mathbb{T}$.

Again, after having constructed the training set $\mathbb{O}$, any suitable neural network training algorithm can be employed for the regression task at hand (e.g. standard backpropagation or the faster Rprop algorithm (Riedmiller and Braun, 1993) we use). Apart from those net training issues, the pseudo-code of OA-NFQ in Figure 5.3 reflects also the policy screening technique (cf. Section 5.2.3): In between individual Q iterations we let the current value function $Q_i^q$ and the corresponding dispatching policy, respectively, undergo an additional evaluation based on simulating a number of screening (scheduling) problems. Via that mechanism, the best Q iteration and its belonging Q function $Q_i^{top}$ is detected and finally returned.

We need to stress that in presence of using a neural value function approximation mechanism to represent Q and providing agents with local view information only, neither the convergence guarantees for certain (averaging) types of fitted Q iteration algorithms (see Ernst et al. (2006) for a thorough discussion), nor the convergence proof of the optimistic assumption-based Q learning algorithm (supporting finite state-action spaces, only) endure. Nevertheless, it is possible to obtain impressive empirical results despite the approximations we employ, as we will show in the next section.

111

## 5 Value Function-Based Solution Approaches

---

**Input:** transition tuple set $\mathbb{T} = \{(s_i^k, a_i^k, r^k, s_i'^k) | k = 1, \ldots, |\mathbb{T}|\}$,
number of Q iterations $N \in \mathbb{N}$
1: $q \leftarrow 0$
2: **initialize** $Q_i^q \leftarrow$ random weight initialization of MLP
3: **while** $q < N$ **do** //Q iterations
4: $\quad \mathbb{O} \leftarrow \emptyset$ //optimistic training set
5: $\quad$ **for** $k = 1$ **to** $|\mathbb{T}|$ **do**
6: $\quad\quad in^k \leftarrow (s_i^k, a_i^k)$
7: $\quad\quad out^k \leftarrow r^k + \gamma \max_{\alpha \in A(s_i^k)} Q_i^q(s_i^k, \alpha)$
8: $\quad\quad \mathbb{K} \leftarrow \{(in^l, out^l) | in^l = (s_i^k, a_i^k)\}$ //$|\mathbb{K}| \in \{0, 1\}$
9: $\quad\quad$ **if** $\mathbb{K} = \emptyset$ **then**
10: $\quad\quad\quad \mathbb{O} \leftarrow \mathbb{O} \cup \{(in^k, out^k)\}$
11: $\quad\quad$ **else**
12: $\quad\quad\quad out_{max} \leftarrow \max\{\ out^k,\ \{out^l | (in^l, out^l) \in \mathbb{K}\}\ \}$
13: $\quad\quad\quad \mathbb{O} \leftarrow \mathbb{O} \cup \{(in^k, out_{max})\}$
14: $\quad\quad\quad \mathbb{O} \leftarrow \mathbb{O} \setminus \mathbb{K}$
15: $\quad\quad$ **endif**
16: $\quad$ **end for**
17: $\quad Q_i^{q+1} \leftarrow$ train MLP given $\mathbb{F}$ using Rprop
18: $\quad$ **perform** policy screening to evaluate $\pi_i(s_i) = \arg\max_{\alpha \in s_i} Q_i^{q+1}(s_i, \alpha)$
$\quad\quad\quad$ and let $Q_i^{top} \leftarrow Q_i^{q+1}$ in case of an improvement
19: $\quad q \leftarrow q + 1$
20: **end while**
21: **return** $Q_i^{top}$

---

**Algorithm 5.3:**
OA-NFQ: An Optimistic Multi-Agent Implementation of NFQ (applied by agent $i$)

## 5.4 Empirical Evaluation

In this section, we evaluate the use of approximate reinforcement learning for the job-shop scheduling benchmark problems that are in the center of our interest. In particular, we want to address the question, if it is possible to utilize the algorithms we have described in the preceding sections, to let the agents acquire high-quality dispatching policies for problem instances of current standards of difficulty. Furthermore, we want to investigate, whether the learned policies generalize to other, similar scheduling benchmark problems, too.

We begin by a comprehensive description of the experimental set-up we use and continue with some results for two standard example benchmark problems. Then, we report on the learning results for a broad collection of larger-sized benchmarks which also allows for a comparison to the performance of policy search-based RL algorithms. Finally, we explore the generalization capabilities of OA-NFQ within two further experiments.

## 5.4.1 Experimental Set-Up

During all experiments to be described in the following, we employ value function-based reinforcement learning to let the scheduling agents adapt their behavior policy, based on repeatedly collecting experience within their environment and on receiving positive or negative feedback (reinforcement signals) from that environment, which, as before, we model as a decentralized Markov decision process with changing action sets. After that *learning* phase, each agent will have obtained a purposive, reactive behavior for the respective environment. Then, during the *application* phase, e.g. during application in a real plant, each agent can make its scheduling decisions very quickly by utilizing its reactive behavior (Gabel and Riedmiller, 2007c). Both phases fit into the general batch-mode RL scheme outlined by Algorithm 5.1. During the latter phase, however, the learned $Q_i$ functions are exploited greedily by all agents. During the former, by contrast, an exploration strategy is pursued which chooses random actions with some probability and which makes updates to $Q_i$ using one of the value function update algorithms we have presented (Algorithm 5.2 or 5.3).

Assuming a typical $m \times n$ job-shop scheduling problem modelled as a DEC-MDP with changing action sets as well as reactively acting agents, it is clear that the transition graph of the system is acyclic and the number of states till reaching $s^f$ is finite. Therefore, all policies are always proper and the problem horizon is finite, which is why the discount factor $\gamma$ can safely be set to one (no discounting).

When considering a single job-shop problem, the number of possible states is, of course, finite. A focal point pursued in this chapter, however, is not to concentrate just on individual problem instances, but on arbitrary ones. Hence, we assume the domain of state-action value functions to be infinite or even continuous (see the discussion on that topic in Section 5.1.1), and employ multi-layer perceptron neural networks as function approximation mechanisms to represent them. Each learning agent utilizes an MLP with one hidden layer (13:9:1 topology, cf. the illustration in Figure 5.2 and the following feature description) to represent its local state-action value function $Q_i$.

**State and Action Features**

When provided with some kind of a "global view" on the entire plant, i.e. when being granted full joint state observability, including information about the situation at all resources and the processing status of all jobs, a classical solution algorithm (like a branch-and-bound method) could be easily applied – even in parallel by each agent – to construct a disjunctive graph for the problem at hand and solve it. In this respect, however, we have introduced a significant aggravation of the problem: First, we require a reactive scheduling decision in each state to be taken in real-time, i.e. we do not allot arbitrary amounts of computation time. Second, the DEC-MDP-based problem interpretation restricts the amount of state information the agents get. Instead of the global view, each agent $i$ has access to local state information $s_i$ only, containing condensed information about its associated resource and the jobs waiting there. On the one hand, this partial observability increases the difficulty in finding an optimal schedule. On the other hand, it allows for complete decentralization in decision-making, since each agent is provided with informa-

## 5 Value Function-Based Solution Approaches

tion only that are relevant for making a local decision at the resource it is responsible for. Apparently, this is particularly useful in applications where no global control can be instantiated and where communication between distributed working centers is impossible (Gabel and Riedmiller, 2007a).

Nevertheless, the characterization of local states by means of several comprehensive features, viz the agents' local view, is still large and forces us tackle a high-dimensional continuous state-action space:

**Feature Vectors** representing states $s_i \in S_i$ and actions (jobs[4]) $a_i \in \mathcal{A}_i^r$, as corresponding to the resources' local view, have to exhibit some relation to the expected rewards, hence to the makespan, and must allow for a comprehensive characterization of the current situation. Moreover, it is advisable to define features that represent properties of typical problem classes instead of single problem instances, so that the dispatching policies acquired during learning are general and can be applied for different, though possibly similar scheduling problems, too. With respect to the desired real-time applicability of the system, the features should also be easy to compute, enabling a maximum degree of reactivity. In the experiments whose results we describe in Section 5.4.3, we made use of seven state features and six action features, thus having 13 inputs to the neural network representing the local state-action value function $Q_i$.

**State Features** depict the current situation of the resource by describing its processing state and the set $s_i = \{\alpha_1, \alpha_2, \dots\}$ of jobs currently waiting at that resource. That job set characterization includes the resource's current workload, an estimation of the earliest possible job completion times, and the estimated makespan. Furthermore, we capture characteristics of $s_i$ by forming relations between minimal and maximal values of certain job properties over the job set (like operation duration times or remaining job processing times).

**Action Features** characterize single jobs $\alpha$ from $s_i$ currently selectable by $i$. Here, we aim at describing makespan-oriented properties of individual jobs (like processing time indices), as well as immediate consequences to be expected when processing that job next, viz the properties of the job's remaining operations (e.g. the relative remaining processing time). Apart from that, action features cover the significance of the next operation $o_{\alpha,k+1}$ of job $\alpha$ (e.g. its relative duration).

**Local and Global Rewards**

Throughout this work we consider cooperative agents. The cooperative nature of the DEC-MDPs we are addressing is expressed in the global reward signal all agents receive. Thus, the reward function $r$ is used to specify the goal of the team of agents and is a function of states, joint actions, and successor states. As emphasized before, a desirable sequence

---
[4] Recall that we identify the set $\mathcal{J}$ of jobs in a job-shop scheduling problem $\mathbb{J}$ (Definition 3.1) with the set $\mathcal{A}^r$ of all actions of a DEC-MDP with changing action sets and partially ordered transition dependencies (cf. Equation 3.1 in Section 3.2.2).

## 5.4 Empirical Evaluation

of joint actions ought to correspond to a high long-term reward, which we formalized as the expected return (cf. Equation 2.1).

In principle, it is also possible to split the reward function into agent-specific components. Then, the global reward can be assembled by amalgamating local rewards that relate to single agents. If this type of factorizing the reward is done in such a manner, that increasing any local reward yields also an increased global reward, too, then the system at hand is considered to be reward independent (cf. Definition 2.11).

Our general specification of decentralized Markov decision processes with changing action sets and partially ordered transition dependencies does not require any further preconditions or assumptions concerning the reward structure. When targeting job-shop scheduling problems with the objective of minimizing maximum makespan of the resulting schedules, however, it is possible to express the global reward as a sum of local ones and, hence, to interpret the learning system as a reward-independent one. The latter point is of interest insofar as it may allow us to entirely decouple the learning agents: Instead of receiving local state observations and taking local actions, the independent agents would then also receive only local rewards. Although this approach might be appealing from a practical point of view in terms of achieving pure decentralization, the selfish consideration of local reward signals only is expected to yield less cooperative, and hence, sub-optimal joint performance.

The application of the general Q learning update rule, which also underlies the NFQ/OA-NFQ algorithms, establishes a relation between the local dispatching decisions as made by agent $i$ and the overall optimization goal, since the global immediate rewards are taken into consideration. As an intuitive example in the realm of production scheduling, large negative immediate rewards (or, equivalently, high costs) may be caused due to tardy jobs, i.e. due to tasks that were not accomplished until their deadline.

Another issue is that in job-shop scheduling, a resource is not allowed to take actions at each discrete time step, after having started some operation $o_{j,k}$ the resource remains busy until that operation is finished. Therefore, we let $\mathcal{R}_{s_i a_i}$ collect the immediate global rewards that arise between $t$ and the next decision time point $t+\delta(o_{j,k})$ of agent $i$ according to

$$\mathcal{R}_{s_i a_i}(t, \Delta t_i) = \sum_{k=t}^{t+\delta(o_{j,k})} r(s(k), a(k), s(k+1)).$$

If we assume convergence of $Q_i$ to the optimal local value function $Q_i^*$, we obtain a predictor of the expected accumulated global rewards that will arise, when in state $s_i$ a job denoted by $a_i$ would be processed next. Then, a policy $\pi$ that exploits $Q_i$ greedily will lead to optimized performance of the scheduling agent. In accordance with our definitions of local policies for decentralized MDPs (cf. Definition 2.9), a local, reactive, and deterministic policy that greedily exploits its value function chooses its next local action as follows

$$\pi(s_i) = \max_{\alpha \in A_i(s_i)} Q_i(s_i, \alpha).$$

Naturally, a crucial precondition for our value function-based RL approach to learning to make sophisticated scheduling decisions is that the global immediate rewards (as feedback to the learning agents) coincide with the overall objective of scheduling. We define the

# 5 Value Function-Based Solution Approaches

global rewards $r$ to be the sum of the rewards that can be associated with the agents (sum over $i \in Ag$) and jobs (sum over $j \in \mathcal{J}$):

$$r(s,a,s') = \sum_{i=1}^{m} u_i(s,a,s') + \sum_{j=1}^{n} v_j(s,a,s'). \tag{5.13}$$

When focusing on minimizing overall tardiness, for instance, it is standing to reason to set $u_i \equiv 0$ and to let $v_j$ capture the tardiness $T_j = max(0, c_j - d_j)$ of the jobs[5] by

$$v_j(s,a,s') = \begin{cases} -T_j, & \text{if } j \text{ is being finished in state } s' \\ 0, & \text{else} \end{cases} \tag{5.14}$$

A disadvantage of that formulation is that the cost function does not reflect when the tardiness actually occurs. Since that information may help the learning algorithm, the following, equivalent formulation is preferable, which assigns costs at each time step during processing:

$$v_j(s,a,s') = \begin{cases} -1, & \text{if } j \text{ is tardy in state } s' \\ 0, & \text{else} \end{cases} \tag{5.15}$$

Equations 5.14 and 5.15 are meant as an example and are no longer useful when the overall objective is to minimize the makespan $C_{max}$ of the resulting schedule. Accordingly, information about tardy jobs or finishing times $c_j$ of individual jobs provide no meaningful indicator relating to the makespan. There is, of course, a lot of work on tardiness-minimizing approaches (Gabel and Riedmiller, 2006b), but as far as the work at hand is considered we stick with aiming at minimizing makespan.

As emphasized in Section 3.2.2, it is known that the makespan of the schedule is minimized, if as many resources as possible are processing jobs concurrently and, accordingly, as few as possible resources with queued jobs are in the system: A high utilization of the resources implies a minimal makespan (Pinedo, 2002). Stated differently, the minimal makespan of a non-delay schedule is obtained when the number of time steps can be minimized during which jobs are waiting for processing at the resources' queues. This argument gives rise to setting

$$v_j \equiv 0 \text{ and}$$
$$u_i(s,a,s') = -|\{j \mid j \text{ queued at } i\}| \tag{5.16}$$

so that high negative rewards are generated when many jobs, that are waiting for further processing, are in the system and, hence, the overall utilization of the resources is poor.

Our definition of global immediate rewards in Equation 5.13 does in general not support reward independence according to Definition 2.11. However, it is worth noting that – for the objective of minimizing maximum makespan we are interested in – the reward formulation given by Equation 5.16 in fact yields reward independence. Although each function $u_i$ (for all $i \in Ag$) is defined over $S \times A \times S$, it actually requires information

---

[5] As defined in Chapter 3, $c_j$ refers to the completion time of job $j$. The deadline that may be associated with that job is denoted by $d_j$.

## 5.4 Empirical Evaluation

relating to the situation of agent $i$ only and, accordingly, we can define local reward functions $r_i : S_i \times A_i \times S_i$ as

$$r_i(\sigma, \alpha, \sigma') = u_i(s, a, s') \; \forall \sigma, \sigma' \in S_i, \alpha \in A_i \text{ and}$$
$$\exists s = (s_1, \ldots, s_m), a = (a_1, \ldots, a_m), s' = (s'_1, \ldots, s'_m) : s_i = \sigma, a_i = \alpha, s'_i = \sigma'.$$

This in turn allows us to interpret the global reward $r$ as a sum of local rewards $r_i$ by

$$r(s, a, s') = \sum_{i=1}^{m} r_i(s_i, a_i, s'_i)$$

for all $s = (s_1, \ldots, s_m)$, $a = (a_1, \ldots, a_m)$, $s' = (s'_1, \ldots, s'_m)$ as demanded in the definition of reward independence (Definition 2.11).

The important point to be noted about the idea to make each agent learn based purely on local rewards $r_i(s_i, a_i, s'_i) = -|\{j \mid j \text{ queued at } i\}|$ is that this in fact recasts the learning objective from reducing the length of the schedule (i.e. makespan) to minimizing the number of jobs waiting at any resource individually. The latter, however, is in conformity with the utilization of the SPT dispatching rule discussed in Section 3.3.2, which always selects that job whose next operation has the shortest processing time. Generally speaking, the SPT rule is one of the rather well-performing dispatching rules, if the goal is to minimize makespan: For many scheduling benchmark problems it yields satisfying or good values of $C_{max}$, but as it is a very simple and static heuristic, it may also fail on certain problem instances. This is, for example, the case for the small educational benchmark problem FT6, where in fact the worst performance possible is brought about, if all agents involved make their decisions based on the SPT dispatching rule ($C_{max}^{SPT} = 88$, cf. Figure 4.8).

As pointed out, our main focus is on conveying a global reward signal to the independently learning agents, but in the next section we also briefly examine the performance loss yielded, when agents receive local rewards only and, thus, learn purely selfishly.

### 5.4.2 Example Benchmarks

Similarly as in the chapter on policy search-based reinforcement learning, we start our empirical analysis with the educational benchmark problem FT6 presented in Section 3.1.1. During the data collection stage of our batch-mode reinforcement learning approach, each agent executes an $\varepsilon$-greedy, reactive, deterministic policy ($\varepsilon = 0.2$) derived from its current Q function. For the problem instances at hand, the value function update procedure (line 11 of Algorithm 5.1) is entered each time an agent has extended its set of transition 4-tuples by 50 additional experience units. As far as the fitted Q iteration part is concerned, we use $N = 20$ Q iterations throughout all our experiments. And, concerning the supervised learning part involved, we employed the Rprop neural network training procedure with 500 epochs and its default parameter settings ($\eta^+ = 1.2$, $\eta^- = 0.5$).

In principle, we distinguish between three different modes of operation for the learning agents.

## 5 Value Function-Based Solution Approaches

- During the learning phase – which we might also call experience collection and processing phase –, a set $\mathcal{S}_L$ of scheduling problem instances is repeatedly processed on the simulated plant, where the agents associated to the $m$ resources follow their $\varepsilon$-greedy policies, sample experience, and at times adapt their policies. This corresponds to the outer loop of the batch-mode reinforcement learning framework sketched in Figure 5.1.

- When adapting their behavior policies using one of the value function update algorithms discussed (in the context of fitted Q iteration, cf. the inner loop within Figure 5.1), the agents may utilize the policy screening technique outlined in Section 5.2.3. In that case, they process scheduling scenarios from a separate screening set $\mathcal{S}_S$ for validation in order to assess the quality of greedy policies induced from intermediately created state-action value functions.

- During the evaluation or application phase, the ensemble of agents processes scheduling benchmark instances from a set $\mathcal{S}_A$ of test problems, employing greedy policies with respect to the local value functions learned.

As far as the example benchmarks are concerned we address next, we let $\mathcal{S}_L = \mathcal{S}_S = \mathcal{S}_A$, thus making the agents learn to make good dispatching decisions for specific problem instances without addressing the issue of generalization.

**FT6 Benchmark** Table 5.1 summarizes the average makespan values plus corresponding standard deviations, when using value function-based batch-mode reinforcement learning agents for the FT6 benchmark. A first observation to be made is that local reward signals indeed make the agents generate selfish behavior which mimics the SPT dispatching priority rule. This effect is most apparent in the table's first row for the OA-NFQ algorithm where maximal makespan (86.17) is attained, very much approaching the performance of SPT (88.0).

Using the policy screening technique in conjunction with local rewards (second row of Table 5.1) represents a somewhat inconsistent course of action: On the one hand, local rewards reinforce SPT-like behavior and, hence, a policy yielding high makespan values. On the other hand, policy screening analyzes the $N = 20$ value functions and corresponding policies generated during the Q iteration process and picks the one with minimal makespan. Needless to say that this contradictory combination of learning goals is, in particular for the FT6 problem, inappropriate and generally yields policies that create average makespan schedules.

Let us more specifically focus on the case of global rewards. If no policy screening is conducted and, hence, the Q value function after the 20th fitted Q iteration is considered, OA-NFQ is only marginally superior to NFQ. The performance achievable in this setting (third row in the result table) features a rather high standard deviation and is inferior to, for example, the gradient-descent policy search algorithms investigated in Section 4.3. This fact points to a potential weakness of the neural value function-based batch-mode learning approach and thus supports the utility of applying policy screening. It also motivates the need for developing other heuristics that might foster convergent learning behavior. We will discuss the latter issue in more detail in Section 5.5.1.

5.4 Empirical Evaluation

| Policy Screening | Reward Signals | NFQ $\mathbb{E}[C_{max}]$ | | OA-NFQ $\mathbb{E}[C_{max}]$ | |
|---|---|---|---|---|---|
| no | local | 68.37 | ±0.56 | 86.71 | ±0.36 |
| yes | local | 62.15 | ±2.35 | 68.86 | ±2.94 |
| no | global | 63.91 | ±1.59 | 63.87 | ±1.94 |
| yes | global | 59.78 | ±1.05 | 58.63 | ±0.38 |

Table 5.1: Neural Value Function-Based Reinforcement Learning Results for the FT6 Benchmark: The average performance of OA-NFQ and NFQ in conjunction with/without using the policy screening technique and the local and global reward signals are contrasted.

Neural networks are known to belong to the class of "exaggerating" value function approximators (Gordon, 1996) which disallow for theoretical guarantees when using them as representation of state-action value functions. More specifically, it may easily happen that, for example, the policy that is represented by the set of value functions $Q_i^{18}$ after the 18th Q iteration within the NFQ algorithm is clearly superior to policy represented by the $Q_i^{20}$ functions. Accordingly, the utilization of the policy screening technique brings about some relief in that respect. So, by far the best results are achieved for the setting with global rewards and policy screening.

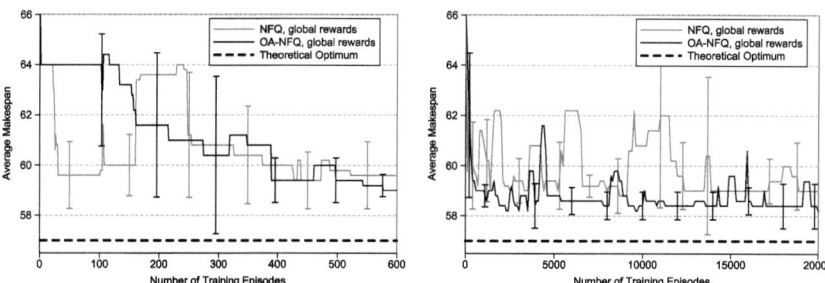

Figure 5.3: Learning with NFQ and OA-NFQ for the FT6 Benchmark: This chart opposes the learning yielded by the NFQ and OA-NFQ algorithm when applied for the FT6 job-shop scheduling benchmark. The reactive policies obtained by the independently learning agents quickly improve (left), the long-term progress is shown in the right part. Policy screening was used throughout this series of experiments.

Plain performance numbers indicate a statistically significant plus for OA-NFQ over its single-agent counterpart NFQ, which also becomes apparent when having a look at corresponding learning progress curves: Averaged over 10 independent repetitions of the same learning experiment, Figure 5.3 visualizes the learning progress when 6 independently learning agents perform value function-based batch-mode RL in parallel. The left part of that figure, which covers the first 600 training episodes of the learning process, shows fast

## 5 Value Function-Based Solution Approaches

learning improvements. Indeed, after 600 repetitions of the simulated scheduling process, for the expected makespan $\mathbb{E}[C_{max}|\pi_{600}] = -J(\pi_{600})$ we obtain a value of $59.6 \pm 1.34$ and $59.0 \pm 0.45$ for NFQ and OA-NFQ, respectively (each with global rewards and policy screening). In any case, the quick improvement of the joint policy supports the data efficiency of the batch-mode approach to value function-based reinforcement learning.

The superiority of the optimistic assumption-based version of neural fitted Q iteration, being applied to in a decentralized Markov decision process, can be more clearly read from the long-term development of the learning curves (right part of Figure 5.3). In the further curse of learning, here up to 20000 training episodes, we observe that both NFQ and OA-NFQ do not steadily converge. Instead, their performance is subject to fluctuations with varying magnitude which are caused by the fact that we allot exactly $N = 20$ Q iterations to the fitted Q iteration loop. Between the 5000th and 20000th training episode there is no more significant improvement in the performance of either method. When comparing the average standard deviations that NFQ and OA-NFQ yield in this setting (1.05 vs. 0.38), we can conclude that the optimistic assumption improves the learning algorithm's stability: From the set of transition four-tuples collected each agent subselects that fraction that previously brought about best performance (i.e. assuming other agents to behave optimally), and in using the corresponding reduced optimistic training pattern set for the supervised value function fitting, near-optimal behavior is enforced.

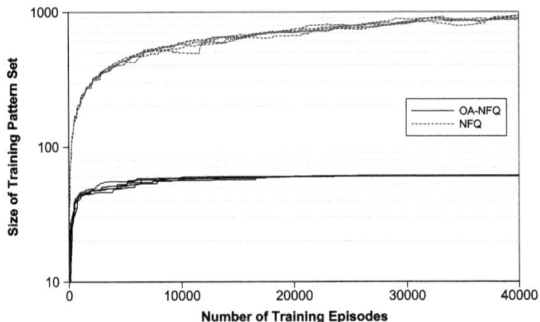

Figure 5.4: Training Data Utilization with NFQ and OA-NFQ for the FT6 Benchmark: For 5 repetitions of the FT6 learning experiment the development of the sizes of the respective training pattern sets used in the scope of fitted Q iteration are plotted. All curves show average values over the pattern sets of the six agents involved.

The consideration of a reduced optimistic training pattern set as specified in Definition 5.2 has also the beneficial effect that learning can be speeded up: For the supervised learning part of a fitted Q iteration algorithm – in our case, training a neural network –, each agent employs only a minor fraction of the experience data it has collected. As a consequence, the required training times will be reduced significantly: Figure 5.4 compares the average sizes of the training pattern sets $\mathbb{F}$ and $\mathbb{O}$ generated and employed by the NFQ

## 5.4 Empirical Evaluation

and OA-NFQ value function update method (cf. Algorithms 5.2 and 5.3), respectively. Obviously, the optimistic training pattern set $\mathbb{O}$ comprises about an order of magnitude less elements than the pattern set $\mathbb{F}$ typically used within fitted Q iteration algorithms. To this end, it is important to note that this type of training data selection has, in fact, no negative effect on the performance of the resulting policy: For the global reward setting we consider, learning on the basis of a reduced pattern set $\mathbb{O}$ and, hence, using OA-NFQ yields better results than the standard (single-agent) NFQ algorithm, as shown in Table 5.1.

**FT10 Benchmark** While the FT6 problem comprises 6 jobs with 6 operations each, the FT10 problem by the same authors (Muth and Thompson, 1963) comprises 100 operations (10 jobs with 10 operations each that must be processed across 10 resources). The latter has been labelled a "notorious" problem, as it had remained unsolved (no optimal schedule found) for more than twenty years after its publication.

Again, we process the same scheduling problem during learning and during policy screening, i.e. $\mathcal{S}_L = \mathcal{S}_S = \{FT10\}$. Here, as well as subsequently, we focus on the OA-NFQ algorithm with global rewards as, in the experiments above, this learning method has proved to be the most reliable and performant one. Apart from the increased problem size, all other settings that relate to the learning algorithm remain the same. This time, however, we focus not only on the final performance, but compare the OA-NFQ-based learning agents with a broader selection of different approaches.

1. While for the FT6 benchmark a set of randomly dispatching agents yields schedules with average makespan of 68.43, for the FT10 benchmark it holds $\mathbb{E}[C_{max}|\pi_{rnd}] = 1253$. This expected makespan serves as a baseline to compare against.

2. Also, simple static dispatching priority rules with local state observability (such as the FIFO, SPT, or LPT rule) ought to be clearly outperformed by our learning approach. Such rules perform reactive scheduling and make their decisions which job to process next based solely on their local view on the respective resource.

3. By contrast, dispatching rules that may access more than just local state information (such as the SQNO or AMCC rule, cf. Section 3.3.2) operate under simplified conditions compared to our reactive agents which we consider to be entities within a DEC-MDP (and not in an MMDP). Consequently, outperforming rules of that type is much harder to accomplish.

4. The optimal schedule for the FT10 problem[6] has a makespan of $C_{max}^{opt} = 930$. Hence, this value serves as lower bound.

Regarding the restrictions OA-NFQ-based learning agents are subject to (DEC-MDP interpretation of a JSSP with local state information) a comparison to group 2 is most self-evident. However, by approaching or even surpassing the performance of algorithms from group 3, we can make a case for the power of our approach.

---

[6]Note that this schedule is a delay schedule, which cannot be yielded by purely reactively acting agents. Thus, the true lower bound achievable by using reactive agents is actually above 930.

# 5 Value Function-Based Solution Approaches

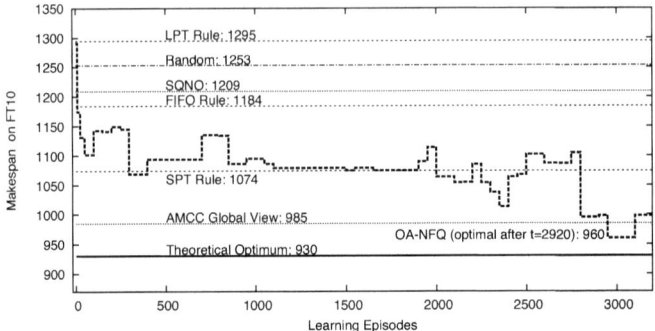

Figure 5.5: Learning Process for the Notorious FT10 Problem: Reactive agents employing OA-NFQ as batch-mode RL algorithm improve their cooperative behavior as learning proceeds.

Figure 5.5 visualizes the makespan yielded by the mentioned scheduling algorithms and shows how OA-NFQ-trained agents perform. The best solution found by the learning approach was discovered after 2920 repeated processings of $\mathcal{S}_L$. The makespan $C_{max} = 960$ of the corresponding non-delay schedule thus has a relative error of 3.2% compared to the optimal schedule. We note that we have detected the optimal learned dispatching policy (represented by the agents' neural networks representing their Q functions) by means of the policy screening method described in Section 5.2.3.

## 5.4.3 Benchmark Suites

Figure 5.6 illustrates the learning progress of OA-NFQ when applied to the same set of 15 job-shop scheduling problems used for the evaluation of the JEPS and GDPS policy search reinforcement learning algorithms (cf. Sections 4.2 and 4.3). Each of these problems involves 100 operations, distributed over 10 jobs with 10 operations each as well as 10 processing resources. We recollect that in Chapter 4 we invariably employed stochastic policies for which we could prove that convergence to a deterministic policy (in general, to a local optimum) is always achieved, which means that the performance $J(\pi)$ (with $-J(\pi) = \mathbb{E}[C_{max}|\pi]$) of the policy converges as learning progresses.

By contrast, within the current part of this book we concentrate on learning local agent-specific value functions that we represent using neural networks. As to be expected and as already observed during the experiments for the FT6 benchmark problem above, the development of $-J(\pi)$ shows the trend of decreasing, but it does not reliably and continuously converge. Fortunately, the utilization of the policy screening technique allows us to detect and remember those state-action value functions from which high-quality policies, i.e. policies yielding a low makespan of the schedule generated, could be induced during screening. The corresponding curve in Figure 5.6, therefore, is steadily decreasing and, after already 25000 training episodes, reaches a value of $-J(\pi_{PS}) = 945.1$ (PS indicates

5.4 Empirical Evaluation

policy screening) and draws level with the average makespan values that are yielded by the policy search-based RL algorithms we investigated in Chapter 4. The remaining error when compared to the theoretical optimum, which is represented by the makespan of an optimal schedule, is 5.2% after that many training episodes. Besides, the development of $C_{max}^{best}$ is shown, which indicates the average (over the set of 15 problems considered) of the best schedule occasionally created during the agents' learning phases, i.e. when they interacted with the DEC-MDP in an $\varepsilon$-greedy manner.

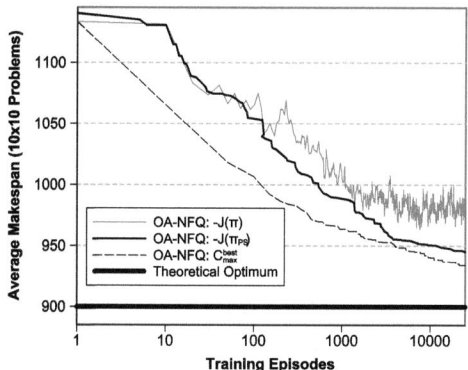

Figure 5.6: Learning Progress of OA-NFQ for a Set of 10x10 JSSPs: The solid line indicates the performance of those top policies that were detected by means of policy screening. All curves are averaged over the 15 problems considered.

Next, we investigate the effectiveness of our agent-based scheduling approach for a large number of different-sized benchmark problem suites, ranging from job-shop scheduling problems with five resources and ten jobs to fifteen resources and twenty jobs. We allow the agents to sample training data tuples in an $\varepsilon$-greedy manner for maximally 25000 processings of $\mathcal{S}_L$ with $\mathcal{S}_L = \mathcal{S}_S$ and permitted intermediate calls to OA-NFQ (again, $N = 20$ iterations of the Q iteration loop) in order to reach the vicinity of a near-optimal Q function as quickly as possible. Here, all resulting value functions and corresponding greedy multi-agent policies are evaluated (tested during the application phase) on the same problems as used during learning ($\mathcal{S}_L = \mathcal{S}_A$).

For a better illustration of the findings we have grouped the results on individual benchmark problems into classes with respect to the numbers of resources and jobs to be processed (Figure 5.7). As before, all benchmark problems are taken from the Operations Research Library[7] (Beasley, 2005). Although these benchmarks are of different sizes, they have in common that no recirculation occurs and that each job has to be processed on each resource exactly once. The results are given relative to the makespan of the optimal schedule (100%, black data series). Data series colored in light gray correspond to

---

[7]Benchmark problems ABZ5-9 were originally generated by Adams et al. (1988), problems ORB01-09 by Applegate and Cook (1991), and finally, problems LA1-20 are due to Lawrence (1984).

## 5 Value Function-Based Solution Approaches

static rules having local state information only (group 2 from the above enumeration of algorithms to compare against), whereas medium gray-colored ones are not subject to that restriction (group 3). The dark gray-colored data series corresponds to our approach using independent batch-mode reinforcement learning agents that determine their value functions using OA-NFQ which is based on the DEC-MDP interpretation of JSSPs and, hence, is restricted to the local view, too.

For the $5 \times 15$ (LA6-10) and $5 \times 20$ (LA11-15) benchmark problems, the optimal solution can be found by our learning approach in all cases. This depicts an impressive result as it means that the optimal schedule in terms of minimal makespan is created for each of these problem instances, if each of the agents exploits its acquired local value function $Q_i$ greedily.

For the $5 \times 10$ (LA1-5) and $10 \times 10$ (LA16-20, ORB1-9) sets, only a small relative error of less than ten percent compared to the optimal makespan remains (3.4/4.0/7.2%). As to be expected, dispatching rules, even those disposing of more than just local state information (AMCC, SQNO), are clearly outperformed. For the larger benchmarks (ABZ) involving 15 resources and 20 jobs per problem instance the relative error increases to 10.6%, but the rule-based schedulers can be outperformed still.

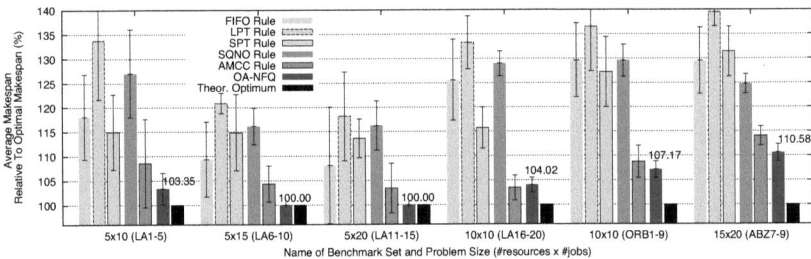

Figure 5.7: Benchmark Results for OA-NFQ: For different sets of benchmark problems with equal size, this figure visualizes the average performance of different approaches in terms of minimized makespan of the resulting schedules. Error bars indicate the standard deviations of the relative errors over the problem instances within the respective benchmark problem sets.

For the purpose of result comparability to the policy search-based approaches proposed in Chapter 4 (cf. Tables 4.1 and 4.2), Table 5.2 summarizes the learning results for identical sets of benchmark problems. To this end, an important difference is that OA-NFQ-based learning was allotted 25000 training episodes only, whereas JEPS and GDPS were allowed to process the considered scenarios 250000 times. The comparison of these algorithms, however, is fair insofar as we employ OA-NFQ in conjunction with policy screening which requires a substantial amount of additional simulated screening runs. As a result, in total approximately the same amount of interaction with the DEC-MDP is granted to all methods.

| Size $m \times n$ | #Prbl | Theor.Opt. | Dispatching Rules ||||||  OA-NFQ ||
|---|---|---|---|---|---|---|---|---|---|---|
| | | | Random | FIFO | LPT | SPT | SQNO | AMCC | $-J(\pi_{PS})$ | Rem.Err. |
| $5 \times 10$ | 5 | 620.2 | 765.4 | 732.4 | 829.6 | 713.0 | 787.6 | 673.4 | 641.0 | 3.4% |
| $5 \times 15$ | 5 | 917.6 | 1052.4 | 1003.6 | 1108.8 | 1054.0 | 1065.4 | 955.6 | 917.6 | 0.0% |
| $5 \times 20$ | 6 | 1179.2 | 1358.4 | 1339.0 | 1435.7 | 1330.7 | 1390.8 | 1241.8 | 1190.8 | 1.0% |
| $10 \times 10$ | 17 | 912.5 | 1158.0 | 1153.0 | 1228.3 | 1106.3 | 1163.1 | 973.7 | 964.3 | 5.7% |
| $10 \times 15$ | 5 | 983.4 | 1285.3 | 1271.0 | 1337.4 | 1263.6 | 1220.4 | 1094.8 | 1042.2 | 6.0% |
| $15 \times 15$ | 5 | 1263.2 | 1640.8 | 1585.4 | 1772.0 | 1573.6 | 1531.0 | 1387.4 | 1333.2 | 5.5% |
| $15 \times 20$ | 3 | 676.0 | 878.0 | 875.3 | 942.7 | 888.3 | 843.3 | 771.0 | 747.7 | 10.6% |
| Average | 46 | 946.5 | 1178.0 | 1157.0 | 1251.4 | 1140.8 | 1166.7 | 1019.0 | 988.1 | 4.4%$_{\pm 3.5}$ |

Table 5.2: Benchmark Result Overview for OA-NFQ: Learning results for scheduling benchmarks of varying size achieved using OA-NFQ. All entries are averaged over #Prbl. The last column denotes the relative remaining error (%) of the makespan achieved by the joint policy (detected by policy screening) compared to the theoretical optimum and, thus, indicates to what extent the globally best schedule could be approximated.

### 5.4.4 Generalization Capabilities

During all previous experiments, the performance of the joint policy the agents induce from their local state-action value functions has been determined on the same JSSP instances that were repeatedly processed during training. Stated differently, we consistently set $\mathcal{S}_L = \mathcal{S}_A$. As pointed out before, this analysis is interesting from the perspective of making independent agents learn to solve a single intricate scheduling problem. The arguments we have provided in the section on the issue of generalization (Section 5.1.1), however, emphasize one particular possible merit of our value function-based multi-agent RL approach, when applied to job-shop scheduling problems: The neural value functions learned and corresponding behavior policies induced from them may be well applicable to situations not covered during training. This includes random disturbances of the production process (e.g. due to processing delays or resource failures) as well as completely new scheduling scenarios.

To empirically investigate the generalization capabilities of the learned dispatching policies, the following experiments are designed differently. Now, the learning agents are presented three sets of scheduling problems:

- the training set $\mathcal{S}_L$ for the learning phase,
- the screening set $\mathcal{S}_S$ for intermediate policy screening rollouts (as before, we set $\mathcal{S}_L = \mathcal{S}_S$),
- and an application set $\mathcal{S}_A$ containing independent problem instances to evaluate the quality of the learning results on problem instances the agents have not seen before ($\mathcal{S}_L \cap \mathcal{S}_A = \emptyset$).

Of course, it would be unrealistic to expect the dispatching policies that were trained using, for instance, a training set with $5 \times 15$ problems, to bring about reasonable scheduling decisions for very different problems (e.g. for $10 \times 10$ benchmarks). Therefore, we

## 5 Value Function-Based Solution Approaches

have conducted experiments for benchmark suites $\mathcal{S}$ consisting of problems with identical sizes that were provided by the same authors. From an applicatory point of view, this assumption is appropriate and purposeful, because it reflects the requirements of a real plant where usually variations in the scheduling tasks to be solved occur according to some scheme and depending on the plant layout, but not in an entirely arbitrary manner.

Moreover, since $|\mathcal{S}|$ is rather small under these premises, we perform $\nu$-fold cross-validation on $\mathcal{S}$, i.e. we disjoint $\mathcal{S}$ into $\mathcal{S}_L$ and $\mathcal{S}_A$, let the agents train by processing problems from $\mathcal{S}_L$ and assess the performance of the learning results on $\mathcal{S}_A$. Finally, we repeat that procedure $\nu$ times to form average values.

Figure 5.8 illustrates the learning process and the learning results for a benchmark suite of $5 \times 15$ problems $\mathcal{S}_{LA}^{5\times15} = \{LA06, \ldots, LA10\}$ (top), as well as for the more challenging suite of $10 \times 10$ problems $\mathcal{S}_{ORB}^{10\times10} = \{ORB1, \ldots, ORB9\}$. For the former, our learning approach succeeds in nearly entirely capturing the characteristics of the training problems in $\mathcal{S}_L$ during training: If the learned dispatching policies process the instances from $\mathcal{S}_L$, the theoretic optimum is almost reached, i.e. scheduling decisions resulting in minimal makespan are yielded (a very low relative error of 0.3% remains). This can be read from the fact that the dashed OA-NFQ curve (for the performance during the learning phase, i.e. when processing scheduling problems from $\mathcal{S}_L$) converges towards the theoretical optimum.

What is, however, more important, is that even on the independent problem instances from $\mathcal{S}_A$ (5-fold cross-validation) that were not experienced during training, excellent results are achieved: The solid thin curve, which corresponds to the performance of the OA-NFQ-trained agents when applied to independent test problems, is improving as learning proceeds. Starting with a randomly initialized policy with an average makespan of 1229.1, the makespan values yielded by the ensemble of trained agents is being reduced continuously. Finally, with an average makespan of 951.6 during the application phase, the acquired policies outperform not just simple dispatching rules, but even those that have full state information (like AMCC). Furthermore, the gap in performance compared to the theoretically best schedules is only 3.7% in terms of average $C_{max}$.

The training (learning phase) and testing (application phase) curves for the $\mathcal{S}_{ORB}^{10\times10}$ benchmark suite are not as steep and the local dispatching rules obtained feature a remaining relative error of 18.6% compared to the theoretic optimum in terms of minimal makespan. Since this set of benchmark problems is known to be more intricate, this depicts a positive result, too. In particular, the learning curve (bottom part of Figure 5.8) shows that standard dispatching rules are clearly outperformed. Concerning the performance on the training problem instances from $\mathcal{S}_L$ (these values are not included in Table 5.3), OA-NFQ achieves a relative remaining error of, as already said, only 0.3% for the $LA$ problems and 13.1% for the $ORB$ problems.

In Table 5.3 we provide a clear summary of the generalization-specific learning results for the considered benchmark suite $\mathcal{S}_{LA}^{5\times15}$ as well as for the more intricate suite of $10\times10$ problems $\mathcal{S}_{ORB}^{10\times10}$. We stress again that the average makespan values reported for OA-NFQ correspond to its performance on independent test problem instances. That means, to scheduling scenarios that were not included in the respective training sets $\mathcal{S}_L$ during cross-validation. The performance values reported correspond to the learning results obtained after the agents had been trained for 2000 training episodes in the case of the LA ($5 \times 15$)

5.4 Empirical Evaluation

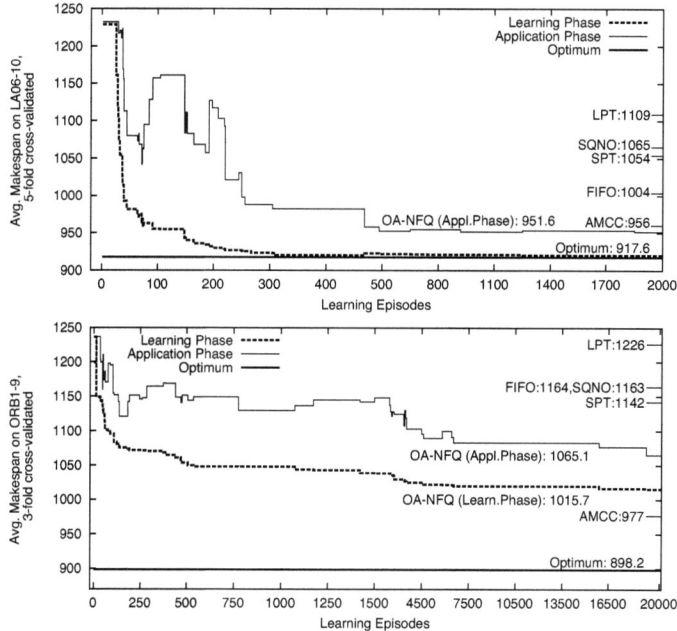

Figure 5.8: Generalization Capabilities of OA-NFQ-Trained Agents: Using $\nu$-fold cross-validation, the adaptive agents' dispatching policies are trained on the $\mathcal{S}_{LA}^{5\times 15}$ (top) and $\mathcal{S}_{ORB}^{10\times 10}$ (bottom) benchmark suites, respectively, and, during the application phase, are evaluated on independent test problems. At the chart's right hand side, the average makespans achieved by several static dispatching rules are given for comparison.

benchmark problems and for 25000 training episodes in the case of the ORB (10 × 10) benchmark set, using the scenarios from $\mathcal{S}_L$, respectively.

From that numbers (average remaining errors of 3.7%/18.6% compared to the theoretic optimum) it is obvious that all static local view dispatchers, to which OA-NFQ must naturally be compared, are clearly outperformed. Interestingly, for the $\mathcal{S}_{LA}^{5\times 15}$ problem suite not just dispatching rules working under the same conditions as OA-NFQ, but even the AMCC rule is beaten, which exhaustively benefits from its global view on the plant. For the $\mathcal{S}_{ORB}^{10\times 10}$ suite, AMCC brings about slightly better performance than OA-NFQ. This is logical since both methods were already nearly head-to-head (cf. Figure 5.7) when we trained OA-NFQ agents for individual 10 × 10 problem instances, as described in the experiment in Section 5.4.3.

The presented results of the series of experiments on generalization properties allow us to draw two empiric conclusions: First, traditional dispatching priority rules that solely

## 5 Value Function-Based Solution Approaches

| Benchmark Suite Name | $S_{LA}^{5\times15}$ | | $S_{ORB}^{10\times10}$ | |
|---|---|---|---|---|
| Problem Instances | $LA06,\ldots,LA10$ | | $ORB1,\ldots,ORB9$ | |
| Local View   Random | 1229.1 | 33.9% | 1235.2 | 37.5% |
| FIFO | 1003.6 | 9.4% | 1164.3 | 29.6% |
| LPT | 1108.8 | 20.9% | 1226.1 | 36.5% |
| SPT | 1054.0 | 14.9% | 1142.6 | 27.1% |
| Global View   AMCC | 955.6 | 4.2% | 977.1 | 8.8% |
| SQNO | 1065.4 | 16.1% | 1163.3 | 29.5% |
| **OA-NFQ** (local view) | **951.6** | **3.7%** | **1065.1** | **18.6%** |
| with Cross-Validation | 5-fold | | 3-fold | |
| Avg. Optimum ($C_{max,opt}^{avg}$) | *917.6* | | *898.2* | |

Table 5.3: Generalization Capabilities: During its application phase, the learned dispatching policies (using OA-NFQ) are used for problems not covered during training. Average makespan and remaining errors relative to the optimum are provided.

employ local state information regarding the respective resource (just as our learning approach does) are clearly outperformed. And, second, the resulting dispatching policies acquired during training feature generalization capabilities and, hence, can effectively be applied to similar, yet unknown, scheduling problem instances.

## 5.5 Discussion

The chapter at hand has been addressing reinforcement learning approaches that aim at acquiring local state-action value functions from which the agents can induce their policies. In so doing, we particularly focused on multi-layer perceptron neural networks as value function approximation mechanism and developed OA-NFQ as an instance of a batch-mode reinforcement learning algorithm tailored for multi-agent learning. This final section is meant to wrap up and discuss our findings: We briefly point to additional related work, devote a section on the convergence properties of approximate fitted RL algorithms, and finally discuss advantages and limitations of OA-NFQ.

### 5.5.1 Related Work

Optimistic assumption-based neural fitted Q iteration (OA-NFQ) is a neural value function-based batch-mode RL algorithm that we developed with the intention of making independently acting and learning agents acquire approximately optimal policies within cooperative multi-agent settings. On the one hand, being an instance of the fitted Q iteration family of RL algorithms, OA-NFQ is of course related to the work by Ernst et al. (2006) on FQI and, even more, to the NFQ algorithm of which it is a direct extension (cf. Section 5.2.2, Riedmiller, 2005). On the other hand, Q learning based on the optimistic assumption is due to the work by Lauer and Riedmiller (2000). Our optimistic batch-mode learning approach is thus related to that piece of work as well, though extended for decentralized MDP settings with partial state observability.

## 5.5 Discussion

Moreover, the idea of using distributed, agent-specific value functions, i.e. local value functions belonging to the agents, originates from the work by Schneider et al. (1999). This approach has thenceforth been applied in the context of different applications, for example for energy distribution networks (Schneider et al., 1998) or for mobile robot planning and intelligent traffic systems (Ferreira and Khosla, 2000).

The issue of local versus global rewards within cooperative multi-agent systems, which we have touched only briefly, is in the center of the research by Agogino and Tumer (2005) and Tumer and Agogino (2004). Their focus is on the design of agent-specific utility functions (cost or reward functions) that are factored in that there is a strong correlation between individual agent rewards and the performance of the team as a whole, and that are highly learnable by each single agent, meaning that any agent's contribution to the success of the team is considered appropriately.

While the exact relations to other researchers' work mentioned afore have been discussed thoroughly in the preceding sections of this chapter, we shall focus on the convergence properties of our approach and corresponding related work, next. Besides, regarding related approaches to solving job-shop scheduling problems using value function-based reinforcement learning we refer to the section on related work in Chapter 3 (Section 3.3). And, for an overview of further model-free RL approaches for learning in cooperative multi-agent systems we point to Section 2.5.

**Convergence Issues and Problems**

The fitted Q iteration learning scheme outlined in Section 5.1.2 tries to iteratively minimize the Bellman error (cf. Equation 5.3) over the set $\mathbb{T}$ of experience tuples. The supervised learning component involved, i.e. the function approximator fitting part, however, makes us raise the question to which extent does Bellman error minimization imply convergence to a (near-)optimal policy when used in conjunction with function approximation?

In general, for several algorithms, it is expected that convergence cannot be achieved and a phenomenon called "chattering" occurs. The space $\mathcal{Q}$ of all Q functions can be divided into regions where a constant policy (given by greedy Q exploitation) is followed. Bertsekas and Tsitsiklis (1996) call these regions greedy regions because each one corresponds to a different greedy policy and has its own greedy point – the point in $\mathcal{Q}$ to which $\tilde{Q}(\cdot)$ moves in the course of learning. If it happens that the greedy point does not lie in its greedy region, the policy learned will fluctuate between two or more greedy policies that share the same boundary in $\mathcal{Q}$. More details and a deeper analysis of the chattering problem can be found in the paper by Gordon (1996) and the book by Bertsekas and Tsitsiklis (1996).

As a matter of fact, much of the literature has focused on gaining insights into the convergence behavior of approximate RL, e.g. on the soundness of approximate value iteration or policy iteration (Munos, 2005, 2003). Nevertheless, there are also various publications reporting on negative results using reinforcement learning approaches with function approximation, many of which head into a specific direction: The policy the learning agent acquires quickly reaches a remarkable quality, but in the further course of learning a significant policy degradation can be observed. So, for instance, Bertsekas and Tsitsiklis (1996) report on attempts to learn a policy for playing the game of Tetris and point out the paradoxical observation that high performance is achieved after relatively few policy iterations, but then the performance drops. Gaskett (2002) has trained a Q controller for the cart pole benchmark and obtained excellent results initially. But, despite trying several approaches in an attempt to reduce policy degradation, these results got lost in the further course of learning. Weaver and Baxter (1999) performed experiments with a backgammon-playing learning agent and observed reduced playing performance while improving the accuracy of value function approximation concurrently. Bertsekas et al. (2000) made similar observations, when applying a neuro-dynamic programming approach to a missile defense problem: The sequence of policies generated during learning did not converge; improvements could be obtained in the initial iterations and once the vicinity of the optimal value function had been reached, oscillations occurred. Munos (2003) divides the learning process into a transitional and a stationary phase. During the former, rapid improvements in policy quality can be made due to a comparatively good value function approximation, when compared to the closeness to the optimality ($|\tilde{Q}^q - T\tilde{Q}^{q-1}|$ is low compared to $|T\tilde{Q}^{q-1} - Q^\star|$)[8]. Therefore, he argues that a greedy policy with respect to $\tilde{Q}^q$ is likely to be superior to the policy represented by greedy exploitation of $T\tilde{Q}^{q-1}$.

Regarding the goal to obtain a more stable learning progress and near-optimal policies there are several related publications. Kakade and Langford (2002) point out to the fact that approximate value function methods suffer from insufficient theoretical results on the performance of a policy based on approximated values. Working with stochastic policies and within an online policy iteration setting, they propose a conservative policy iteration method which seeks to find "approximately" optimal solutions by stopping to iterate when the estimated policy advantage from one iteration to the next drops below some threshold. Boyan and Moore (1995) stress that dynamic programming approaches in combination with function approximation can bring about wrong policies even in very benign cases. They suggest an algorithm, called GrowSupport, that uses simulations with the current greedy policy (roll-outs) to determine state values and successively adds elements to a set of state values whose final value has been determined. Weaver and Baxter (1999) have introduced an extended version of $TD(\lambda)$ that is based on state-value differences and demonstrated its successful applicability for a toy problem and for the acrobot benchmark.

As pointed out in Section 5.2.3, neural networks belong to the class of "exaggerating" value function approximation mechanisms (Gordon, 1996) and as such feature the potential risk of diverging. This problem concerns NFQ as well and, accordingly, a number of extensions have been proposed that aim at stabilizing this algorithm's learning performance. For example, monitored Q iteration has been suggested as an approach to circumvent effects of policy degradation during advanced stages of learning (Gabel and Riedmiller, 2006b). Here, the basic idea is to define an alternative error measure which more directly relates to a policy's actual performance, to create the conditions that this error measure can be effectively calculated during learning, and to continuously monitor the learning process utilizing the alternative error measure. In so doing, top-performing policies are remembered and also an early stopping of learning is facilitated.

As stressed before, in the context of this work we mostly relied on the – admittedly time-consuming, but simple and effective – policy screening technique (Section 5.2.3) in

---

[8]The operator $T$ is the Bellman operator which was introduced in Section 2.1.5.

order to evaluate the trained policies. Improving this technique is also the topic of current research. For example, Kietzmann and Riedmiller (2009) argue that it is possible to select the most promising policies out of the set of all intermediately created policies and to do the screening only for that subset. The resulting method, offline policy evaluation, helps in avoiding an extensive simulated evaluation of all generated policies and, thus, saves computational resources, while it still allows for figuring out a nearly optimal policy.

### 5.5.2 Advantages and Limitations of OA-NFQ

The learning of optimal value functions with the succeeding derivation of a policy represents the predominant approach to tackle reinforcement learning problems. In this chapter, we have explored batch-mode RL approaches and, specifically, suggested a novel multi-agent batch RL algorithm, OA-NFQ.

The approach we have taken has proved to be very powerful when employed for learning joint dispatching policies for job-shop scheduling problems modelled as decentralized Markov decision processes. When compared to the default approach to solving JSSPs in a centralized manner, we benefit from the idea of "distribute and conquer". The trained agents can quickly, independently, and with minimal computational effort decide for their action (calculating $Q_i(s_i, \alpha \forall \alpha \in A(s_i))$ suffices, i.e. basically $|s_i|$ forward sweeps through the neural net that represents $Q_i$ are necessary).

Of course, in this manner the optimal joint action will not always be executed, but our experimental studies confirm that the decisions made by the agents are of high quality, yielding near-optimal schedules in terms of minimizing makespan after all. Equally important, the corresponding policies learned are acquired after little training time, i.e. after little interaction with the simulated scheduling plant. This can be mainly tributed to the data-efficient nature of batch-mode reinforcement learning algorithms.

The probably most convincing and outstanding characteristic of our value function-based approach to finding near-optimal joint policies for DEC-MDPs is that the OA-NFQ algorithm features excellent generalization capabilities. Of course, during the training phase it entails the requirement of learning in a deterministic environment, but after the agents have acquired their local policies, they may apply them for stochastic and, more importantly, completely different scheduling problems. In so doing, standard approaches that perform reactive scheduling with local observations (like dispatching priority rules) can be outperformed clearly.

While the RL approaches based on policy search examined in Chapter 4 exhibit a rather strong dependency on several learning parameters, we stress that the combination of methods involved in the development of the OA-NFQ algorithm, resulted in a very low parameter sensitivity. Relatively straightforward design decisions with respect to parameters as well as state and action features already brought about convincing learning results and varying them had only a minor impact on learning performance. To this end, for instance, investing more feature engineering effort might even further increase the capabilities of OA-NFQ.

Value function-based reinforcement learning is also afflicted with certain limitations. Policy search RL approaches are capable of significantly restricting the space of policies to be considered during learning (given that adequate task knowledge is available). By

## 5 Value Function-Based Solution Approaches

contrast, value function-based RL more strongly suffers from the "curse of dimensionality", i.e. from the exponential increase of the state space as the problem dimension grows. In principle, they have to take into account each state-action pair separately and, hence, would consume an exponential amount of memory to store the value function. We have tackled this issue in two different ways: First, we have restricted ourselves to factored state representations, where the global state can be broken up into $m$ smaller local ones. Second, we avoided a table-based exact representation of the value function and instead employed multi-layer perceptrons as a value function approximation scheme that is known to be powerful and to feature good generalization capabilities.

Applying value function approximation, however, generally comes with the cost that convergence guarantees of various RL algorithms no longer hold. Furthermore, the use of neural networks for that task brings the risk of "exaggerating" certain state-action value estimates (Section 5.4.2). To this end, we relied on the policy screening technique in order to select the best-performing policies generated during learning.

Having spoken about possibly enormous memory requirements for value function-based RL, this issue also concerns the batch-mode learning part of our approach. Working with growing transition tuple sets, of course, the training times when fitting a function approximator for the pattern set generated increases. At this, our interpretation and integration of the optimistic assumption into OA-NFQ has yielded some relief. Thus, the OA part of this algorithm serves two purposes: It enables improved (optimistic) inter-agent coordination and at the same time reduces learning times as only a fraction of the data collected is actually exploited when doing fitted Q iteration.

Our approach to model the scheduling task as a sequential decision problem and to make reactive scheduling decisions features the disadvantage that, in the form presented, the resulting schedules correspond to solutions from the set of non-delay schedules, only: If a resource has finished processing one operation and has at least one job waiting, the dispatching agent immediately continues processing by picking one of the waiting jobs. Our approach does not allow a resource to remain idle, if there is more work to be done.

From scheduling theory, however, it is well-known that for certain scheduling problem instances the optimal schedule may very well be a delay schedule (cf. Section 3.1.1). As visualized in Figure 3.2 on page 38, the following subset inclusion holds for three sub-classes of non-preemptive schedules

$$\mathbb{S}_{nondelay} \subsetneq \mathbb{S}_{active} \subsetneq \mathbb{S}_{semiactive} \subsetneq \mathbb{S}$$

where $\mathbb{S}$ denotes the set of all possible schedules (Pinedo, 2002). The optimal schedule for a particular problem, however, is always within $\mathbb{S}_{active}$, but not necessarily within $\mathbb{S}_{nondelay}$. As a consequence, our approach will fail to find the optimal solution for many problem instances, but is capable of generating near-optimal schedules from $\mathbb{S}_{nondelay}$. For these reasons, one of our main goals to be pursued in the next chapter is to extend our learning framework to allow for the generation of delay schedules. In so doing, we are going to refrain from making the agents behave purely reactively (as we did up to here) and, moreover, we will allow them to employ a limited form of communication in order to resolve certain inter-agent dependencies.

# 6 Communicating Agents and Optimal Schedules

In the previous two chapters, we were concerned with approximate solution approaches for DEC-MDPs with changing action sets that basically relied on *reactively* acting and learning independent agents. We have emphasized that this kind of reactivity does not always allow for finding optimal policies because the learners are memoryless and unable to take inter-agent dependencies into account properly. By contrast, the notion of jointly optimal team behavior will shift into our focus in the chapter at hand.

In particular, we will investigate two orthogonal approaches that enable the learners to execute optimal local policies – based on state history information as well as on communication – and we will integrate these concepts with (some of) the reinforcement learning methods we developed in Chapter 4 and 5.

We start by providing some foundations on reactive policies and their limitations as well as on the relevance of an agent's interaction history. In Section 6.2, we describe the two mentioned approaches that are meant to enhance the learning agents' capabilities in yielding optimal joint policies. Subsequently, we evaluate certain combinations of these approaches with the distributed reinforcement learning algorithms proposed in earlier chapters for various job-shop scheduling problems. And, finally, in Section 6.4 we conclude with a discussion of our findings and related work.

## 6.1 Foundations

The agents we are considering do not possess a model of the environment, but have to learn good behavior by repeatedly interacting with their environment. As we have seen, the learning task within decentralized Markov decision processes is aggravated, when compared to learning within single-agent MDPs, mainly by two complicating factors: the inability of each agent to fully observe the global system state as well as the presence of multiple, independently acting agents.

Moreover, a third factor that complicates the finding of jointly optimal policies must be attributed to us: Within the scope of the policy search-based and value function-based reinforcement learning methods that we developed in Chapter 4 and 5, we always made the learning agents employ reactive local policies. This kind of memorylessness, of course, impedes the task of learning good behavior within an environment that each agent perceives as non-Markovian due to the former two reasons mentioned.

## 6.1.1 Reactive Policies and Their Limitations

An agent taking its action based solely on its most recent local observation $s_i \subseteq \mathcal{A}_i$ will in general not be able to contribute to optimal corporate behavior. In particular, it will have difficulties in assessing the value of taking its idle action $\alpha_0$. Taking $\alpha_0$, the local state remains unchanged except when it is influenced by dependent actions of other agents. Since a purely reactive agent, however, has no information related to other agents and dependencies at all, it is incapable of properly distinguishing when it is favorable to remain idle and when not. For these reasons, we have excluded $\alpha_0$ from all $\mathcal{A}_i$ for purely reactive agents.

**Definition 6.1** (Reactive Policy).
*For a factored m-agent DEC-MDP with changing action sets and partially ordered transition dependencies, a* reactive policy $\pi^r = \langle \pi_1^r \ldots \pi_m^r \rangle$ *consists of m reactive local policies with* $\pi_i^r : S_i \to \mathcal{A}_i^r$ *where* $S_i = \mathcal{P}(\mathcal{A}_i^r)$.

That is, purely reactive policies always take an action $\alpha \in \mathcal{A}_i(s_i) = s_i$ (except for $s_i = \emptyset$), even if it was more advisable to stay idle and wait for a transition from $s_i$ to some $s_i' = s_i \cup \{\alpha'\}$ induced by another agent, and then execute $\alpha'$ in $s_i'$.

## 6.1.2 Interaction Histories

Oliehoek et al. (2008a) have shown that there exists at least one optimal deterministic joint policy for each DEC-POMDP. Thus, although the utilization of stochastic policies can be beneficial during learning, it is basically sufficient to restrict attention to deterministic policies while still allowing for jointly optimal behavior.

For decentralized MDPs with changing action sets and partially ordered transition dependencies there are, after $D$ decision stages, at maximum $(2^{|\mathcal{A}_i^r|})^D$ possible local state histories for agent $i$. As a consequence, there are a total of

$$\sum_{d=0}^{D-1} (2^{|\mathcal{A}_i^r|})^d = \frac{(2^{|\mathcal{A}_i^r|})^D - 1}{2^{|\mathcal{A}_i^r|} - 1}$$

such sequences for agent $i$. However, when taking into account the execute-once property of the class of DEC-MDPs we are addressing (cf. Lemma 1), we obtain a total number of

$$\sum_{d=0}^{|\mathcal{A}_i^r|-1} (|\mathcal{A}_i^r| - d)^{(2^{|\mathcal{A}_i^r|})^d}$$

of possible local policies for agent $i$, which is doubly exponential in the number of decision stages and, hence, in the number of available actions for that agent.

When not using reactive agents, but those that base their action choices on the full interaction history, we enable the team as a whole to acquire optimal behavior. Unfortunately, the local policies must then be defined over sequences of local states $\bar{s}_i \in \bar{S}_i$ which brings about an exponential blow-up in the size of the domain over which $\pi_i$ is defined. Needless to say that such an approach quickly renders infeasible as the problem size considered grows. Having in mind that we intend to work with rather intricate and larger-scaled scheduling problems, we refrain from pursuing this straightforward approach. Instead, in what follows we

- seize the idea of using a highly compact representation of an agent's interaction history which we developed in Section 2.4.3. In so doing, we exploit properties of DEC-MDPs with changing action sets in a purposeful manner. While this approach still forces us to handle a clearly increased state space, we do not have to face the exponential increase just mentioned.

- As a second, orthogonal approach, we intend to resolve some of the state transition dependencies between agents. From an agent's point of view, this yields an at least partial reconstitution of the Markov property as the effect of the inter-agent dependencies – as modelled by means of dependency functions $\sigma_i$ (cf. Definition 2.13) – are made explicit. Moreover, the agents' policies remain reactive ones which keeps the state space to be considered at a moderate size.

From an applicatory perspective, both approaches are intended as a mean to create optimal policies. In terms of job-shop scheduling tasks, this specifically addresses the capability to create delay schedules. As a reminder, delay schedules arise, if at some point of processing at least one resource remains idle although currently at least one job is waiting for further processing at the resource considered. By contrast, a reactive dispatching agent would pick one of the waiting jobs, immediately continue its processing, and in so doing, yield a non-delay schedule. As described in Section 5.5.2, however, the optimal schedule for a given JSSP is always within the class $\mathbb{S}_{active}$ of delay schedules. Since reactive agents produce schedules from the class of non-delay schedules and because $\mathbb{S}_{nondelay} \subsetneq \mathbb{S}_{active}$, they can miss the optimal solution of a job-shop scheduling problem. We have illustrated that issue in detail in Section 3.1.1 and, subsequently, expect the two extension approaches mentioned to result in a performance boost, when combined with the learning methods presented in earlier chapters.

## 6.2 Resolving Transition Dependencies

Each agent in a DEC-MDP observes its local state fully. What brings about the aggravation of its decision-making problem, when compared to an MDP setting, is that it can influence other agents' local states and that its local state can also be influenced by the actions other agents execute. Stated differently, we do *not* consider transition-independent decentralized decision problems (cf. Definition 2.10). The methods to be discussed now aim at revealing (some of) the transition dependencies and, thus, allow the agents to face an environment that is, informally speaking, more Markovian.

### 6.2.1 Interaction History Encodings

In Section 2.4.3, we have investigated the question of the complexity of solving decentralized MDPs with changing action sets and partially ordered transition dependencies.

6 Communicating Agents and Optimal Schedules

The crucial step in showing that this class of DEC-MDPs is NP-hard (as opposed to the NEXP-hardness of general DEC-MDPs) was the definition of a compact encoding of an agent's interaction history. We have proved that our definition of an encoding function $Enc_i : \overline{S}_i \to E_i$ (Definition 2.14)

- is capable of compressing the information of the history $\overline{s}_i$ of local states to an exponentially smaller amount of data,
- allows for defining a policy on top of $Enc_i$ that yields optimal joint behavior,
- and, as a consequence, that DEC-MDPs with changing action sets and partially ordered transition dependencies are NP-hard.

The compression realized by $Enc_i$ is descriptively visualized in Figure 2.7 on page 27: While the size of stored full interaction histories scales exponentially with $|S_i|$ and doubly exponentially with $|\mathcal{A}_i^r|$, the encoded history requires only space polynomial in $|S_i|$ and exponential in $|\mathcal{A}_i^r|$. The latter also holds for reactive agents that consider and remember their most recent state observation only. However, while reactive agents are in general incapable of yielding jointly optimal behavior, an agent that picks its action based on an encoded interaction history is not.

As a reminder, in essence the encoding function guarantees that each agent always knows whether some local action has not yet been in its action set, whether it currently is, or whether it had already been. This piece of information may, for example, enable an agent to wait, i.e. execute its idle action $\alpha_0$, until some desired action enters its action set, as caused by a state transition dependency on another agent. Accordingly, we define a policy based on encoded interaction histories, which chooses actions from $\mathcal{A}_i$ (instead of $\mathcal{A}_i^r = \mathcal{A}_i \setminus \{\alpha_0\}$) as follows.

**Definition 6.2** (Encoding-Based Policy).
*For a factored m-agent DEC-MDP with changing action sets and partially ordered transition dependencies, an* encoding-based policy $\pi^e = \langle \pi_1^e \ldots \pi_m^e \rangle$ *consists of m encoding-based local policies with* $\pi_i^e : E_i \to \mathcal{A}_i$ *where* $E_i = \times_{|\mathcal{A}_i|} \{0, 1, 2\}$ *and the encoding function* $Enc_i : \overline{S}_i \to E_i$ *is defined in accordance with Definition 2.14.*

### Integration with JEPS and GDPS

An integration of the encoding-based approach with our policy search-based reinforcement learning methods is only in part possible. The basic variant of joint equilibrium policy search (JEPS) which employs a policy parameter vector for each local state encountered, can easily be extended to work on top of $Enc(\overline{s}_i)$ instead of on the recent local state $s_i$. All that is required is to define a separate policy parameter vector $\theta_L^i$ for each encoded interaction history $Enc_i(\overline{s}_i)$. Moreover, each parameter vector $\theta_L^i(Enc_i(\overline{s}_i))$ must contain one more entry corresponding to the action execution probability of $\alpha_0$.

Unfortunately, in Section 4.2.4, we found that the main limitation of JEPS are its enormous memory requirements for storing the policy parameter vectors. By increasing the size of the state space (from $2^{|\mathcal{A}_i^r|}$ to $3^{|\mathcal{A}_i|}$) to be considered, we would magnify this

## 6.2 Resolving Transition Dependencies

problem even more. For this reason, we will not consider the combination of the basic version of JEPS with encoded interaction histories any further.

JEPS$_G$ employs a single policy parameter vector $\theta_G^i$ containing one single entry for each $\alpha \in \mathcal{A}_i^r$. Given the current state $s_i$, action probabilities for each available action are inferred using $\theta_G^i$ (specified in Definition 4.4). While this representation is highly compact and beneficial for a policy search technique, it is fundamentally tuned to select one out of the set of currently available actions regardless of the agent's history. An extension towards the consideration of an agent's interaction history, or a compact encoding thereof, would require the introduction of additional history-specific parameter vectors and, basically, yield an entirely new learning method. Although this may be an interesting issue for future work, we will explore that option no further. Note that the arguments just made also transfer to the gradient-descent policy search algorithm GDPS (Section 4.3) as this one also essentially relies on a policy parameterization with one global parameter vector.

**Integration with OA-NFQ**

In value function-based reinforcement learning we aim at acquiring the optimal state-action value function. More specifically, for the decentralized problems we are addressing we employed distributed Q value functions where each local value function $Q_i$ provides agent $i$ with an estimate – as far as OA-NFQ is concerned with an optimistic estimate – of the expected rewards when executing a local action in a certain local state. In Chapter 5, the domains over which the $Q_i$ functions were defined were the cross product of $S_i$ and $\mathcal{A}_i^r$, giving rise to reactive agents that consider only the most recent local state.

The idea of encoding the contents of an agent's interaction history can be easily integrated with a value function-based RL method. For this to happen, we have to extend the definition of $Q_i$ so as to being defined over encoded state histories and local actions, i.e. from $Q_i : S_i \times \mathcal{A}_i^r \to \mathbb{R}$ to $Q_i : E_i \times \mathcal{A}_i \to \mathbb{R}$. Note that now the idle action $\alpha_0 \in \mathcal{A}_i$ is also covered which indicates that the value function must be capable of assessing the value of the decision to remain idle even if there are other actions available. A greedy, encoding-based local policy can be induced from $Q_i : E_i \times \mathcal{A}_i$ as usual.

In the context of this book we employ neural net-based representations of local value functions. Hence, the question remains how to properly incorporate a neural net over the extended domain $E_i \times \mathcal{A}_i$. In Section 5.4.1, we have depicted how to employ a number of descriptive features for describing local states and actions for a reactive agent. When focusing on encodings of an agent's interaction history now, we extend the mentioned feature descriptions of local states such that they contain at least as much information as an encoding comprises. Practically, we

- recall that an encoded interaction history $Enc_i(\overline{s}_i)$ comprises basically the trinary information, whether an action has already been executed, is available, or is not yet available. In order to capture this information we expand the set of state features (previously, i.e. for reactive agents: six features) by three additional features that characterize the set of actions already executed by an agent. For the JSSP scenarios we are addressing, this includes the sum of operation durations already processed, the sum of the remaining processing times of the jobs already processed at the considered resource, as well as the relation of the processing time of the shortest and longest operation already processed.

- Moreover, the value of the idle action $\alpha_0$ in conjunction with the current $Enc_i(\overline{s}_i)$ must also be covered by $Q_i$. To this end, we characterize the idle action with the same set of action features we employ for "normal" actions. As a specialty with respect to our feature sets for JSSPs, however, we assume the idle action to be an operation of a job which contains only one single operation with a duration of one time step. Accordingly, the features derived for the idle action are considerably different from the features describing real actions. This line of action places the idle action at a place in feature space that is very distant from real actions and, hence, supports their differentiation.

Some care must be taken with respect to the allowance of the idle action. In principle, if an agent decides to remain idle, it is defined to do so until its local state is changed by an external event, i.e. due to the influence exerted by other agents, which means until its local action set is extended by some other agent. This way of proceeding, however, may be dangerous when multiple agents execute $\alpha_0$ in parallel, for example, due to exploration or also if the idle action yields the highest Q value given the current local value function of the considered agent. Then, it may easily happen that the team gets trapped in a deadlock situation where a number of agents constantly remain idle and refrain from executing any further actions.

In order to prevent the collective from getting trapped in such deadlocks, we impose a timeout for the execution of the idle action $\alpha_0$, requiring that each agent may execute $\alpha_0$ for maximally $d_{max}$ consecutive time steps. Of course, the value of $d_{max}$ should be set with respect to the problems addressed and, in particular, with regard to the duration of other actions. While we will discuss suitable choices for that parameter below, we note already that setting $d_{max} = 0$ reestablishes purely reactive agent behavior as then the idle action can be selected at no times.

### 6.2.2 Communication-Based Awareness of Inter-Agent Dependencies

The definition of an encoding function of an agent's interaction history as discussed in Section 6.2.1 represents just one way to exploit the regularities in the transition dependencies of the class of DEC-MDPs we identified. Next, we suggest a communication-based approach that also aims at utilizing these properties and that is at least capable of providing approximately optimal solutions.

In Definition 2.14, we stated that the probability that agent $i$'s local state moves to $s'_i$ depends three factors: on that agent's current local state $s_i$, on its action $a_i$, as well as on the set $\Delta_i := \{a_j \in \mathcal{A}_j | i = \sigma_j(a_j), i \neq j\}$, i.e. on the local actions of all agents that may influence agent $i$'s transition. Let us for the moment assume that agent $i$ always knows $\Delta_i$. Then, all transition dependencies would be resolved as they would be known to each agent. As a consequence, all local transitions would be Markovian and local states would represent a sufficient statistic for each agent to behave optimally.

Unfortunately, fulfilling the assumption of all $\Delta_i$ to be known conflicts with the idea of decentralized decision-making. In fact, knowing $\sigma_j$ and relevant actions $a_j$ of other

## 6.2 Resolving Transition Dependencies

agents, enables agent $i$ to determine their influence on its local successor state and to best select its local action $a_i$. This action, however, generally also influences another agent's transition and, hence, that agent's action choice if it knows its set $\Delta_j$, as well. Thus, it can be seen that even in the benign case of a two-agent system, there may be circular dependencies, which is why knowing all $\Delta_i$ entirely would only be possible, if a central decision maker employing a joint policy and deciding for joint actions were used.

**Enhancing a Reactive Agent**

Although knowing $\Delta_i$ in general is not feasible, we may enhance the capabilities of a reactive agent $i$ by allowing it to get at least some partial information about this set. For this, we extend a reactive agent's local state space from $S_i = \mathcal{P}(\mathcal{A}_i^r)$ to $\hat{S}_i$ such that for all $\hat{s}_i \in \hat{S}_i$ it holds $\hat{s}_i = (s_i, z_i)$ with $z_i \in \mathcal{P}(\mathcal{A}_i^r \setminus s_i)$. So, $z_i$ is a subset of the set of actions currently *not* in the action set of agent $i$.

**Definition 6.3** (Transition Dependency Resolving).
*Let $1, \ldots, m$ be reactive agents acting in a DEC-MDP, as specified in Definition 2.13, whose local state spaces are extended to $\hat{S}_i$. Assume that current local actions $a_1, \ldots, a_m$ are taken consecutively. Given that agent $j$ decides for $a_j \in A_j(s_j)$ and $\sigma_j(a_j) = i$, let also $s_i$ be the local state of $i$ and $\hat{s}_i$ its current extended local state with $\hat{s}_i = (s_i, z_i)$. Then, the transition dependency between $j$ and $i$ is said to be resolved, if $z_i := z_i \cup \{a_j\}$.*

The resolving of a transition dependency according to Definition 6.3 corresponds to letting agent $i$ know some of those current local actions of other agents by which the local state of $i$ will soon be influenced. Note that in order to fully comply with Definition 2.13 the influence one dependent action $a_j$ now exerts on agent $i$ yields not just an extension of $i$'s action set ($s_i = A_i(s_i) := A_i(s_i) \cup \{a_j\}$), but also a removal from $z_i$, i.e. $z_i := z_i \setminus \{a_j\}$.

Because, for the class of problems we are dealing with, inter-agent interferences are always exerted by changing (extending) another agent's action set, in this way agent $i$ gets to know which further action(s) will soon be available in its action set. By integrating this piece of information into $i$'s extended local state description $\hat{S}_i$, this agent obtains the opportunity to willingly stay idle (execute $\alpha_0$) until the announced action $a_j \in z_i$ enters its action set and can finally be executed.

Thus, because local states $\hat{s}_i$ are extended by information relating to transition dependencies between agents, such policies are normally more capable than purely reactive ones, since at least some information about future local state transitions induced by teammates can be regarded during decision-making. Figure 6.1 provides an intuitive example for that mechanism: It is centered around meeting the deadline for finishing action $\alpha_4$, and it opposes the behavior of purely reactively acting agents (left) with agents that are informed about future state transitions that will occur due to actions taken by other agents.

Obviously, $\hat{S}_i$ has the same size as $E_i$ ($|\hat{S}_i| \in O(3^k)$ with $k = |\mathcal{A}_i^r|$). Given the above definition of $z_i$, however, it is clear that a policy $\hat{\pi} = \langle \hat{\pi}_1 \ldots \hat{\pi}_m \rangle$ whose components $\hat{\pi}_i$ are defined over extended local state spaces $\hat{S}_i$ is generally not an encoding for agent $i$'s interaction history (except for the theoretical case when $\Delta_i$ is entirely known) and thus not capable of optimizing the global value. Yet, because local states $\hat{s}_i$ are extended by information relating to transition dependencies between agents, such policies are normally

# 6 Communicating Agents and Optimal Schedules

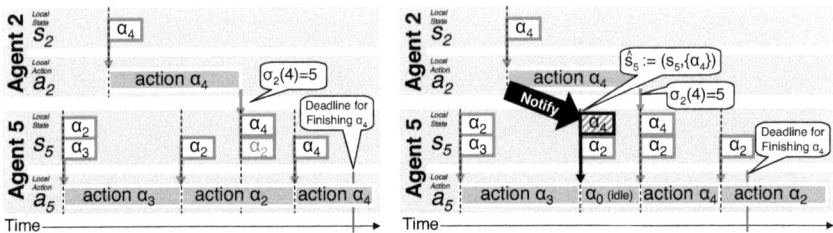

Figure 6.1: Communication-Based Awareness of State Transition Dependencies: In the left part, both agents behave purely reactively. Agent 5 executes $\alpha_2$ as soon as it can. In the right, a notification from agent 2 allows for resolving a dependency: agent 5 may stay willingly idle, execute $\alpha_4$ prior to $\alpha_2$, and meet its deadline.

more capable than purely reactive ones, since at least some information about future local state transitions induced by teammates can be regarded during decision-making.

Since, as argued before, in practice not all transition dependencies can be resolved, $z_i$ will adopt only few values from its domain, which is why $O(3^k)$ represents the worst-case size of $\hat{S}_i$, but generally $\hat{S}_i$ will be sized only marginally beyond $O(2^k)$.

The notification of agent $i$, which instructs him to extend its local state component $z_i$ by $\alpha$, may easily be realized by a simple message passing scheme (assuming cost-free communication between agents) that allows agent $j$ to send a single directed message to agent $\sigma_j(\alpha)$ upon the local execution of $\alpha$. Obviously, this kind of partial resolving of transition dependencies is particularly useful in applications where the execution of atomic actions takes more than a single time step and where, hence, decision-making proceeds asynchronously across agents. Under those conditions, up to half of the dependencies in $\Delta_i$ (over all $i$) may be resolved.

For completeness, we also provide a formal definition of a policy that allows for partial transition dependency resolvings via communication:

**Definition 6.4** (Communication-Based Policy).
*For a factored $m$-agent DEC-MDP with changing action sets and partially ordered transition dependencies, a* communication-enhanced policy $\pi^c = \langle \pi_1^c \ldots \pi_m^c \rangle$ *consists of $m$ local policies with $\pi_i^c : \hat{S}_i \to \mathcal{A}_i$ that are defined over the extended state space $\hat{S}_i$ where for all $\hat{s}_i \in \hat{S}_i$ it holds $\hat{s}_i = (s_i, z_i)$ with $s_i \in \mathcal{P}(\mathcal{A}_i^r)$ and $z_i \in \mathcal{P}(\mathcal{A}_i^r \setminus s_i)$. For each agent $i$ the contents of $z_i$ is defined to be determined by messages coming from other agents $j \in Ag \setminus \{i\}$.*

For legibility, we have defined all policies in Definitions 6.1, 6.2, and 6.4 to be deterministic ones. Of course, redefining them as stochastic policies (e.g. as required for applying the JEPS or GDPS algorithm) is easily possible which we will show exemplarily below. What matters are basically the differences in the local state spaces ($S_i$, $E_i$, or $\hat{S}_i$) and action spaces ($\mathcal{A}_i^r$ or $\mathcal{A}_i$) over which they are defined.

## 6.2 Resolving Transition Dependencies

**Integration with JEPS, GDPS, and OA-NFQ**

The communication-based approach to partially resolving state transition dependencies can be easily combined with all learning methods that are in the center of our interest. Essentially, we require each agent $j$ that executes an action $\alpha \in \mathcal{A}_j^r$ to send a single directed message to agent $i := \sigma_j(\alpha)$ ($\sigma_j$ denotes agent $j$'s dependency function according to Definition 2.13), thus notifying agent $i$ that its local state will soon be changed due to the influence of agent $j$. Upon receiving this information, agent $i$ changes its local state from $(s_i, z_i) \in \hat{S}_i$ to $(s_i, z_i \cup \{\alpha\}) \in \hat{S}_i$. What is more important, however, is that when executing an action (hence, starting an operation of a job in the job-shop scheduling domain), agent $i$

- may either select an action $\alpha' \in s_i$ in the usual manner,

- but may also pick an action $\alpha'' \in z_i$ which has been announced to become available soon, but which is currently not yet executable. In this case, agent $i$ executes in fact the idle action $\alpha_0$ until the announced action $\alpha''$ truly enters its action set (i.e. $\alpha'' \in s_i$), and then immediately continues with the "real" execution of $\alpha''$.

Summing up, we might say that the suggested communication scheme with its corresponding communication-enhanced policy make the learning agents act in a reactive manner – however, reactivity is here defined over an extended local state space and also enables the usage of the idle action. The latter point is of importance with respect to the generation of schedules from beyond the class of non-delay schedules.

Working with stochastic policies as done, for example, for GDPS, we define the stochastic communication-enhanced local policy by

$$\pi_{\theta^i}^c(\hat{s}_i, \alpha) = \begin{cases} \dfrac{e^{-\theta_\alpha^i}}{\sum_{x \in s_i} e^{-\theta_x^i} + \sum_{x \in z_i} e^{-\theta_x^i}} & \text{if } \alpha \in s_i \cup z_i \\ 0 & \text{else} \end{cases} \quad (6.1)$$

for all $\alpha \in \mathcal{A}_i^r$ and extended local states $\hat{s}_i = (s_i, z_i) \in \hat{S}_i$ which depicts an extension of the Gibbs policy provided in Definition 4.13. If, however, an element $\alpha \in z_i$ is selected during execution given the probabilities defined by $\pi_{\theta^i}^c$, then in fact agent $i$ remains idle, i.e. it executes $\alpha_0$, until $\alpha$ enters its local state $s_i$, and after this immediately continues to process $\alpha$. To which extend this approach brings about improvements when compared to purely reactively acting agents shall be explored with the help of empirical experiments in the domain of job-shop scheduling that we present next.

Regarding the use of limited inter-agent communication in order to overcome the agents' limitation of being capable of generating non-delay schedules only, it must be acknowledged that this enhancement brings about an aggravation of the learning problem. Since it holds $|\hat{S}_i| \gg |S_i|$, the agents must handle a clearly increased number of local states. Also, the number of actions to be considered in each extended state is equal or larger than in its non-extended counterpart $s_i$. In order to be able to trade off between the goal of learning policies superior to reactive policies and the rising of the difficulty of the learning task, we employ the parameter $d_{max} \geq 0$ already mentioned in Section 6.2.1, which stands for the maximal number of time steps an agent is allowed to remain idle. Given the current local state $\hat{s}_i(t) = (s_i(t), z_i(t))$, agent $i$ is allowed to execute an $\alpha \in z_i$ (by executing $\alpha_0$ in fact) only, if the notification regarding $\alpha$ has announced that $\alpha$ enters $s_i$ after maximally $d_{max}$ time steps, i.e. if $\exists \tau > t : \alpha \in s_i(\tau)$ and $\tau - t \leq d_{max}$. This restriction can easily be realized by adapting the first case of Equation 6.1 appropriately. Thus, when setting $d_{max}=0$, we again arrive at purely reactive agents, which for job-shop scheduling problems could generate non-delay schedules only, whereas for $d_{max} \geq \max_{x \in \mathcal{A}} \delta(x)$ (with $\delta$ denoting the operations' durations) the communication-based resolving of transition dependencies is fully activated. For the experiments whose results we report in the next section, we either made use of purely reactive agents ($d_{max}=0$) or used a value of $d_{max}=20$.

## 6.3 Empirical Evaluation

The goal of this chapter's experimental study is to investigate the influence of the two approaches for overcoming the limitations of purely reactive agents that we have proposed in the previous section. We note that we refrain from analyzing the effects of the combination of every learning method developed with every extension approach suggested. Nevertheless, we intend to cover a meaningful selection of methodological combinations. As before, we start with comparative experiments using the educational FT6 benchmark before we proceed with the results obtained for a selection of larger-scaled JSSP instances.

### 6.3.1 Example Benchmark

In this experiment, the issue of optimality shifts into our focus. We recall that during all experiments in this book that addressed the FT6 benchmark we employed reactive agents that yielded non-delay schedules. Accordingly, the lower bound in terms of performance (measured in terms of minimizing makespan $C_{max}$) was at $C_{max}^{nd-opt} = 57$ which denotes the makespan of the best non-delay schedule. Besides, we know that the true theoretical optimum for this problem is represented by a schedule with a makespan of $C_{max}^{opt} = 55$, which represents a delay schedule that requires some idleness from some of the agents in order to be generated. Thus, in previous chapters we typically aimed at achieving joint policies for the team of agents that brought about a schedule with $C_{max} = 57$. By contrast, a makespan of 55 is what we would like to achieve now.

Our primary concern is on analyzing the following three approaches when integrated with a value function-based reinforcement learning method that utilizes the OA-NFQ algorithm at its core. We employ the optimistic assumption-based neural fitted Q iteration algorithm in the same manner as in Section 5.4.2 and compare agents that independently learn

- purely reactive policies $\pi_i^r$ defined over $S_i = \mathcal{P}(\mathcal{A}_i^r)$ (cf. Definition 6.1) that never remain idle when their action set is not empty [**RCT**],

- policies $\pi_i^e : E_i \to \mathcal{A}_i$ using full information about the agents' histories (cf. Definition 6.2), where $E_i$ is a compact encoding of that agent $i$'s observation history $\overline{S}_i$ [**ENC**],

## 6.3 Empirical Evaluation

- reactive policies $\pi_i^c$ that are partially aware of their dependencies on other agents (notified about forthcoming influences exerted by other agents, cf. Definition 6.4) [COM].

In job-shop scheduling problems, it typically holds that $d(o_{j,k}) > 1$ for all $j$ and $k$, i.e. the processing of a single operation lasts more than one time step. Since most of such durations are not identical, decision-making usually proceeds asynchronously across agents. We assume that a COM-agent $i$ sends a message to agent $\sigma_i(\alpha)$ when it starts the execution of an operation from job $\alpha$, announcing to that agent the arrival of $\alpha$, whereas the actual influence on agent $\sigma_i(\alpha)$ (its action set extension) occurs $d(o_{\alpha,\cdot})$ steps later (after $o_{\alpha,\cdot}$ has been finished).

With regard to the parameter setting $d_{max} = 20$ mentioned above, we note that – as far as the FT6 benchmark problem is concerned where all jobs' operations have a duration of maximally 10 time steps – this setting results in that all agents do always consider all communicated jobs for "virtual" execution, i.e. they are allowed to stay idle and wait for them to become available, at all times.

For a problem with $m$ resources and $n$ jobs consisting of $m$ operations each, there are $(n!)^m$ possible schedules (also called set of active schedules, $\mathbb{S}_{active}$). Considering purely reactive agents, the number of policies and corresponding schedules that can be represented is usually dramatically reduced. Unfortunately, only schedules from the class of non-delay schedules $\mathbb{S}_{nondelay}$ can be created by applying reactive policies. Since $\mathbb{S}_{nondelay} \subsetneq \mathbb{S}_{active}$ and because it is known that the optimal schedule is always in $\mathbb{S}_{active}$ (for more explanations refer to Section 3.1.1 and Figure 3.1 on page 37), but not necessarily in $\mathbb{S}_{nondelay}$, RCT-agents can at best learn the best solution from $\mathbb{S}_{nondelay}$. By contrast, learning with ENC-agents, in principle the optimal solution can be attained, but we expect that the time required by our learning approach for this to happen will increase significantly.

We hypothesize that the awareness of inter-agent dependencies achieved by partial dependency resolutions via communication may in fact realize a good trade-off between the former two approaches. On the one hand, when resolving a transition dependency according to Definition 6.3, an agent $i$ can become aware of an incoming job. Thus, $i$ may decide to wait for that arrival, instead of starting to execute another job. Hence, also delay schedules can be created. On the other hand, very poor policies with unnecessary idle times can be avoided, since a decision to stay idle will be taken very dedicatedly, viz only when a future job arrival has been announced. This falls into place with the fact that the extension of an agent's local state to $\hat{s}_i = (s_i, z_i)$ is rather limited and, consequently, the number of local states is only slightly increased.

Figure 6.2 summarizes the learning curves for OA-NFQ in conjunction with the three approaches listed above. Note that the SPT/FIFO/AMCC dispatching priority rules yield $C_{max} = 88/77/55$, here, and are not drawn for clarity. The figure also shows the makespan of an optimal schedule (55) and of an optimal non-delay schedule (57). All results are averaged over 10 experiment repetitions and indicators for best/worst runs are provided. Furthermore, in order to blind out the potentially uneven convergence behavior when using neural network-based value function approximation (cf. Figure 5.3 and the belonging discussion on page 119), in this series of experiments we employed a simple pocket algorithm that broadens the scope of policy screening such that the best policy

## 6 Communicating Agents and Optimal Schedules

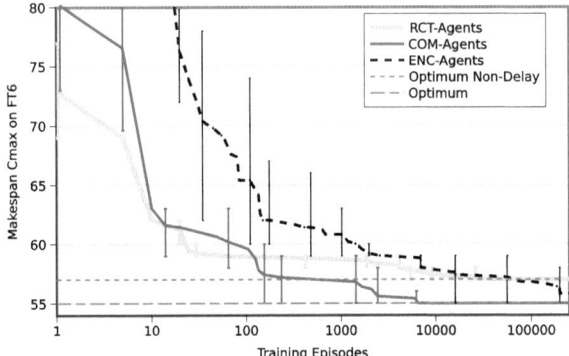

Figure 6.2: Beyond Pure Reactivity: Learning curves using encoding-based and communicating agents for the FT6 Benchmark.

ever (across all training episodes) is remembered. Since Figure 6.2 plots the makespan which the joint policy yields that is stored in the pocket, the learning curves show a better convergence behavior than those drawn in Figure 5.3.

First of all, this experiment stresses once more the general effectiveness of our learning approach, since each type of learning agents considered manages to attain its respective optimum. The steepest learning curve emerges for purely reactive agents that achieve the best non-delay solution, hence little interaction with the process is required for those agents to obtain high-quality policies. By contrast, ENC- and COM-agents are capable of learning the optimal policy (with $C_{max} = 55$), where the former require significantly more training time than the latter (note the log scale abscissa in Figure 6.2). This can be tributed to the clearly increased number of local states of ENC-agents, which have to cover the agents' state histories, and to the fact that they may take idle actions in principle in any state, while COM-agents do so only when a notification regarding forthcoming externally influenced state transitions has been received.

### 6.3.2 Benchmark Suites

We continue with experiments that are centered around the OA-NFQ algorithm, yet focus on larger-scaled JSSPs of varying problem sizes now.

For all the benchmark suites we are considering (except for the FT6 problem) it holds $\delta(o_{j,k}) \in [1, 99]$ for all operations within all jobs $j$, that is the processing of individual operations requires between one and ninety-nine time steps. Accordingly, the $d_{max}$ parameter (when set to a value of 20) actually constrains the use of the idle action, if a job's future availability has been announced via a notification. Empirically, if we set $d_{max}$ such that

$$d_{max} \geq \max_{j,k} \delta(o_{j,k})$$

for the JSSP considered (here: $d_{max} \geq 99$)) and, hence, do not restrict the usage of the $\alpha_0$ at all, we obtain, for the example of the FT10 problem, an average of 36.11 local situations (during a single processing of this $10 \times 10$ problem with purely random action choices) in which a local state of some agent has been extended from $(s_i, z_i)$ to $(s_i, z_i')$ with $z_i \subsetneq z_i'$ and $s_i \neq \emptyset$, i.e. where a deliberate decision to remain idle despite the existence of currently waiting jobs may be taken. By contrast, with the setting of $d_{max} = 20$, which we will utilize subsequently, this number drops to an average of 15.95.

**Value Function-Based Reinforcement Learning: OA-NFQ**

As can be read from Figure 5.7 on page 124, there are a number of benchmarks for which even a team of purely reactively acting OA-NFQ-trained agents manages to collectively create the optimal schedule. Naturally, for those benchmarks it holds that the respective optimal schedules are to be found within the class $\mathbb{S}_{nondelay}$ of non-delay schedules. And, consequently, using ENC- or COM-agents, no further improvement in terms of finding a policy that yields schedules with lower makespan is possible.

Since we want to explore the influence of using encoded local state histories as well as of resolved transition dependencies due to communication – as opposed to reactive learners –, we consciously put aside those benchmark problems. Instead we focus on 24 more intricate JSSPs (involving up to 15 agents and 20 jobs, i.e. 300 operations) for which the RCT version of our OA-NFQ learning agents did not succeed in acquiring the optimal joint policy.

| Problem Size | #Prbl | Dispatch Rules | | Theor. | Learning Agents Using **OA-NFQ** | | | | | |
| $m \times n$ | | SPT | AMCC | Opt. | RCT | Err | ENC | Err | COM | Err |
|---|---|---|---|---|---|---|---|---|---|---|
| $6 \times 6$ | 1 | 88 | 55 | 55 | 57.4 | 4.4% | 57.8 | 5.1% | 55.0 | 0.0% |
| $5 \times 10$ | 3 | 734.7 | 702.7 | 614.0 | 648.7 | 5.7% | 648.3 | 5.6% | 642.0 | 4.6% |
| $10 \times 10$ | 17 | 1106.3 | 973.7 | 912.5 | 964.3 | 5.7% | 992.1 | 8.7% | 954.1 | 4.6% |
| $5 \times 20$ | 1 | 1267.0 | 1338.0 | 1165.0 | 1235.0 | 6.0% | 1244.0 | 6.8% | 1183.0 | 1.5% |
| $15 \times 20$ | 3 | 888.3 | 771.0 | 676.0 | 747.7 | 10.6% | 818.0 | 21.0% | 733.7 | 8.5% |
| Average | 25 | 1001.2 | 894.7 | 824.1 | 875.0 | 6.2% | 902.7 | 9.5% | 863.4 | 4.8% |

Table 6.1: Beyond Pure Reactivity: Learning results using encoding-based and communicating agents for scheduling benchmarks of varying size. All entries are average makespan values achieved after 25000 training episodes. *Err* columns shows the relative remaining error (%) of the RCT-, ENC-, and COM-agents compared to the theoretical optimum.

Table 6.1 provides an overview of the results for the mentioned benchmark problems, grouped by problem sizes $(m \times n)$. It is important to note that – to be consistent with the experiments whose results we reported in Section 5.4.3 – this summary gives the quality of policies obtained after 25000 training episodes. Because, as shown in Section 6.3.1, ENC-agents require substantially longer to acquire high-quality policies, the results in the corresponding column are expectedly poor (remaining average error of 9.5%). To this end, a substantial increase in the training time allotted would have been necessary in order to achieve results that are comparable to the quality of the schedules created by the policies learned with reactive agents. When opposing the average error yielded by RCT agents (6.2%) with the average error reported in Table 5.2 (4.4%), it must be kept in mind that the former value was determined over a different set of benchmark problems, namely over those only for which reactively learning agents failed to acquire optimal joint policies. Accordingly, different average values are listed in these two tables.

The key observation with respect to the utilization of inter-agent communication is that our notification scheme helps the agents in learning policies of higher quality. In terms of the average makespan values, a clear improvement can be achieved: While in the communication-free case the resulting schedules have an average length of 875.0 (remaining error of 6.2%), the use of limited inter-agent notifications reduces this value to 863.4 (error of 4.8%).

**Policy Search-Based Reinforcement Learning: GDPS**

In Chapter 4, we have developed and evaluated different policy search RL algorithms for DEC-MDPs with changing action sets. Our empirical analysis showed a slight advantage for gradient descent policy search over joint equilibrium policy search. For this reason, in the following we consider an extension of GDPS that utilizes our proposed inter-agent communication mechanism and compare it to the basic (reactive and communication-free) variant of GDPS.

Within the following series of experiments, we focus on the same selection of job-shop scheduling benchmark problems from the OR Library as in Section 4.3.5 (ranging from 5 resources and 10 jobs to 15 resources and 30 jobs).

As before, for any specific $m \times n$ job-shop scheduling benchmark instance, we initialize all agents' policies by $\theta^i_\alpha = 0$ for all $i \in \{1, \ldots, m\}$ and all $\alpha \in \mathcal{A}^r_i$ such that initially the agents dispatch all waiting jobs with equal probability (such a policy, hence, represents a baseline). Recall that using the modelling and policy representation we have suggested (and assuming the JSS problem instance features no recirculations), there are $n$ policy parameters to be stored per agent, which makes a total of $mn$ real-valued policy parameters for the probabilistic joint policy. Throughout all our experiments, we allow the agents to update their local policies $b_{max} = 2500$ times, where we use a constant learning rate $\beta = 0.01$ (cf. Equation 4.9) that has been settled empirically. Estimating the gradient $g_\alpha = \nabla_{\theta^i_\alpha} J(\theta^i)$ in a Monte-Carlo manner according to Equation 4.14, we allot $e = 100$ scheduling roll-outs to be performed.

The main goal of this evaluation is to compare purely reactively learning agents with those that are enhanced by means of communication. As indicated above, we do so by setting $d_{max} = 0$ for reactive agents (this corresponds to the results reported in Section 4.3.5, which we mirror here) and by letting $d_{max} = 20$ otherwise.

Pursuing the overall goal of minimizing maximum makespan, we focus on the following three different evaluation criteria. First, we are interested in the makespan $C^{best}_{max}$ of the best schedule that has been produced occasionally by the set of probabilistic policies during ongoing learning. Second, we are interested in the value of the makespan $C_{max}(\mu)$ of the maximum likelihood schedule (cf. Definition 4.6 in Section 4.3.5) that arises when all of the agents select jobs greedily, i.e. choose the action $\arg\max_{\alpha \in \mathcal{A}^r_i} \pi^c_{\theta^i}(\hat{s}_i, \alpha)$, at all decision points. Our third concern is the convergence behavior and speed of the algorithm. By

## 6.3 Empirical Evaluation

convergence we here refer to MLS convergence as introduced in Section 4.3.5, i.e. to the number of policy updates from which on the maximum likelihood schedule changes no further.

Figure 6.3 visualizes an exemplary learning run for the FT10 benchmark problem. Besides the development of the makespan $C_{max}(\mu)$ of the maximum likelihood schedule, here also the makespan of the best schedule encountered intermediately ($C_{max}^{best} = 964$) is shown. Furthermore, the relation to the starting point of learning (initial, random policies with average makespan of $C_{max}^{init} = 1229$) and to the theoretical optimum ($C_{max}^{opt} = 930$) are highlighted.

Drawn in gray, the corresponding $C_{max}(\mu)$ and $C_{max}^{best}$ curves for communicating agents with $d_{max} = 20$ are plotted which obviously outperform the RCT-agents, but require more learning time to achieve that result. The remaining percentual error of the acquired joint policy (converged to the maximum likelihood schedule with $C_{max}(\mu) = 993$ after $\hat{b} = 429$ updates) relative to the optimum is thus 6.8%.

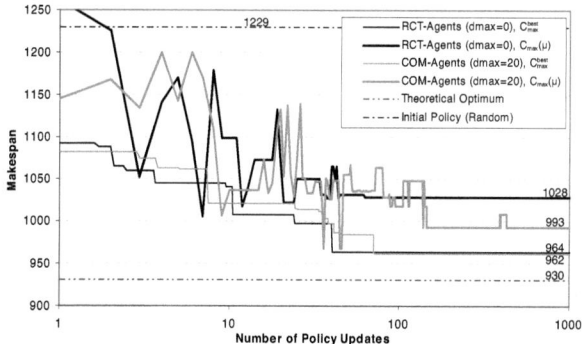

Figure 6.3: GDPS Learning Progress for the FT10 Problem: Purely reactive and communicating agents are opposed with respect to $C_{max}^{best}$ and, more importantly, the makespan $C_{max}(\mu)$ of the maximum likelihood schedule.

Table 6.2 summarizes the learning results for GDPS-based learning over various jobshop scheduling benchmarks averaged over problems of different $m \times n$ sizes. In any case, the starting point of learning is represented by the initial, random dispatching policy (all $\theta_\alpha^i = 0$) whose relative error $Err_{init} = 100\% \cdot (C_{max}^{init}/C_{max}^{opt} - 1)$ is typically in the range of 20-30%. Starting from this baseline, the error values $Err_{best} = 100\% \cdot (C_{max}^{best}/C_{max}^{opt} - 1)$ for the best intermediate schedule found as well as $Err_\mu = 100\% \cdot (C_{max}(\mu)/C_{max}^{opt} - 1)$ for the maximum likelihood schedule (obtained after $b_{max} = 2500$ policy updates) can be decreased significantly. Note that the results in the left half of the table's main part (RCT, $d_{max} = 0$) are identical to those reported in Section 4.3.5.

The theoretical optimum is achieved ($Err = 0\%$) only occasionally which is to be expected since the policy gradient learning algorithm in general converges to a local optimum. The time to arrive at that local optimum is given by the average number $\hat{b}$ of policy updates necessary until $C_{max}(\mu)$ does not change any further. For the communicating

## 6 Communicating Agents and Optimal Schedules

agents, in some cases, in particular for the larger-sized benchmark problems, convergence could not be obtained within $b_{max} = 2500$ updates which is denoted by a '-' in Table 6.2. From this fact as well as from a comparison of both $\hat{b}$ columns we can conclude that the problem aggravation introduced by setting $d_{max} > 0$ brings about a clear reduction of the learning speed.

The average remaining error values for both non-communicating and communicating agents given in the table's last row seem to indicate only a marginal advantage for the latter. These results, however, correspond to the policies acquired after $b_{max} = 2500$ policy updates. As a matter of fact, COM-agents require generally longer learning times due to the extended state space on the basis of which they are operating and we have observed that MLS convergence can not be obtained within that amount of learning time for all benchmarks considered. Thus, if we calculate the average remaining error with respect to the makespan of the optimal schedule only those (tendentially smaller-sized) benchmarks for which MLS convergence was achieved after less than $b_{max}$ policy update steps, then the gain resulting from the use of communication gets more apparent, as COM-agents yield $Err_\mu = 3.8\%$ and RCT-agents only 4.4% over the delineated subset of benchmark problems.

| Size $m \times n$ | #Prbl | Theor. Opt. $C_{max}^{opt}$ | Initial Policy | | Learning Agents Using **GDPS** | | | | | | | |
|---|---|---|---|---|---|---|---|---|---|---|---|---|
| | | | | | **RCT** ($d_{max} = 0$) | | | | **COM** ($d_{max} = 20$) | | | |
| | | | $-J(\pi_{\theta_{init}})$ | $Err_{init}$ | $C_{max}^{best}$ | $Err_{best}$ | $C_{max}(\mu)$ | $Err_\mu$ | $\hat{b}$ | $C_{max}^{best}$ | $Err_{best}$ | $C_{max}(\mu)$ | $Err_\mu$ | $\hat{b}$ |
| 5 × 10 | 5 | 620.2 | 765.4 | 23.4% | 631.8 | 1.9% | 640.4 | 3.3% | 229 | 632.0 | 1.9% | 643.6 | 3.8% | 367 |
| 5 × 15 | 5 | 917.6 | 1052.4 | 14.7% | 917.6 | 0.0% | 918.4 | 0.1% | 69 | 917.6 | 0.0% | 917.6 | 0.0% | 670 |
| 5 × 20 | 6 | 1179.2 | 1358.4 | 15.2% | 1181.3 | 0.2% | 1181.7 | 0.2% | 226 | 1180.8 | 0.1% | 1183.3 | 0.3% | 2067 |
| 10 × 10 | 17 | 912.5 | 1158.0 | 26.9% | 951.2 | 4.2% | 968.5 | 6.1% | 158 | 933.5 | 2.3% | 954.7 | 4.6% | 494 |
| 10 × 15 | 5 | 983.4 | 1285.3 | 30.7% | 1029.0 | 4.6% | 1041.6 | 5.9% | 948 | 1008.6 | 2.6% | 1024.8 | 4.2% | 973 |
| 15 × 15 | 5 | 1263.2 | 1640.8 | 29.9% | 1338.6 | 6.0% | 1367.2 | 8.2% | 159 | 1323.0 | 4.7% | 1355.8 | 7.3% | 624 |
| 15 × 20 | 3 | 676.0 | 878.0 | 29.9% | 713.0 | 5.4% | 729.0 | 7.8% | 678 | 717.7 | 6.2% | 763.3 | 12.9% | - |
| Average | 46 | 946.5 | 1178.0 | 24.5% | 977.9 | 3.4%±2.8 | 990.9 | 4.7%±3.5 | 285 | 967.2 | 2.3%±2.1 | 985.5 | 4.3%±3.8 | |
| 10 × 20 | 5 | 1236.2 | 1608.2 | 30.1% | 1272.0 | 2.9% | 1284.6 | 3.9% | 556 | 1266.2 | 2.4% | 1294.2 | 4.7% | 1738 |
| 10 × 30 | 5 | 1792.4 | 2118.6 | 18.2% | 1792.4 | 0.0% | 1792.8 | 0.0% | 1634 | 1792.4 | 0.0% | 1814.4 | 1.2% | - |
| Average | 56 | 1050.3 | 1300.4 | 23.8% | 1076.9 | 3.1%±2.8 | 1088.7 | 4.3%±3.6 | 429 | 1068.0 | 2.1%±2.1 | 1087.1 | 4.1%±3.7 | |

Table 6.2: Communication-Based Learning Results Using GDPS for Varying Benchmarks: This table opposes communication-free reactive learning with communication-enhanced learning for the gradient descent policy search reinforcement learning algorithm. The results in the left half of the table's main part (RCT) are a reprint from the evaluation in Section 4.3.5. The $\hat{b}$ columns refer to the number of policy updates till MLS convergence. In the case of COM agents, MLS convergence could not always be achieved within $\lambda_{max} = 250000$ episodes of interaction with the environment (indicated by a '-' entry in that column). In that case the value $C_{max}(\mu)$ refers to the maximum likelihood schedule yielded by the joint policy acquired after $\lambda_{max}$ episodes.

## 6.4 Discussion

In this chapter, we proposed and evaluated two extensions to the distributed learning algorithms proposed throughout this work. Our investigations were driven by the goal of learning optimal joint policies. While in Chapter 4 and 5 we restricted ourselves to purely reactive agents and, hence, were interested in finding the best reactive joint policies, in the chapter at hand we focused on two approaches that enabled the independent agents to take into account at least some of the dependencies on other agents during decision-making.

The first of these approaches (the encoding-based one, ENC) implemented the straightforward idea of extending the agents' local states by making them consider not just their recent local observations, but the entire history of local states encountered. Although we employed a compact encoding of the interaction history (as proposed in Section 2.4.3), the number of states to be considered by each agent is clearly increased, likewise the learning time required for acquiring (near-)optimal joint policies.

The second approach (the communication-based one, COM) turned out to realize a good trade-off between the former one and purely reactive agents. It interprets communication as a very scarce resource, makes very dedicated use of notifications exchanged between the agents, and allows the learners to partially get to know future incoming jobs (i.e. actions that will become available) such that they are enabled to willingly remain idle and, hence, are capable of creating solutions corresponding to delay schedules. Our experiments in the scope of which, as before, we interpreted job-shop scheduling problems as decentralized Markov decision processes with changing action sets and partially ordered transition dependencies confirmed that both approaches suggested are capable of improving the learning agents' joint performance.

**Related Work**

The notification scheme that we have suggested in the scope of this chapter has turned out to be a straightforward and effective technique for enhancing the capabilities of purely reactively acting agents. In so doing, we touched the issue of communication only briefly as our COM-agents make a very limited and dedicated use of this instrument, exploiting the structural properties and dependencies that exist in the scope of DEC-MDPs with changing action sets and partially ordered transition dependencies. As far as our learning algorithms are concerned, the restricted use of communication is convenient as, especially in practice, the establishment of communication must be assumed to come along with some costs.

The topic of inter-agent communication has been frequently addressed in the literature on research on learning and coordination in multi-agent systems. A very natural approach to communication is to allow all agents to continually broadcast their local states to all teammates. In the case of decentralized MDPs, this essentially renders the problem an MMDP, as each agent gets aware of the global system state at all times. When imposing the restriction that such communication is allowed only every $k$ time steps, we arrive at the DEC-POMDP-based framework of synchronizing communication by Becker et al. (2005). In contrast to Bernstein's DEC-POMDP framework, the COM-MTDP framework for modelling multi-agent problems (Pynadath and Tambe, 2002b) contains communicative actions at its heart. It has been employed to enable learning agents to willingly decide to communicate by interpreting communication as an additional action whose meaningful utilization must be learned (Nair et al., 2004). Similarly, in an early work, Xuan et al. (2001) define communicative acts as central elements in their framework for distributed control, and Goldman and Zilberstein (2003) define the DEC-POMDP-COM framework in which the explicit learning of communication decisions is targeted. However, as shown by Goldman and Zilberstein (2004), the explicit consideration of communication in the modelling of distributed decision problems does not bring about more representational power.

Another interesting line of research deals with the learning of the semantics of sent messages. While transmitting local states, experience tuples, or value function estimates requires the agents involved to speak the same language, here the communication partners additionally have to learn and recognize the meaning of messages received (Spaan et al., 2006). By contrast, in this chapter we have coped with a message passing scheme that utilizes communication as a scarce resource and whose meaning is fixed. Thus, our work is more related to the research of Szer and Charpillet (2004) who enforce coordination in MMDPs using a fixed utility-based communication strategy, to the work by Aras et al. (2004) and Schneider et al. (1999) who let the agents exchange local rewards and do Q updates depending on communicated rewards of neighboring agents, as well as to the research by Riedmiller et al. (2000) who permit communication between neighboring agents only, but also allow for learning to communicate and to react to received messages.

# 7 Conclusion

Decision-making in cooperative multi-agent systems has emerged as an important topic of research in artificial intelligence. In distributed systems, coordinated cooperation between individually acting agents is of crucial importance if it is desired to accomplish a certain common goal. The behavior policies of individually acting agents must be well-aligned with one another in order to achieve this. In this spirit, the focus of the book at hand has been laid on multi-agent reinforcement learning methods which allow for automatically acquiring cooperative policies based solely on a specification of the desired joint behavior of the whole system.

Likewise, many larger-scale applications are well-suited to be formulated in terms of spatially or functionally distributed entities, i.e. using a multi-agent approach. One such application area is represented by production planning and optimization problems. To this end, our particular interest has been on distributed job-shop scheduling problems which are known to be computationally very difficult and which naturally allow for decentralized solution approaches.

## 7.1 Summary

The research described in this dissertation has been conducted along three complementary lines and has thus brought about contributions within three different, yet related areas.

### Modelling of Distributed Decision-Making Problems

Research on distributed control of cooperative multi-agent systems has received a lot of attention during the past years. While Markov decision processes (MDP) have proven to be a suitable tool for solving problems involving a single agent, a number of extensions of these models to multi-agent systems have been suggested. Among those, the DEC-MDP framework (Bernstein et al., 2002), that is characterized by each agent having only a partial view of the global system state, has been frequently investigated. However, it has been shown that the complexity of general DEC-MDPs is NEXP-complete, even for the benign case of two cooperative agents.

In this regard, a first contribution of this work is that we have identified a class of cooperative decentralized MDPs that features a number of regularities in the way agents influence the state transitions of other agents (Section 2.4). Exploiting the knowledge about these correlations, we have proven that this class of problems – called factored $m$-agent decentralized Markov decision processes with changing action sets and partially ordered transition dependencies – is easier to solve (NP-hard) than general DEC-MDPs (NEXP-hard).

# 7 Conclusion

Interestingly, this subclass of DEC-MDPs covers a wide range of practical problems. In practice, distributed problem-solving is often characterized by a larger number of agents involved and by a factored system state description where the agents base their decisions on local observations. Also, the assumptions we made, namely that local actions may influence the state transitions of maximally one other agent and that any action has to be performed only once, are frequently fulfilled. Sample real-world applications include scenarios from manufacturing, production planning, or assembly line optimization, where typically the production of a good involves a number of processing steps that have to be performed in a specific order and where an appropriate scheduling of single operations is crucial to maximize joint productivity. We have shown that our class of factored $m$-agent DEC-MDPs with changing action sets and partially ordered transition dependencies covers a various scheduling problems, for example flow-shop and job-shop scheduling scenarios (Pinedo, 2002), even scheduling problems with recirculating tasks can be modelled.

**Model-Free Multi-Agent Reinforcement Learning Algorithms**

Despite the mitigation in terms of reduced problem complexity just summarized, the class of decentralized problems we have been focusing on is NP-hard. Accordingly, it has not been our goal to develop new optimal solution algorithms which would be doomed by computational intractability with growing problem sizes. Instead, we have tackled distributed decision-making problems by utilizing model-free reinforcement learning techniques. When employing these techniques, we interpret the agents as being independent adaptive entities that learn to improve their behavior by trial and error-based interaction with the environment. Based on this idea of decentralized model-free learning, we have developed three novel multi-agent reinforcement learning algorithms.

On the one hand, in Chapter 4, we have proposed two policy search-based reinforcement learning algorithms that are geared to finding near-optimal joint policies for the agents within the DEC-MDP.

- Joint equilibrium policy search (JEPS, Section 4.2) turned out to be an effective method for enforcing coordination between the agents in order to achieve optimal joint policies or good approximations thereof. Furthermore, an enhanced variant of this algorithm adheres to a number of nice theoretical convergence guarantees.

- Policy gradient methods have recently gained much popularity within the RL and distributed AI community. So, as a second implementation of a policy search-based RL approach, we have shown how to apply a gradient-descent policy search (GDPS, Section 4.3) method to distributed problems. Although policy gradient algorithms generally do not allow for finding the best joint policy, they facilitate discovering near-optimal approximations, as represented by local optima in the search space, within little time.

On the other hand, we have utilized the more traditional, i.e. value function-based approach to reinforcement learning for the problem settings of our interest (Chapter 5). Additionally, we have aimed at learning agent-specific policies that feature good generalization capabilities, meaning that they should be applicable to problem instances not covered during the learning process and that, hence, incorporate general problem knowledge.

- To this end, we have presented a new distributed RL algorithm for learning in deterministic multi-agent environments, optimistic assumption-based neural fitted Q iteration (OA-NFQ). This algorithm realizes a combination of data-efficient batch-mode reinforcement learning in conjunction with neural value function approximation, and the utilization of an optimistic inter-agent coordination.

It makes quite a difference whether an agent in a DEC-MDP makes its local decisions based solely on its most recent local observation, i.e. in a purely reactive, memoryless manner, or whether it remembers its entire history of interaction with the environment and, thus, with other agents. Alternatively, other agents may be endowed to reveal, for example via communication, some of their local information to teammates so as to attenuate the potentially detrimental effects of inter-agent dependencies. We have studied these issues in the preceding chapter of this book, essentially proposing a limited inter-agent notification scheme for DEC-MDPs with changing action sets and empirically confirming the benefits of explicitly considering and resolving inter-agent dependencies.

**Application for Distributed Job-Shop Scheduling Problems**

A third, and final line of research embedded in this dissertation has dealt with the application of the proposed modelling approaches and learning algorithms to distributed job-shop scheduling problems.

Job-shop problems are NP-hard. In contrast to classical analytical scheduling approaches, we have pursued an alternative approach to scheduling, where each resource is assigned a decision-making agent that decides which job to process next, based on its partial view of the production plant. More specifically, we have shown how scheduling problems can be cast (and subsequently solved) as decentralized Markov decision processes and how this matches with the subclass of general DEC-MDPs identified before.

Although it is possible to adopt a global view on a given scheduling problem – as is done in analytical scheduling –, to model it as a single MDP, we preferred to interpret and solve it as a multi-agent learning problem using our learning approach relying on reinforcement learning. On the one hand, we therefore arrive at the challenge of a problem complication due to independently learning agents. But, on the other hand, we derive the benefit of being enabled to perform reactive scheduling, including the capability to react to unforeseen events. Furthermore, a decentralized view on a scheduling task is of higher relevance to practice since a central control cannot always be instantiated.

We have turned to a variety of established job-shop scheduling benchmark problems for the purpose of validating and evaluating the performance of all learning algorithms proposed throughout this work. Despite certain restrictions of these algorithms, as well as approximations introduced by these methods, the empirical parts within the methodological chapters (Chapters 4-6) contain several convincing results for classical Operations Research job-shop scheduling benchmarks. Our experiments for such large-scale benchmark problems let us come up with the conclusion that problems of current standards of

# 7 Conclusion

difficulty can very well be effectively solved by the learning method we suggest: The dispatching policies our learning agents acquire clearly surpass traditional dispatching rules and, in some cases, are able to reach the theoretically optimal solution. Notwithstanding the inherent difficulties in facing partial state observability and agent independent learning, the dispatching policies acquired do also generalize to unknown situations without retraining, i.e. they are adequate for similar scheduling problems not covered during the learning phase.

## 7.2 Outlook

The work performed and described in the scope of this book opens a number of opportunities for interesting directions of future research. In this section, we concentrate on both possible extensions of our work as well as on alternative research directions.

### Applicability and Stochasticity

In Chapter 3, we have shown that the class of decentralized problems identified in Section 2.4 and focused on subsequently matches well with job-shop scheduling problems. We have also pointed to the fact that this class' usability is not restricted to this application area, but can be employed for different scheduling problems and application domains beyond manufacturing as well. Accordingly, an interesting avenue for future work is represented by employing and assessing the learning algorithms developed to different tasks, e.g. to network routing or traffic control problems.

Classical job-shop scheduling problems (cf. Section 3.1), which we used as benchmark throughout this work, are deterministic in nature. There are also stochastic versions of job-shop scheduling problems (Pinedo, 2002). Stochasticity may arise, for example, if the durations of a job's operations are randomly perturbed or if (adopting a practice-oriented perspective) the execution of some operation to some product has failed, thus requiring a repetition of that operation. We stress once more that our modelling framework allows for stochasticity by definition. The distributed learning algorithms we have suggested do so in part: While GDPS is immediately applicable to stochastic JSSPs (see Gabel and Riedmiller (2008b) for corresponding experimental results), the versions of JEPS proposed in this document are not, because of their straightforward implementation of the heuristic function (we elaborate more on this point below). OA-NFQ requires a deterministic environment during learning in order to fully exploit the power of the optimistic assumption it uses, whereas NFQ is not bothered by a stochastic environment. Both of these value function-based RL algorithms can handle non-determinism in their application phase, i.e. when exploiting their learned dispatching policies for some new scheduling problem. Although we did not explicitly test these algorithms for stochastic JSS problems, we in fact challenged them even more by testing the acquired joint policies for entirely different scheduling problem instances (not just for noisified ones). After all, however, the further development of those components of the learning approaches mentioned that prohibit their use in stochastic systems (e.g. the optimistic assumption or JEPS' heuristic function implementation) represents a major and very interesting challenge for future work.

## 7.2 Outlook

**Extensions and Alternatives**

In Chapter 4, we have applied our policy search-based RL solution approaches consistently with constant learning rates. However, adaptive methods exist (e.g. the Rprop method, Riedmiller and Braun, 1993) that allow for dynamically changing learning rate vectors as learning proceeds. As such adaptations typically result in a significant speed-up of the learning progress (Kocsis et al., 2006), a combination of JEPS and GDPS with Rprop is a promising idea.

Such a speed-up may be very desirable, especially if an extension of the proposed policy search methods towards the consideration of interaction histories, and hence the consideration of much larger state spaces, is desired. The latter represents a promising idea in itself since, as shown theoretically in Section 2.4 and empirically in Section 6.3, memory-based learning agents have a clear advantage over memoryless ones, although this extension will significantly increase the amount of experience to be collected through interaction with the environment.

Another important issue for future work concerns particularly the JEPS algorithm (Section 4.2). We have investigated its theoretical properties, assuming the existence of an optimal heuristic function $H$ that tells whether a joint equilibrium has been attained. In practice, of course, an optimal heuristic cannot be expected to be known and, in fact, for our experiments around JEPS we employed a straightforward, $R_{max}$-based implementation of $H$. To this end, the performance of JEPS can supposedly be improved if more sophisticated realizations of the heuristic are utilized. For instance, the explorative capabilities of JEPS may be increased if an $\epsilon$-$R_{max}$-based heuristic with vanishing $\epsilon$ is used, that returns true if the current policy performance is within an $\epsilon$-vicinity of $R_{max}$.

In the context of the experiments around our OA-NFQ approach, we have also compared local and global reward schemes. While the former allow for a higher degree of decentralization of the entire learning process, they enforce selfish agent behavior and yield a poor degree of cooperation. Concerning job-shop scheduling using cooperative agents, global rewards obviously brought about best performance. But, using the notion of Tumer and Agogino (2004), such reward functions feature a high degree of learnability and, at the same time, a low factoredness. To this end, it would be an interesting idea to integrate and analyze different utility functions, such as the wonderful life utility scheme (Tumer et al., 2002).

With respect to our value function-based approaches (Chapter 5), we invested a moderate effort in the task of feature engineering, i.e. in finding and crafting comprehensive and general features that describe individual actions (in our JSS application: available jobs) or local states (sets of waiting jobs). There exist, however, powerful mechanisms that aid the system designer in creating or removing certain features (Guyon and Elisseeff, 2003). Hence, the use of state-of-the-art feature engineering methods, such as clustering methods, singular value decomposition, or principal component analysis, may enhance the applicability and performance, and eventually even the already excellent generalization capabilities of our learning approach.

In our model-free batch-mode reinforcement learning algorithms (Sections 5.2 and 5.3), we focussed on the use of artificial neural networks as a tool for approximating value functions over high-dimensional continuous state-action spaces in the context of the fitted

## 7 Conclusion

Q iteration algorithm. Of course, there are also other powerful machine learning algorithms that might be employed for this purpose, for example, decision trees (Ernst et al., 2006), support vector regression (Csaji and Monostori, 2008), or Gaussian processes (Deisenroth et al., 2008). A comparison of NFQ and OA-NFQ against FQI variants using other function approximation mechanisms depicts a further interesting topic.

Multi-layer perceptron neural networks are well-known for their representational power, their good generalization capabilities, and, when used in batch-mode, for their combinability with advanced network training methods. A drawback when using them in the scope of value function-based RL is their lack of convergence guarantees (Gordon, 1996). In order to enforce stable learning results, we relied on the straightforward, but computationally expensive policy screening technique (Bertsekas et al., 2000) which selects high-quality policies in spite of oscillations in the learning process. Research on more efficient methods that foster robust learning behavior for neural value function-based RL depicts an important open issue.

Finally, we have employed a restricted inter-agent notification scheme to enable the learning agents to resolve some of their dependencies on one another. While this turned out to be a highly effective and efficient approach, another interesting direction is to study the learning of when and with whom to communicate (Riedmiller et al., 2000), given that communication is no longer free of charge, but modelled as an action that incurs some cost.

# Glossary

| | |
|---|---|
| AI | Artificial Intelligence |
| AMCC | Avoid maximum current makespan |
| COM-MTDP | Communicating multi-agent team decision problem |
| DEC-MDP | Decentralized Markov decision process |
| DEC-POMDP | Decentralized partially observable Markov decision process |
| DPR | Dispatching priority rule |
| EA | Evolutionary algorithm |
| ESS | Earliest start schedule |
| FIFO | First in first out |
| FQI | Fitted Q iteration |
| FT6, FT10 | Job-shop scheduling benchmark problem instances proposed by Fisher and Thompson (Muth and Thompson, 1963) |
| GDPS | Gradient-descent policy search |
| IL | Independent learner |
| IPL | Incremental policy learning |
| JAL | Joint-action learner |
| JEPS | Joint equilibrium policy search |
| JSS | Job-shop scheduling |
| JSSP | Job-shop scheduling problem |
| LPT | Longest processing time |
| MDP | Markov decision process |
| MLP | Multi-layer perceptron |
| MLS | Maximum likelihood schedule |
| MMDP | Multi-agent Markov decision process |
| NDP | Neuro-dynamic programming |
| MTDP | Multi-agent team decision problem |
| NEXP | Complexity class of problems solvable in exponential time by a non-deterministic Turing machine |
| NFQ | Neural fitted Q iteration |
| NP | Complexity class of problems solvable in polynomial time by a non-deterministic Turing machine |
| OA-NFQ | Optimistic assumption-based neural fitted Q iteration |
| P | Complexity class of problems solvable in polynomial time by a Deterministic Turing machine |
| PG | Policy gradient |
| POIPSG | Partially observable identical payoff stochastic game |
| POMDP | Partially observable Markov decision process |
| POSG | Partially observable stochastic game |

| | |
|---|---|
| PSPACE | Complexity class of problems solvable in by a deterministic Turing machine with polynomial space requirements |
| RL | Reinforcement learning |
| SPT | Shortest processing time |
| SQNO | Shortest queue for next operation |
| TD | Temporal difference |

# Bibliography

D. Aberdeen and O. Buffet. Concurrent Probabilistic Temporal Planning with Policy-Gradients. In *Proceedings of the Seventeenth International Conference on Automated Planning and Scheduling (ICAPS 2007)*, pages 10–17, Providence, USA, 2007. AAAI Press.

J. Adams, E. Balas, and D. Zawack. The Shifting Bottleneck Procedure for Job Shop Scheduling. *Management Science*, 34(3):391–401, 1988.

A. Agogino and K. Tumer. Multi-agent Reward Analysis for Learning in Noisy Domains. In *Proceedings of the 4th International Joint Conference on Autonomous Agents and Multiagent Systems (AAMAS 2005)*, pages 81–88, Utrecht, The Netherlands, 2005. ACM Press.

C. Amato, D. Bernstein, and S. Zilberstein. Optimizing Memory-Bounded Controllers for Decentralized POMDPs. In *Proceedings of the 23rd Conference on Uncertainty in Artificial Intelligence (UAI 2007)*, Vancouver, Canada, 2007.

D. Applegate and W. Cook. A Computational Study of the Job-Shop Scheduling Problem. *ORSA Journal on Computing*, 3:149–156, 1991.

R. Aras, A. Dutech, and F. Charpillet. Cooperation through Communication in Decentralized Markov Games. In *Proceedings of the International Conference on Advances in Intelligent Systems – Theory and Applications (AISTA 2004)*, Luxembourg, Luxembourg, 2004. IEEE Press.

K. Arrow and L. Hurwicz. Stability of the Gradient Process in $n$-Person Games. *Journal of the Society of Industrial and Applied Mathematics*, 8(2):280–295, 1960.

M. Aydin and E. Öztemel. Dynamic Job-Shop Scheduling Using Reinforcement Learning Agents. *Robotics and Autonomous Systems*, 33:169–178, 2000.

J. Bagnell and A. Ng. On Local Rewards and Scaling Distributed Reinforcement Learning. In *Advances in Neural Information Processing Systems 18 (NIPS 2005)*, Vancouver, Canada, 2005.

L. Baird and A. Moore. Gradient Descent for General Reinforcement Learning. In *Advances in Neural Information Processing Systems 11 (NIPS 1998)*, pages 968–974, Denver, USA, 1999. The MIT Press.

A. Baker. A Survey of Factory Control Algorithms which Can Be Implemented in a Multi-Agent Heterarchy: Dispatching, Scheduling, and Pull. *Journal of Manufacturing Systems*, 17(4):297–320, 1998.

A. Barto and R. Crites. Improving Elevator Performance using Reinforcement Learning. In *Advances in Neural Information Processing Systems 8 (NIPS 1995)*, pages 1017–1023, Denver, USA, 1996. MIT Press.

A. Barto, R. Sutton, and C. Anderson. Neuron-Like Elements that Can Solve Difficult Learning Control Problems. *IEEE Transactions on Systems, Man, and Cybernetics*, 13: 835–846, 1983.

J. Baxter and P. Bartlett. Direct Gradient-Based Reinforcement Learning: I. Gradient Estimation Algorithms. Technical report, Research School of Information Sciences and Engineering, Australian National University, 1999.

J. Bean. Genetics and Random Keys for Sequencing and Optimization. *ORSA Journal of Computing*, 6:154–160, 1994.

J. Beasley. OR-Library, 2005. http://people.brunel.ac.uk/~mastjjb/jeb/info.html.

R. Becker, S. Zilberstein, and V. Lesser. Decentralized Markov Decision Processes with Event-Driven Interactions. In *Proceedings of the 3rd International Conference on Autonomous Agents and Multi-Agent Systems (AAMAS 2004)*, pages 302–309, New York, USA, 2004a. ACM Press.

R. Becker, S. Zilberstein, V. Lesser, and C. Goldman. Solving Transition Independent Decentralized MDPs. *Journal of Artificial Intelligence Research*, 22:423–455, 2004b.

R. Becker, V. Lesser, and S. Zilberstein. Analyzing Myopic Approaches for Multi-Agent Communication. In *Proceedings of the 2005 IEEE/WIC/ACM International Conference on Intelligent Agent Technology (IAT 2005)*, pages 550–557, Compiegne, France, 2005. IEEE Computer Society.

R. E. Bellman. *Dynamic Programming*. Princeton University Press, USA, 1957.

D. Bernstein, R. Givan, N. Immerman, and S. Zilberstein. The Complexity of Decentralized Control of Markov Decision Processes. In *Proceedings of the 16th Conference in Uncertainty in Artificial Intelligence (UAI'00)*, pages 32–37, Stanford, CA, June 2000. Morgan Kaufmann.

D. Bernstein, D. Givan, N. Immerman, and S. Zilberstein. The Complexity of Decentralized Control of Markov Decision Processes. *Mathematics of Operations Research*, 27(4): 819–840, 2002.

D. Bernstein, E. Hansen, and S. Zilberstein. Bounded Policy Iteration for Decentralized POMDPs. In *Proceedings of the 19th International Joint Conference on Artificial Intelligence (IJCAI 2005)*, pages 1287–1292, Edinburgh, United Kingdom, 2005. Professional Book Center.

D. Bertsekas and J. Tsitsiklis. *Neuro Dynamic Programming*. Athena Scientific, Belmont, USA, 1996.

D. Bertsekas, M. Homer, D. Logan, S. Patek, and N. Sandell. Missile Defense and Interceptor Allocation by Neuro-Dynamic Programming. *IEEE Transactions on Systems, Man, and Cybernetics*, 30(1):42–51, 2000.

A. Beynier and A. Mouaddib. A Polynomial Algorithm for Decentralized Markov Decision Processes with Temporal Constraints. In *Proceedings of the 4th International Joint Conference on Autonomous Agents and Multiagent Systems (AAMAS 2005)*, pages 963–969, Utrecht, The Netherlands, 2005. ACM Press.

A. Beynier and A. Mouaddib. An Iterative Algorithm for Solving Constrained Decentralized Markov Decision Processes. In *Proceedings, The Twenty-First National Conference on Artificial Intelligence (AAAI 2006)*, Boston, USA, 2006. AAAI Press.

K. Bhaskaran and M. Pinedo. Dispatching. In G. Salvendy, editor, *Handbook of Industrial Engineering*, pages 2184–2198. John Wiley, New York, USA, 1977.

B. Bikramjit, S. Sen, and J. Peng. Fast Concurrent Reinforcement Learners. In *Proceedings of the 17th International Joint Conference on Artificial Intelligence (IJCAI 2001)*, pages 825–830, Seattle, WA, August 2001. Morgan Kaufmann.

S. Binato, W. Hery, D. Loewenstern, and M. Resende. A GRASP for Job Shop Scheduling. In P. Hansen and C. Ribeiro, editors, *Essays and Surveys in Metaheuristics*, pages 177–293. Kluwer Academic Publishers, New York, USA, 2001.

J. Blazewicz, K. Ecker, G. Schmidt, and J. Weglarz. *Scheduling in Computer and Manufacturing Systems*. Springer, Berlin, Germany, 1993.

C. Boutilier. Sequential Optimality and Coordination in Multiagent Systems. In *Proceedings of 16th International Joint Conference on Artificial Intelligence (IJCAI 1999)*, pages 478–485, Stockholm, Sweden, 1999. Morgan Kaufmann.

D. Bovet and P. Crescenzi. *Introduction to the Theory of Complexity*. Prentice Hall, Hertfordshire, United Kingdom, 1994.

M. Bowling. Convergence Problems of General-Sum Multiagent Reinforcement Learning. In *Proceedings of the Seventeenth International Conference on Machine Learning (ICML 2000)*, pages 89–94, Stanford, USA, 2000. Morgan Kaufmann.

J. Boyan and M. Littman. Packet Routing in Dynamically Changing Networks – A Reinforcement Learning Approach. In *Advances in Neural Information Processing Systems 6 (NIPS 1993)*, pages 671–678, Denver, USA, 1994. Morgan Kaufmann.

J. A. Boyan and A. W. Moore. Generalization in Reinforcement Learning: Safely Approximating the Value Function. In *Advances in Neural Information Processing Systems 7*, pages 369–376, Cambridge, USA, 1995. MIT Press.

R. Brafman and M. Tennenholtz. Learning to Cooperate Efficiently: A Model-Based Approach. *Journal of Artificial Intelligence Research*, 19:11–23, 2003.

## Bibliography

R. Brafman and M. Tennenholtz. R-MAX - A General Polynomial Time Algorithm for Near-Optimal Reinforcement Learning. In *Proceedings of the 17th International Joint Conference on Artificial Intelligence (IJCAI 2001)*, pages 953–958, Seattle, USA, 2001. Morgan Kaufmann.

P. Brucker and S. Knust. *Complex Scheduling*. Springer, Berlin, Germany, 2005.

P. Brucker, B. Jurisch, and B. Sievers. A Branch and Bound Algorithm for the Job-Shop Scheduling Problem. *Discrete Applied Mathematics*, 49(1-2):107–127, 1994.

J. Carlier and E. Pinson. An Algorithm for Solving the Job-Shop Problem. *Management Science*, 35(2):164–176, 1989.

I. Chades and B. Bouteiller. Solving Multiagent Markov Decision Processes: A Forest Management Example. In *Proceedings of the International Congress on Modelling and Simulation (MODSIM 2005)*, pages 1594–1600, Canberra, Australia, 2005. Modelling and Simulation Society of Australia and New Zealand.

Y. Chang, T. Ho, and L. Kaelbling. All Learning Is Local: Multi-Agent Learning in Global Reward Games. In *Advances in Neural Information Processing Systems 16 (NIPS 2003)*, Vancouver and Whistler, Canada, 2003.

Y. Chang, T. Ho, and L. Kaelbling. Mobilized Ad-Hoc Networks: A Reinforcement Learning Approach. In *Proceedings of the First International Conference on Autonomic Computing (ICAC 2004)*, pages 240–247, New York, USA, 2004. IEEE Computer Society.

K. Chellapilla and D. Fogel. Evolution, Neural Networks, Games, and Intelligence. *Proceedings of the IEEE*, 87(9):1471–1496, 1999.

C. Claus and C. Boutilier. The Dynamics of Reinforcement Learning in Cooperative Multiagent Systems. In *Proceedings of the Fifteenth National Conference on Artificial Intelligence (AAAI-98)*, pages 746–752, Menlo Park, USA, 1998. AAAI Press.

B. Csaji and L. Monostori. Adaptive Stochastic Resource Control: A Machine Learning Approach. *Journal of Artificial Intelligence Research*, 32:453–486, 2008.

B. Csaji and L. Monostori. Adaptive Algorithms in Distributed Resource Allocation. In *Proceedings of the 6th International Workshop on Emergent Synthesis (IWES 2004)*, pages 69–75, Kashiwa, Japan, 2004.

B. Csaji and L. Monostori. Adaptive Sampling Based Large-Scale Stochastic Resource Control. In *Proceedings of the 21st National Conference on Artificial Intelligence (AAAI 2006)*, Boston, USA, 2006. AAAI Press.

M. Deisenroth, J. Peters, and C. Rasmussen. Approximate Dynamic Programming with Gaussian Processes. In *Proceedings of the 2008 American Control Conference (ACC 2008)*, pages 4480–4485, Seattle, USA, 2008. IEEE Press.

M. Dell'Amico and M. Trubian. Applying Tabu Search to the Job-Shop Scheduling Problem. *Annals of Operations Research*, 41(1-4):231–252, 1993.

D. Ernst, P. Geurts, and L. Wehenkel. Tree-Based Batch Mode Reinforcement Learning. *Journal of Machine Learning Research*, 6(1):503–556, 2006.

H. Ferra, K. Lau, C. Leckie, and A. Tang. Applying Reinforcement Learning to Packet Scheduling in Routers. In *Proceedings of the Fifteenth Innovative Applications of Artificial Intelligence Conference (IAAI-03)*, pages 79–84, Acapulco, Mexico, 2003. AAAI Press.

E. Ferreira and P. Khosla. Multi Agent Collaboration Using Distributed Value Functions. In *Proceedings of the IEEE Intelligent Vehicle Symposium 2000 (IV 2000)*, pages 404–409, Dearborn, USA, 2000. IEEE Press.

J. Filar and O. Vrieze. *Competitive Markov Decision Processes – Theory, Algorithms, and Applications*. Springer-Verlag, New York, USA, 1996.

D. Fudenberg and J. Tirole. *Game Theory*. MIT Press, Boston, USA, 1991.

N. Fulda and D. Ventura. Incremental Policy Learning: An Equilibrium Selection Algorithm for Reinforcement Learning Agents with Common Interests. In *Proceedings of the 2004 IEEE International Joint Conference on Neural Networks (IJCNN)*, pages 1121–1125, Budapest, Hungary, 2004. IEEE Press.

T. Gabel and M. Riedmiller. Adaptive Reactive Job-Shop Scheduling with Learning Agents. *International Journal of Information Technology and Intelligent Computing*, 2(4), 2007a.

T. Gabel and M. Riedmiller. Multi-Agent Case-Based Reasoning for Cooperative Reinforcement Learners. In *Proceedings of the 8th European Conference on Case-Based Reasoning (ECCBR 2006)*, pages 32–46, Fethiye, Turkey, 2006a. Springer.

T. Gabel and M. Riedmiller. Reducing Policy Degradation in Neuro-Dynamic Programming. In *Proceedings of ESANN2006*, pages 653–658, Bruges, Belgium, 2006b.

T. Gabel and M. Riedmiller. On a Successful Application of Multi-Agent Reinforcement Learning to Operations Research Benchmarks. In *Proceedings of the IEEE Symposium on Approximate Dynamic Programming and Reinforcement Learning (ADPRL 2007)*, pages 68–75, Honolulu, USA, 2007b. IEEE Press.

T. Gabel and M. Riedmiller. Scaling Adaptive Agent-Based Reactive Job-Shop Scheduling to Large-Scale Problems. In *In Proceedings of the IEEE Symposium on Computational Intelligence in Scheduling (CI-Sched 2007)*, pages 259–266, Honolulu, USA, 2007c. IEEE Press.

T. Gabel and M. Riedmiller. Reinforcement Learning for DEC-MDPs with Changing Action Sets and Partially Ordered Dependencies. In *Proceedings of the 7th International Joint Conference on Autonomous Agents and Multiagent Systems (AAMAS 2008)*, pages 1333–1336, Estoril, Portugal, 2008a. IFAAMAS.

## Bibliography

T. Gabel and M. Riedmiller. Gradient Descent Policy Search for Distributed Job-Shop Scheduling Problems. In *Online Proceedings of the 18th International Conference on Planning and Scheduling (ICAPS 2008)*, Sydney, Australia, 2008b. AAAI Press.

T. Gabel and M. Riedmiller. Joint Equilibrium Policy Search for Multi-Agent Scheduling Problems. In *Proceedings of the 6th Conference on Multiagent System Technologies (MATES 2008)*, pages 61–72, Kaiserslautern, Germany, 2008c. Springer.

T. Gabel and A. Stahl. Exploiting Background Knowledge when Learning Similarity Measures. In *Proceedings of the 7th European Conference on Case-Based Reasoning (ECCBR 2004)*, pages 169–183, Madrid, Spain, 2004. Springer.

T. Gabel, R. Hafner, S. Lange, M. Lauer, and M. Riedmiller. Bridging the Gap: Learning in the RoboCup Simulation and Midsize League. In *Proceedings of the 7th Portuguese Conference on Automatic Control (Controlo 2006)*, Porto, Portugal, 2006. Portuguese Society of Automatic Control.

Chris Gaskett. *Q-Learning for Robot Control.* Ph.D. Thesis, Australian National University, 2002.

P. Gmytrasiewicz and P. Doshi. A Framework for Sequential Planning in Multiagent Settings. *Journal of Artificial Intelligence Research*, 24:49–79, 2005.

C. Goldman and S. Zilberstein. Decentralized Control of Cooperative Systems: Categorization and Complexity Analysis. *Journal of Artificial Intelligence Research*, 22: 143–174, 2004.

C. Goldman and S. Zilberstein. Optimizing Information Exchange in Cooperative Multi-Agent Systems. In *Proceedings of the Second International Conference on Autonomous Agents and Multi-Agent Systems (AAMAS 2003)*, pages 137–144, Melbourne, Australia, 2003. ACM Press.

M. González, C. Vela, and R. Varela. A New Hybrid Genetic Algorithm for the Job Shop Scheduling Problem with Setup Times. In *Proceedings of the 18th International Conference on Automated Planning and Scheduling (ICAPS 2008)*, pages 116–123, Sydney, Australia, 2008. AAAI Press.

G. Gordon. Stable Fitted Reinforcement Learning. In *Advances in Neural Information Processing Systems 9 (NIPS 1995)*, pages 1052–1058, Denver, USA, 1996. The MIT Press.

E. Greensmith, P. Bartlett, and J. Baxter. Variance Reduction Techniques for Gradient Estimates in Reinforcement Learning. *Journal of Machine Learning Research*, 5:1471–1530, 2004.

A. Greenwald and K. Hall. Correlated Q-Learning. In *Proceedings of the 20th International Conference on Machine Learning (ICML 2003)*, pages 242–249, Washington, USA, 2003. AAAI Press.

C. Guestrin, M. Lagoudakis, and R. Parr. Coordinated Reinforcement Learning. In *Proceedings of 19th International Conference on Machine Learning (ICML 2002)*, pages 227–234, Sydney, Australia, 2002. Morgan Kaufmann.

I. Guyon and A. Elisseeff. An Introduction to Variable and Feature Selection. *Journal of Machine Learning Research*, 3:1157–1182, 2003.

E. Hansen, D. Bernstein, and S. Zilberstein. Dynamic Programming for Partially Observable Stochastic Games. In *Proceedings of the 19th National Conference on Artificial Intelligence (AAAI 2004)*, pages 709–715, San Jose, USA, 2004. AAAI Press.

V. Heidrich-Meisner, M. Lauer, C. Igel, and M. Riedmiller. Reinforcement Learning in a Nutshell. In *Proceedings of the 15th European Symposium on Artificial Neural Networks (ESANN 2007)*, pages 277–288, Bruges, Belgium, 2007. d-side publications.

J. Holland. *Adaptation in Natural and Artificial Systems*. The University of Michigan Press, 1975.

K. Hornick, M. Stinchcombe, and H. White. Multilayer Feedforward Networks Are Universal Approximators. *Neural Networks*, 2:359–366, 1989.

J. Hu and M. Wellman. Multiagent Reinforcement Learning: Theoretical Framework and an Algorithm. In *Proceedings of the 15th International Conference on Machine Learning (ICML 1998)*, pages 242–250, Madison, USA, 1998. Morgan Kaufmann.

J. Hu and M. P. Wellman. Nash Q-Learning for General-Sum Stochastic Games. *Journal of Machine Learning Research*, 4:1039–1069, 2003. Special Issue on Neural Networks.

D. Joslin and D. Clements. Squeaky Wheel Optimization. *Journal of Artificial Intelligence Research*, 10:353–373, 1999.

L. Kaelbling, M. Littman, and A. Cassandra. Planning and Acting in Partially Observable Stochastic Domains. *Artificial Intelligence*, 101(1-2):99–134, 1998.

S. Kakade and J. Langford. Approximately Optimal Approximate Reinforcement Learning. In *Proceedings of the Nineteenth International Conference (ICML 2002)*, pages 267–275, Sydney, Australia, 2002. Morgan Kaufman.

T. Kietzmann and M. Riedmiller. "selecting the right patterns and policies in rl for a real world application". In *Proceedings of the Twenty-sixth International Conference on Machine Learning (ICML 2009)*, Montreal, Canada, 2009. to appear.

L. Kocsis, C. Szepesvári, and M. Winands. Rspsa: Enhanced parameter optimization in games. In *Proceedings of the 11th International Conference Advances in Computer Games (ACG 2006)*, pages 39–56, Taipei, Taiwain, 2006. Springer.

J. Kok and N. Vlassis. "sparse cooperative q-learning". In *Proceedings of the Twenty-first International Conference on Machine Learning (ICML 2004)*, Banff, Canada, 2004. ACM Press.

# Bibliography

M. Lauer and M. Riedmiller. An Algorithm for Distributed Reinforcement Learning in Cooperative Multi-Agent Systems. In *Proceedings of the Seventeenth International Conference on Machine Learning (ICML 2000)*, pages 535–542, Stanford, USA, 2000. Morgan Kaufmann.

J. Laumonier and B. Chaib-draa. Agent Neighbourhood for Learning Approximated Policies in DEC-MDP. In *Proceedings of Evolutionary Models of Collaboration (EMC 2007), Workshop of the Int. Joint Conf. on AI (IJCAI 2007)*, Hyderabad, India, 2007.

E. Lawler, J. Lenstra, A. Rinnooy-Kan, and D. Shmoys. Sequencing and Scheduling: Algorithms and Complexity. In *Handbooks in Operations Research and Management Science*, pages 445–522. Elsevier, New York, USA, 1993.

S. Lawrence. Supplement to Resource Constrained Project Scheduling: An Experimental Investigation of Heuristic Scheduling Techniques. Technical report, Graduate School of Industrial Administration, Carnegie Mellon University, Pittsburgh, USA, 1984.

M. Littman. Markov Games as a Framework for Multi-Agent Reinforcement Learning. In *Proceeding of the 11th International Conference on Machine Learning (ICML 1994)*, pages 157–163, New Brunswick, USA, 1994. Morgan Kaufmann.

M. Littman. Friend-or-Foe Q-Learning in General-Sum Games. In *Proceedings of the 18th International Conference on Machine Learning (ICML 2001)*, pages 322–328, Williamstown, USA, 2001. Morgan Kaufmann.

J. Liu and K. Sycara. Coordination of Multiple Agents for Production Management. *Annals of Operations Research*, 75(1):235–289, 1997.

J. Liu and K. Sycara. Exploiting Problem Structure for Distributed Constraint Optimization. In *Proceedings of the First International Conference on Multiagent Systems (ICMAS 1995)*, pages 246–253, San Francisco, USA, 1995. The MIT Press.

W. Lovejoy. A Survey of Algorithmic Methods for Partially Observable Markov Decision Processes. *Annals of Operations Research*, 28(1-4):47–66, 1991.

K. Low, J. Dolan, and P. Khosla. Adaptive Multi-Robot Wide-Area Exploration and Mapping. In *Proceedings of the 7th International Joint Conference on Autonomous Agents and Multiagent Systems (AAMAS 2008)*, pages 23–30, Estoril, Portugal, 2008. IFAAMAS.

O. Madani, S. Hanks, and A. Condon. On the Undecidability of Probabilistic Planning and Related Stochastic Optimization Problems. *Artificial Intelligence*, 147(1-2):5–34, 2003.

S. Mahadevan, N. Marchalleck, T. Das, and A. Gosavi. Self-Improving Factory Simulation Using Continuous-Time Average-Reward Reinforcement Learning. In *Proceedings of the 14th International Conference on Machine Learning (ICML 1997)*, pages 202–210, Nashville, USA, 1997. Morgan Kaufmann.

# Bibliography

J. Marecki and M. Tambe. On Opportunistic Techniques for Solving Decentralized Markov Decision Processes with Temporal Constraints. In *Proceedings of the 6th International Joint Conference on Autonomous Agents and Multiagent Systems (AAMAS 2007)*, page 219, Honolulu, USA, 2007. IFAAMAS.

J. Marecki, T. Gupta, P. Varakantham, M. Tambe, and M. Yokoo. Not All Agents Are Equal: Scaling up Distributed POMDPs for Agent Networks. In *Proceedings of the 7th International Joint Conference on Autonomous Agents and Multiagent Systems (AAMAS 2008)*, pages 485–492, Estoril, Portugal, 2008. IFAAMAS.

A. Mascis and D. Pacciarelli. Job-Shop Scheduling with Blocking and No-Wait Constraints. *European Journal of Operational Research*, 143(3):498–517, 2002.

J. Metzen, M. Edgington, Y. Kassahun, and F. Kirchner. Towards Efficient Online Reinforcement Learning Using Neuroevolution. In *Proceedings of the 10th Genetic and Evolutionary Computation Conference (GECCO-2008)*, pages 1425–1426, Atlanta, USA, 2008. ACM.

N. Meuleau, L. Peshkin, K. Kim, and L. Kaelbling. Learning Finite-State Controllers for Partially Observable Environments. In *Proceedings of the 15th Conference on Uncertainty in Artificial Intelligence (UAI 1999)*, pages 427–436, Stockholm, Sweden, 1999. Morgan Kaufmann.

P. Modi, W. Shen, M. Tambe, and M. Yokoo. Adopt: Asynchronous Distributed Constraint Optimization with Quality Guarantees. *Artificial Intelligence*, 161(1–2):149–180, 2005.

T. Mora, A. Sesay, J. Denzinger, H. Golshan, G. Poissant, and C. Konecnik. Cooperative Search for Optimizing Pipeline Operations. In *Proceedings of the 7th International Joint Conference on Autonomous Agents and Multiagent Systems (AAMAS 2008)*, pages 115–122, Estoril, Portugal, 2008. IFAAMAS.

D. Moriarty, A. Schultz, and J. Grefenstette. Evolutionary Algorithms for Reinforcement Learning. *Journal of Artificial Intelligence Research*, 11:199–229, 1999.

M. Mundhenk, J. Goldsmith, C. Lusena, and E. Allender. Complexity of Finite-Horizon Markov Decision Process Problems. *Journal of the ACM*, 47(4):681–720, 2000.

R. Munos. Error Bounds for Approximate Policy Iteration. In *Proceedings of the 20th International Conference Machine Learning (ICML 2003)*, pages 560–567, Washington, USA, 2003. AAAI Press.

R. Munos. Error Bounds for Approximate Value Iteration. In *Proceedings of the 20th National Conference on Artificial Intelligence (AAAI 2005)*, pages 1006–1011, Pittsburgh, USA, 2005. AAAI Press.

J. Muth and G. Thompson. *Industrial Scheduling*. Kluwer Academic Publishers, Dordrecht, The Netherlands, 1963.

## Bibliography

R. Myerson. *Game Theory: Analysis of Conflict.* Harvard University Press, Massachussetts, USA, 1991.

R. Nair, M. Tambe, M. Roth, and M. Yokoo. Communication for Improving Policy Computation in Distributed POMDPs. In *Proceedings of the 3rd International Joint Conference on Autonomous Agents and Multiagent Systems (AAMAS 2004)*, pages 1098–1105, New York, USA, 2004. IEEE Computer Society.

R. Nair, P. Varakantham, M. Tambe, and M. Yokoo. Networked Distributed POMDPs: A Synthesis of Distributed Constraint Optimization and POMDPs. In *Proceedings of the 20th National Conference on Artificial Intelligence (AAAI 2005)*, pages 133–139, Pittsburgh, USA, 2005. AAAI Press.

E. Nowicki and C. Smutnicki. A Fast Taboo Search Algorithm for the Job Shop Problem. *Management Science*, 42(6):797–813, 1996.

E. Nowicki and C. Smutnicki. Some New Ideas in Tabu Search for Job-Shop Scheduling. *Operations Research / Computer Science Interfaces Series*, 30:165–190, 2005.

F. Oliehoek, M. Spaan, and N. Vlassis. Optimal and Approximate Q-Value Functions for Decentralized POMDPs. *Journal of Artificial Intelligence Research*, 32:289–353, 2008a.

F. Oliehoek, M. Spaan, S. Whiteson, and N. Vlassis. Exploiting Locality of Interaction in Factored Dec-POMDPs. In *Proceedings of the 7th International Joint Conference on Autonomous Agents and Multiagent Systems (AAMAS 2008)*, pages 517–524, Estoril, Portugal, 2008b. IFAAMAS.

B. Ombuki and M. Ventresca. Local Search Genetic Algorithms for the Job Shop Scheduling Problem. *Applied Intelligence*, 21(1):99–109, 2004.

P. Ow and T. Morton. Filtered Beam Search in Scheduling. *International Journal of Production Research*, 26:297–307, 1988.

S. Panwalkar and W. Iskander. A Survey of Scheduling Rules. *Operations Research*, 25: 45–61, 1977.

C. Papadimitriou and J. Tsitsiklis. The Complexity of Markov Decision Processes. *Mathematics of Operations Research*, 12(3):441–450, 1987.

L. Peshkin and V. Savova. Reinforcement Learning for Adaptive Routing. In *Proceedings of the International Joint Conference on Neural Networks (IJCNN 2002)*, pages 1825–1830, Hawaii, USA, 2002. IEEE Press.

L. Peshkin, K. Kim, N. Meuleau, and L. Kaelbling. Learning to Cooperate via Policy Search. In *Proceedings of the Sixteenth Conference on Uncertainty in Artificial Intelligence*, pages 489–496, Stanford, USA, 2000. Morgan Kaufmann.

J. Peters, S. Vijayakumar, and S. Schaal. Natural Actor-Critic. In *Proceedings of the 16th European Conference on Machine Learning (ECML 2005)*, pages 280–291, Porto, Portugal, 2005. Springer.

Bibliography

M. Pinedo. *Scheduling. Theory, Algorithms, and Systems*. Prentice Hall, USA, 2002.

E. Pinson. The Job Shop Scheduling Problem: A Concise Survey and Some Recent Developments. In P. Chretienne, E. Coffman, J. Lenstra, and Z. Liu, editors, *Scheduling Theory and Applications*, pages 177–293. John Wiley, New York, USA, 1995.

J. Pita, M. Jain, J. Marecki, F. Ordóñez, C. Portway, M. Tambe, C. Western, P. Paruchuri, and S. Kraus. Deployed ARMOR protection: the application of a game theoretic model for security at the Los Angeles International Airport. In *Industry Track Proceedings of the 7th International Joint Conference on Autonomous Agents and Multiagent Systems (AAMAS 2008)*, pages 125–132, Estoril, Portugal, 2008. IFAAMAS.

M. Puterman. *Markov Decision Processes: Discrete Stochastic Dynamic Programming*. Wiley-Interscience, USA, 2005.

D. Pynadath and M. Tambe. The Communicative Multiagent Team Decision Problem: Analyzing Teamwork Theories and Models. *Journal of Artificial Intelligence Research*, 16:389–423, 2002a.

D. Pynadath and M. Tambe. Multiagent Teamwork: Analyzing the Optimality and Complexity of Key Theories and Models. In *Proceedings of the 1st International Joint Conference on Autonomous Agents & Multiagent Systems (AAMAS 2002)*, pages 873–880, Bologna, Italy, 2002b. ACM.

Z. Rabinovich, C. Goldman, and J. Rosenschein. The Complexity of Multiagent Systems: The Price of Silence. In *Proceedings of the 2nd International Joint Conference on Autonomous Agents & Multiagent Systems (AAMAS 2003)*, pages 1102–1103, Melbourne, Australia, 2003. ACM.

M. Riedmiller. Concepts and Facilities of a Neural Reinforcement Learning Control Architecture for Technical Process Control. *Neural Computation and Application Journal*, 8:323–338, 1999.

M. Riedmiller. Neural Fitted Q Iteration – First Experiences with a Data Efficient Neural Reinforcement Learning Method. In *Machine Learning: ECML 2005, 16th European Conference on Machine Learning*, pages 317–328, Porto, Portugal, 2005. Springer.

M. Riedmiller and H. Braun. A Direct Adaptive Method for Faster Backpropagation Learning: The RPROP Algorithm. In *Proceedings of the IEEE International Conference on Neural Networks (ICNN)*, pages 586–591, San Francisco, USA, 1993. IEEE Press.

M. Riedmiller and T. Gabel. On Experiences in a Complex and Competitive Gaming Domain: Reinforcement Learning Meets RoboCup. In *Proceedings of the 3rd IEEE Symposium on Computational Intelligence and Games (CIG 2007)*, pages 68–75, Honolulu, USA, 2007. IEEE Press.

M. Riedmiller and A. Merke. Using Machine Learning Techniques in Complex Multi-Agent Domains. In I. Stamatescu, W. Menzel, M. Richter, and U. Ratsch, editors, *Adaptivity and Learning*. Springer, 2003.

M. Riedmiller, A. Moore, and J. Schneider. Reinforcement Learning for Cooperating and Communicating Reactive Agents in Electrical Power Grids. In *Proceeding of the ECAI 2000 Workshop on Balancing Reactivity and Social Deliberation in Multi-Agent Systems*, pages 137–149, Berlin, Germany, 2000. Springer.

M. Riedmiller, M. Montemerlo, and H. Dahlkamp. Learning to Drive a Real Car in 20 Minutes. In *Proceedings of Frontiers in the Convergence of Bioscience and Information Technologies (FBIT 2007)*, pages 645–650, Jeju Island, South Korea, 2007a. IEEE Computer Society.

M. Riedmiller, J. Peters, and S. Schaal. Evaluation of Policy Gradient Methods and Variants on the Cart-Pole Benchmark. In *Proceedings of IEEE Symposium on Approximate Dynamic Programming and Reinforcement Learning (ADPRL 2007)*, pages 254–261, Honolulu, USA, 2007b. IEEE Press.

M. Riedmiller, T. Gabel, R. Hafner, and S. Lange. Neural Batch Reinforcement Learning: Three Case Studies in Robotic Soccer. *Autonomous Robots*, page to appear, 2009.

S. Riedmiller and M. Riedmiller. A Neural Reinforcement Learning Approach to Learn Local Dispatching Policies in Production Scheduling. In *Proceedings of 16th International Joint Conference on Artificial Intelligence (IJCAI 1999)*, pages 764–771, Stockholm, Sweden, 1999. Morgan Kaufmann.

B. Roy and B. Sussmann. Les Problemes d'Ordannancement avec Constraintes Disjonctives. Note DS No. 9 bis, SEMA, Montrouge, France, 1964.

S. Russell and P. Norvig. *Artificial Intelligence – A Modern Approach*. Prentice Hall, Englewood Cliffs, USA, 2003.

H. Santana, G. Ramalho, V. Corruble, and B. Ratitch. Multi-Agent Patrolling with Reinforcement Learning. In *Proceedings of the 3rd International Joint Conference on Autonomous Agents and Multiagent Systems (AAMAS 2004)*, pages 1122–1129, New York, USA, 2004. IEEE Computer Society.

J. Schneider, J. Boyan, and A. Moore. Value Function Based Production Scheduling. In *Proceedings of the 15th International Conference on Machine Learning (ICML 1998)*, pages 522–530, Madison, USA, 1998. Morgan Kaufmann.

J. Schneider, W. Wong, A. Moore, and M. Riedmiller. Distributed Value Functions. In *Proceedings of 16th International Conference on Machine Learning (ICML 1999)*, pages 371–378, Bled, Slovenia, 1999. Morgan Kaufmann.

G. Settembre, P. Scerri, A. Farinelli, K. Sycara, and D. Nardi. A Decentralized Approach to Cooperative Situation Assessment in Multi-Robot System. In *Proceedings of the 7th International Joint Conference on Autonomous Agents and Multiagent Systems (AAMAS 2008)*, pages 31–38, Estoril, Portugal, 2008. IFAAMAS.

S. Seuken and S. Zilberstein. Formal Models and Algorithms for Decentralized Decision Making Under Uncertainty. *Journal of Autonomous Agents and Multi-Agent Systems*, 17(2):190–250, 2008.

S. Seuken and S. Zilberstein. Improved Memory-Bounded Dynamic Programming for Decentralized POMDPs. In *Proceedings of the 23rd Conference on Uncertainty in Artificial Intelligence (UAI 2007)*, Vancouver, Canada, 2007a.

S. Seuken and S. Zilberstein. Memory-Bounded Dynamic Programming for DEC-POMDPs. In *Proceedings of the 20th International Joint Conference on Artificial Intelligence (IJCAI 2007)*, pages 2009–2015, Hyderabad, India, 2007b.

J. Shen, R. Becker, and V. Lesser. Agent Interaction in Distributed POMDPs and Implications on Complexity. In *Proceedings of the Fifth International Conference on Autonomous Agents and Multi-Agent Systems (AAMAS 2006)*, pages 529–536, Hakodate, Japan, 2006. ACM Press.

S. Singh and D. Bertsekas. Reinforcement Learning for Dynamic Channel Allocation in Cellular Telephone Systems. In *Advances in Neural Information Processing Systems 9 (NIPS 1996)*, pages 974–980, Denver, USA, 1997. MIT Press.

M. Smith, S. Lee-Urban, and H. Muñoz-Avila. RETALIATE: Learning Winning Policies in First-Person Shooter Games. In *Proceedings of the Twenty-Second AAAI Conference on Artificial Intelligence (AAAI 2007)*, pages 1801–1806, Vancouver, Canada, 2007. AAAI Press.

M. Spaan and F. Melo. Interaction-Driven Markov Games for Decentralized Multiagent Planning Under Uncertainty. In *Proceedings of the 7th International Joint Conference on Autonomous Agents and Multiagent Systems (AAMAS 2008)*, pages 525–532, Estoril, Portugal, 2008. IFAAMAS.

M. Spaan, G. Gordon, and N. Vlassis. Decentralized Planning under Uncertainty for Teams of Communicating Agents. In *Proceedings of the 5th International Joint Conference on Autonomous Agents and Multiagent Systems (AAMAS 2006)*, pages 249–256, Hakodate, Japan, 2006. ACM Press.

K. Stanley and R. Miikkulainen. Evolving Neural Networks through Augmenting Topologies. *Evolutionary Computation*, 10(2):99–127, 2002.

P. Stone and M. Veloso. Multiagent Systems: A Survey from a Machine Learning Perspective. *Autonomous Robots*, 8(3):345–383, 2000.

M. Strens and A. Moore. Direct Policy Search using Paired Statistical Tests. In *Proceedings of the 18th International Conference on Machine Learning (ICML 2001)*, pages 545–552, Williamstown, USA, 2001. Morgan Kaufmann.

R. Sutton and A. Barto. *Reinforcement Learning. An Introduction.* MIT Press/A Bradford Book, Cambridge, USA, 1998.

*Bibliography*

R. Sutton, D. McAllester, S. Singh, and Y. Mansour. Policy Gradient Methods for Reinforcement Learning with Function Approximation. In *Advances in Neural Information Processing Systems 12 (NIPS 1999)*, pages 1057–1063, Denver, USA, 2000. MIT Press.

D. Szer and F. Charpillet. Coordination through Mutual Notification in Cooperative Multiagent Reinforcement Learning. In *Proceedings of the 3rd International Joint Conference on Autonomous Agents and Multiagent Systems (AAMAS 2004)*, pages 1254–1255, New York, USA, 2004. IEEE Computer Society.

D. Szer and F. Charpillet. An Optimal Best-First Search Algorithm for Solving Infinite Horizon DEC-POMDPs. In *Machine Learning: Proceedings of the 16th European Conference on Machine Learning (ECML 2005)*, pages 389–399, Porto, Portugal, 2005. Springer.

D. Szer and F. Charpillet. Point-Based Dynamic Programming for DEC-POMDPs. In *Proceedings of the 21st National Conference on Artificial Intelligence (AAAI 2006)*, Boston, USA, 2006. AAAI Press.

D. Szer, F. Charpillet, and S. Zilberstein. MAA*: A Heuristic Search Algorithm for Solving Decentralized POMDPs. In *Proceedings of the 21st Conference in Uncertainty in Artificial Intelligence (UAI 2005)*, pages 576–590, Edinburgh, United Kingdom, 2005. AUAI Press.

M. Tan. Multi-Agent Reinforcement Learning: Independent vs. Cooperative Learning. In *Proceedings of the 10th International Conference on Machine Learning (ICML 1997)*, pages 330–337, Amherst, USA, 1993. Morgan Kaufmann.

N. Tao, J. Baxter, and L. Weaver. A Multi-Agent Policy-Gradient Approach to Network Routing. In *Proceedings of the Eighteenth International Conference on Machine Learning (ICML 2001)*, pages 553–560, Williamstown, USA, 2001. Morgan Kaufmann.

M. Taylor, S. Whiteson, and P. Stone. Comparing Evolutionary and Temporal Difference Methods in a Reinforcement Learning Domain. In *Proceedings of the Genetic and Evolutionary Computation Conference (GECCO 2006)*, pages 1321–1328, Seattle, USA, 2006. ACM.

G. Tesauro. TD-Gammon, a Self-Teaching Backgammon Program, Achieves Master-Level Play. *Neural Computation*, 6:215–219, 1995.

G. Tesauro. Extending Q-Learning to General Adaptive Multi-Agent Systems. In *Advances in Neural Information Processing Systems 16 (NIPS 2003)*, Vancouver and Whistler, Canada, 2003. MIT Press.

G. Tesauro, R. Das, W. Walsh, and J. Kephart. Utility-Function-Driven Resource Allocation in Autonomic Systems. In *Proceedings of the Second International Conference on Autonomic Computing (ICAC 2005)*, pages 342–343, Seattle, USA, 2005. IEEE Computer Society.

# Bibliography

S. Timmer. *Reinforcement Learning with History Lists*. Ph.D. Thesis, University of Osnabrück, 2008.

K. Tumer and A. Agogino. Time-Extended Policies in Multi-Agent Reinforcement Learning. In *Proceedings of the 3rd International Joint Conference on Autonomous Agents and Multiagent Systems (AAMAS 2004)*, pages 1338–1339, New York, USA, 2004. IEEE Computer Society.

K. Tumer and J. Lawson. Collectives for Multiple Resource Job Scheduling Across Heterogeneous Servers. In *Proceedings of the Second International Joint Conference on Autonomous Agents and Multiagent Systems (AAMAS 2003)*, pages 1142–1143, Victoria, Australia, 2003. ACM Press.

K. Tumer, A. Agogino, and D. Wolpert. Learning Sequences of Actions in Collectives of Autonomous Agents. In *Proceedings of the First International Joint Conference on Autonomous Agents & Multiagent Systems (AAMAS 2002)*, pages 378–385, Bologna, Italy, 2002. ACM Press.

R. Vaessens, E. Aarts, and J. Lenstra. Job Shop Scheduling by Local Search. *Informs Journal on Computing*, 8(3):302–317, 1996.

P. van Laarhoven, E. Aarts, and J. Lenstra. Job Shop Scheduling by Simulated Annealing. *Operations Research*, 40(1):113–125, 1992.

D. Vengerov and N. Iakovlev. A Reinforcement Learning Framework for Dynamic Resource Allocation: First Results. In *Proceedings of the Second International Conference on Autonomic Computing (ICAC 2005)*, pages 339–340, Seattle, USA, 2005. IEEE Computer Society.

G. Wang and S. Mahadevan. Hierarchical Optimization of Policy-Coupled Semi-Markov Decision Processes. In *Proceedings of the Sixteenth International Conference on Machine Learning (ICML 1999)*, pages 464–473, Bled, Slovenia, 1999. Morgan Kaufmann.

C. Watkins and P. Dayan. Q-Learning. *Machine Learning*, 8:279–292, 1992.

Lex Weaver and Jonathan Baxter. Learning From State Differences: $STD(\lambda)$. Technical report, Department of Computer Science, Australian National University, 1999.

G. Weiss. Intelligent Agents. In Gerhard Weiss, editor, *Multi Agent Systems*. MIT Press, 1999.

S. Whiteson and P. Stone. Evolutionary Function Approximation for Reinforcement Learning. *Journal of Machine Learning Research*, 7:877–917, 2006.

R. Williams. Simple Statistical Gradient-Following Algorithms for Connectionist Reinforcement Learning. *Machine Learning*, 8(4):229–256, 1992.

J. Wisner. How Does Your Shop Stack Up? *Modern Machine Shop*, 66(2):86–90, 1993.

I. Witten and M. Corbin. Human Operators and Automatic Adaptive Controllers: A Comparative Study on a Particular Control Task. *International Journal of Man-Machine Studies*, 5:75–104, 1973.

D. Wolpert and K. Tumer. Collective Intelligence, Data Routing and Braess' Paradox. *Journal of Artificial Intelligence Research (JAIR)*, 16:359–387, 2002.

J. Wu and E. Durfee. Mixed-Integer Linear Programming for Transition-Independent Decentralized MDPs. In *Proceedings of the 5th International Joint Conference on Autonomous Agents and Multiagent Systems (AAMAS 2006)*, pages 1058–1060, Hakodate, Japan, 2006. ACM Press.

T. Wu, N. Ye, and D. Zhang. Comparison of Distributed Methods for Resource Allocation. *International Journal of Production Research*, 43(3):515–536, 2005.

P. Xuan, V. Lesser, and S. Zilberstein. Communication Decisions in Multi-Agent Cooperation: Model and Experiments. In *Proceedings of the 5th International Conference on Autonomous Agents (Agents 2001)*, pages 616–623, Montreal, Canada, 2001. ACM Press.

D. Yagan and C. Tham. Coordinated Reinforcement Learning for Decentralized Optimal Control. In *Proceedings of the IEEE Symposium on Approximate Dynamic Programming and Reinforcement Learning (ADPRL 2007)*, pages 296–302, Honolulu, USA, 2007. IEEE Press.

D. Zeng and K. Sycara. Using Case-Based Reasoning as a Reinforcement Learning Framework for Optimization with Changing Criteria. In *Proceedings of the 7th International Conference on Tools with Artificial Intelligence (ICTAI 1995)*, pages 56–62, Takamatsu, Japan, 1995. IEEE Press.

W. Zhang and T. Dietterich. A Reinforcement Learning Approach to Job-Shop Scheduling. In *Proceedings of the 14th International Joint Conference on Artificial Intellience (IJCAI 1995)*, pages 1114–1120, Montreal, Canada, 1995. Morgan Kaufmann.

# List of Figures

| | | |
|---|---|---|
| 1.1 | The Big Picture: Overview of this Book | 5 |
| 2.1 | Schematic View on Reinforcement Learning | 8 |
| 2.2 | The Actor-Critic Architecture | 10 |
| 2.3 | Modelling Frameworks for Learning in Single- and Multi-Agents Systems | 16 |
| 2.4 | DEC-MDPs with Changing Action Sets: Local State of Agent $i$ | 24 |
| 2.5 | Exemplary Dependency Functions | 25 |
| 2.6 | Exemplary Dependency Graphs | 26 |
| 2.7 | Interaction History and Encoding Function | 27 |
| 3.1 | Example of a Classical Job-Shop Scheduling Problem | 37 |
| 3.2 | Classes of Schedules | 38 |
| 3.3 | Optimal Schedule for the Scheduling Problem FT6 | 38 |
| 3.4 | The Disjunctive Graph Model | 40 |
| 4.1 | Joint Equilibrium Policy Search with Local Policy Parameterization | 56 |
| 4.2 | Joint Equilibrium Policy Search with Global Policy Parameterization | 59 |
| 4.3 | Learning Performance of Joint Equilibrium Policy Search for the FT6 Benchmark | 64 |
| 4.4 | Policy Development within a Single Agent Using $JEPS_G$ | 66 |
| 4.5 | Learning Progress for JEPS and $JEPS_G$ on 10x10 Problems | 67 |
| 4.6 | Visualization of Possibilities of Convergence and Optimality of GDPS | 79 |
| 4.7 | Probabilistic Disjunctive Graph | 82 |
| 4.8 | Makespan Distribution for a Random Dispatcher on the FT6 Problem | 83 |
| 4.9 | Learning Performance of Gradient Descent Policy Search for the FT6 Benchmark | 85 |
| 4.10 | Gradient Descent Policy Search Learning Performance from a Single Agent's Point of View | 86 |
| 4.11 | Gradient-Descent Policy Search Applied to a Selection of 10x10 Problems | 88 |
| 5.1 | The Batch-Mode Reinforcement Learning Framework | 97 |
| 5.2 | System Architecture for Value Function-Based Reinforcement Learning | 99 |

## List of Figures

5.3 Learning with NFQ and OA-NFQ for the FT6 Benchmark . . . . . . . . . 119
5.4 Training Data Utilization with NFQ and OA-NFQ for the FT6 Benchmark 120
5.5 Learning Process for the Notorious FT10 Problem . . . . . . . . . . . . . 122
5.6 Learning Progress of OA-NFQ for 10x10 Job-Shop Scheduling Problems . . 123
5.7 Benchmark Results for OA-NFQ . . . . . . . . . . . . . . . . . . . . . . . 124
5.8 Generalization Capabilities of OA-NFQ-Trained Agents . . . . . . . . . . 127

6.1 Communication-Based Awareness of Inter-Agent Dependencies . . . . . . 140
6.2 Learning Curves Using Encoding-Based and Communicating Agents for the FT6 Benchmark . . . . . . . . . . . . . . . . . . . . . . . . . . . . . . . . 144
6.3 Communication-Based GDPS Learning Progress for the FT10 Problem . . 147

## I want morebooks!

Buy your books fast and straightforward online - at one of the world's fastest growing online book stores! Environmentally sound due to Print-on-Demand technologies.

Buy your books online at
## www.get-morebooks.com

Kaufen Sie Ihre Bücher schnell und unkompliziert online – auf einer der am schnellsten wachsenden Buchhandelsplattformen weltweit!
Dank Print-On-Demand umwelt- und ressourcenschonend produziert.

Bücher schneller online kaufen
## www.morebooks.de

OmniScriptum Marketing DEU GmbH
Bahnhofstr. 28
D - 66111 Saarbrücken
Telefax: +49 681 93 81 567-9

info@omniscriptum.com
www.omniscriptum.com

Printed by Books on Demand GmbH, Norderstedt / Germany